THE PRIEST AND THE FÜHRER

The Ministry and Martyrdom of a Peacemaker

A Biography Honoring the Life and Legacy of Father Max Josef Metzger

Leonard Swidler

Cormac O'Duffy

PRAISE FOR *THE PRIEST AND THE FÜHRER*

"*The Priest and The Führer* tells the fascinating story of a man who engaged with major challenges of the first half of the twentieth century, always seeking common sense solutions to issues such as war and peace, interfaith relations, and a democratic and just society worldwide. Despite his convincing, thoughtful approach to problems in the pursuit of truth and justice, he was martyred at the hands of an autocratic regime not open to either. The book provides a tour through Europe of the time and how one man used thoughtful analysis, engagement, and dialogue that had an impact on Christianity and European culture into the contemporary era. He left a blueprint for what a civil society should be and formed organizations and communities that continue to work toward that end."

—Joseph Stoutzenberger, PhD, professor emeritus at Holy Family University, author of *Mystery and Tradition: Catholicism for Today's Spiritual Seekers*

"Max Josef Metzger is a hero of the faith. A priest known for his love and kindness, he gave his life for "the peace of the world and the unity of the Church of Christ" at the hands of one of the most evil regimes the world has ever known. We should be grateful to Leonard Swidler and Cormac O'Duffy for helping bring his story to light in a way which gives glory to the Lord Fr. Metzger served so faithfully."

—Revd Nicky Gumbel, Pioneer of Alpha

"Cormac O'Duffy adds a unique perspective to Leonard Swidler's account of Father Max Joseph Metzger's life and work. He shows us the depth and holiness of Fr. Metzger's life and soul relationship with Christ in the wholeness of body and soul that enabled such a surrender to the point of acceptance of the reality he faced. Metzger's life and work enriched the Roman Church in its ecumenical outreach and will ever be grateful to Fr. Metzger who gave his life for Christ and the Church. May we each discover our call to this unity the Lord Himself desired."

—Fr. Joseph Tedesco OCSO, Superior, Mepkin Abbey

"*The Priest and The Führer* will captivate you with its intense and detailed description of the life and work of Father Max Josef Metzger, a German Catholic priest born in 1887 who lived an amazing life. He was an extremely talented linguist and musician. He founded the Ecumenical movement, 'Una Sancta' and formed multiple prayer groups throughout Europe. His contributions in the area of world peace eventually attracted the attention of the Gestapo and the entire Nazi Party who had him beheaded in 1944 for High Treason. This book is a testimony to an incredible person of saintly behavior and example, and Dr. Swidler's and Dr. O'Duffy's comprehensive and engaging style of writing brings this life of inspiration and sacrifice to the page."

—William Levay, Distinguished Toastmaster and Award-Winning Public Speaker

"A fascinating and instructive introduction to the life of a unique figure in modern German Catholic history."

—George Weigel, Distinguished Senior Fellow and William E. Simon Chair in Catholic Studies, Ethics and Public Policy Center

"A fascinating and enlightening encounter with an ecumenist and martyr who in many ways was a man ahead of his time. Father Max Josef Metzger and the foxhole ecumenism he practiced during the reign of Hitler and the Third Reich is a story not often told, but worth hearing. Swidler and O'Duffy bring to life the triumphs and struggles of this Catholic priest who was willing to lay down his life for the cause of the Una Sancta, planting the seeds for the ecumenism of Vatican II and the Pontifical Council for Promoting Christian Unity. While he seemed to share a commonality with the socialism of the early twentieth century Europe in which he lived, the courage he demonstrated in prison for his faith and ideals was, and continues to be, an inspiration to Christians in counting the cost. In 1943 Metzger paid the ultimate price, the kind of costly discipleship that fellow Lutheran martyr Dietrich Bonhoeffer knew only too well."

—Joel Elowsky, Concordia Seminary, St. Louis, MO

"Whether you are deeply familiar with the theological struggles in Europe or encountering Max Josef Metzger's story for the first time, this book promises to educate and inspire. It was incredible to get to know Metzger through his own writings—his eloquence, conviction, charisma, and courage—alongside the larger geopolitical context of early twentieth century Europe. Metzger's voice rings as a refreshingly *modern* ecumenical—even as he calmly awaited the ultimate 'cancelation' of the Nazis' death penalty—in terms that have never been more important for Christendom."

—Brittany Burgeson O'Duffy, Oxford,
MSc Social Science of the Internet

"Max Josef Metzger was a man of very remarkable personal qualities, deep personal piety, and prophetic vision. His life was one of unstinting work in the service of causes—world peace, ecumenism, and interreligious dialogue. Metzger had been a rebel from a young age— "he danced out of line" as a fellow priest put it—a trait that would result in conflict with his superiors (often as a result of his commitment to abstinence from alcohol), accusations of utopianism ("my exuberant Max who always has his head in the clouds" as his bishop would put it when Metzger was on trial for his life), and endless displacements from one diocese to another in search of episcopal support for his foundations and commitments. These struggles nevertheless led him to draw ever more deeply on an inner reserve of perseverance and an increasingly total dependence on God, which would serve him well when he found himself face to face, in 1943, with the diabolical Nazi judge Roland Freisler (originally a communist who took his inspiration from Andrei Vishinski, the legal instrument of Stalin's Great Terror)."

—Professor Ronan Sharkey, Institute Catholique in Paris

"A thoughtful, and well-written portrait of Central Europe in the first half of the twentieth century, and a timely reminder of how much Catholic priests suffered under the Nazis, and indeed, just how much the good can suffer in times of great turbulence.

Fr. Metzger's work in promoting temperance should awaken echoes in those interested in the history of Alcoholics Anonymous, the Temperance movement of Fr. Theobald Mathew and the Pioneer Total Abstinence Society, and his contribution to the development of a distinctively lay spirituality will engage those countless people involved with Secular Institutes and Personal

Prelatures—one thinks of Frank Duff and the Legion of Mary, for example. Finally, his pioneering work in the areas of ecumenism and interreligious dialogue will be of great interest to those who study Vatican II and the theology of Josef Ratzinger."

—Catherine Kavanagh, PhD (U. of Notre Dame), Senior Lecturer, Department of Philosophy, Mary Immaculate College, South Circular Road, Limerick

"Committed to both the Catholic Church and the cause of ecumenism during a particularly dark time in Europe, Father Metzger and those he inspired worked tirelessly—and effectively—to achieve their goals and objectives. Tragically, Father Metzger was executed before he could see the results of his hard work and dedication. I will add my prayers to those who are striving to have him beatified."

—James R. O'Brien, Colonel, U.S. Air Force (Retired)

"Two Americans pay tribute to the life's work of a German priest—the universal-minded Max Josef Metzger would certainly have liked that.

Why am I so impressed by the *The Priest and the Führer*? Leonard Swidler does not allow Max Josef Metzger and his life's work to freeze into a statue. In a scholarly and at the same time warmhearted and lively manner, he tells the story of a man who devoted his life to peace between peoples and denominations. We encounter Fr. Metzger not only as a scholar and priest with outstanding abilities and talents, but also as a fellow human being with faults and limitations. It is precisely this that brings him closer to us as a companion.

Cormac O'Duffy continues Swidler's remarks into the present day by impressively setting Metzger's texts to music, making his message resonate anew. O'Duffy also points out how much the Una Sancta movement founded by Metzger contributed to the emergence of a political party that overcame the boundaries of denominations and was involved in the democratic reconstruction of Germany after the horrors of the Second World War—the Christian Democratic Union (CDU)."

—Father Christian Hess, Diocese of Freiburg

iPub Global Connection LLC

1050 W Nido Ave

Mesa, AZ 85210-7660

ipubglobalconnection.com

Copyright © 2024 by Leonard Swidler and Cormac O'Duffy

All rights reserved. This book or any portion thereof may not be reproduced or used in any manner whatsoever without the express written permission of the publisher except for the use of brief quotations in a book review.

Library of Congress Control Number: 2023944802

ISBN: 978-1-948575-64-5 (paperback)

ISBN: 978-1-948575-63-8 (ebook)

DEDICATION

This book is dedicated to our collective future—

one where people like Father Metzger are *not* celebrated as heroes

because kindness to our neighbors is so familiar and commonplace,

tightly woven into the fabric of our societies and our minds.

Peace!

How humanity hungers to enjoy the blessings of peace!

There is no land in which there is not the same longing

for the cessation of this frightful pouring out of blood,

for the return of joyous peace.

Indeed, it is like a single outcry

from the depths of all men and women's hearts,

a cry for the peacemaker,

a Savior!

You heavens rain down the just one!

You clouds pour him forth!

Father Max Josef Metzger

CONTENTS

PREFACE 1
IN THE NAME OF THE GERMAN *VOLK* 5
BEGINNINGS 9
   Schooling 13
   Theological Studies 15
   Temperance 19
EARLY PASTORAL WORK 21
WORLD WAR I 25
SOCIAL AND APOSTOLIC WORK 29
   Graz Temperance Work 29
   Renewal of Society Through Religion 31
   Founding of the White Cross 32
   Support from Rome—Not from Home 35
   Growth of the White Cross 38
   The "Time of Troubles" 40
   Priests and South America 44
WORLD PEACE 49
   The Role of the World Peace League of the White Cross ... 51
   Internationale Katholische Liga "Ika" 58
   The World Congress of Christ the King 60
   The Esperanto Movement 61
   International Peace Conferences 63
   Christian Pacifism and Parallels to Communist Ideals 69
   Writings on World Peace 72
ECUMENISM 81
   Beginnings of a Liturgical and Ecumenical Movement ... 83
   The Contributions of Father Metzger 85
   Ecumenical Writings 89
   Ecumenism in Germany 90

 The Una Sancta Brotherhood 92
 Resistance to the Una Sancta Brotherhood Activities 97
 Una Sancta Conferences and Gatherings 100
 Lecturing on Una Sancta 102
 The Flourishing of Una Sancta in Berlin 103
CONFLICT WITH TOTALITARIANISM 107
BETWEEN THE FALL OF THE GAVEL AND THE AXE 131
FINAL REFLECTIONS 151
FOREWORD TO PART 2: "STANDING ON THE SHOULDERS OF GIANTS" 153
 Special Acknowledgements 155
POSTWAR DEVELOPMENT OF UNA SANCTA 156
 Displacement of Populations 157
 Growth of Una Sancta to a People's Movement 157
 Karl Adam on the Reassessment of Luther 160
 Guiding Principles of Una Sancta 161
 Youth Gatherings and Publications 163
 Visibility of Una Sancta and Konrad Adenauer 164
 The Growth of Christian Democracy: Stegerwald to the CDU 167
 The Founding of the CDU in Bad Godesberg, December 1945 170
 The CDU Meeting in Berlin 1946 to Honor Fr. Max Metzger 171
 The Address of Pastor Walter Dress 174
 Reaction to the Meeting at Mercedes Palast and St. Joseph's Parish, Berlin 177
 The Achievement of Una Sancta and the CDU/CSU 178
 The Legacy of Fr. Max Josef Metzger 179
UNA SANCTA IN GERMANY TODAY 181
 The Example of the Munich Una Sancta Circle 181
 The 1960 Munich Eucharistic Conference and Una Sancta 183
 Una Sancta in Munich 185
 Guidelines for Ecumenical Encounter, by Josef Tomé (1941) 187

AFTERWORD.. 189
METZGER'S LEGACY LIVES ON IN MUSIC 189
    The Search for Christian Unity.. 189
    The Prophet of Ecumenism? 190
    "Freundschaft"... 191
    The Meitingen Concert, November 3, 2019 192
    American Premiere at St. Matthew's Lutheran Church, Charleston, February 2020 194
    The Making of the Metzger Oratorio 197
    Further Texts of Metzger from Sister Gertraud, Christ the King Institute 199
    Hymns and Songs from the Community of the White Cross, 1924 201
    The Institute in Meitingen and Its Members 202
    Oratorio Structure: Parts One and Two 204
    The Prison Poems 205
THE FUTURE 209
    The "Alleluia" Memorial, Brandenburg, April 17, 2024................. 209
ABOUT THE AUTHORS 213

PREFACE

This is the story of an *extraordinary man*, who lived an *extraordinary life*, died an *extraordinary death*, and left a most *extraordinary legacy*—Max Josef Metzger. As the title of the book indicates, Metzger's years-long endeavors promoting dialogue and cooperation, working toward unity among Christians and world peace, were his most influential efforts. For the latter, he literally gave his life on the German guillotine.

Metzger's work had consequences 1) on the German national level, 2) toward the creation of the European Union, and 3) reshaping the Catholic—hence the Christian—global religious worlds! His groundbreaking work in building the Catholic-Protestant bridge reshaped the Christian Church in Germany, leading from centuries-long division toward unity.

However, he was also heavily involved in other efforts aimed at the betterment of humankind, such as promoting vegetarianism. Today, we are aware that humanity's continued massive addiction to meat-eating contributes more damage to the Earth's warming atmosphere and melting ice caps than the burning of fossil fuel! He was a pioneer in establishing vegetarian restaurants that served drinks other than alcohol, the excessive consumption of which leads to the destruction of hundreds of millions of lives and families.

In addition to all of that, Metzger had incipient, influential impact on two other major global movements: 1) the Second Vatican Council of the Catholic Church (1962-65), which has been the major force drawing the world into fundamental dialogue among religions and cultures, and 2), the shaping of a joint Catholic-Protestant drive toward a democratic Germany, which contributed to the formation of the European Union.

His was an adventuresome spirit, willing to try and fail, until success began to arise—or not. A prominent example was his very serious advocacy of Esperanto, an artificial language intended to be a universal second language used across the world, in the service of both of his major goals: human worldwide unity, first religiously, but also politically. He was a dynamo within Catholicism, working not only for ecumenical unity among Christians (interreligious dialogue was then only just around the corner of the turning away from religious navel-gazing to turning toward the Other, which then reaches out for endless unity—and also automatically enhances each individual Person). One foretaste of that outreach to the Other Individual manifested itself in the form of his "smuggling of Jews" to safety from the hands of the Gestapo.

I first learned about Max Josef Metzger in the late 1950s while doing three years' research on the Catholic-Protestant rapprochement in post-World War II Germany known as the Una Sancta Movement. That investigation finally saw the light of day as *The Ecumenical Vanguard* (Pittsburgh: Duquesne University Press, 1966). As founder of the Una Sancta Brotherhood in 1938, Metzger's ecumenical activities were the subject of one chapter in that work. But there was so much more depth and drama to Metzger's life than could be encompassed in that single chapter. I felt drawn back to Germany in the summer of 1963 to dig further into Metzger's story. My wife Arlene Anderson Swidler and I spent that summer filling in the gaps in our earlier research of Metzger's life. We interviewed Metzger's sister, friends, colleagues, and acquaintances, and visited the places where he studied, worked, and lived. Much time was spent carefully going through the voluminous archival material on Metzger in the diocesan files of Freiburg im Breisgau and Graz, Austria, the diocesan seminary of Regensburg, Metzger's foundations in Graz and Meitingen bei Augsburg, and the many newspapers and booklets Metzger edited and wrote over the years.

Meitingen Community Brothers in the print room.

For the most part I have avoided using footnotes since most of the information was taken from the above unpublished or largely inaccessible sources. Often, however, I did indicate in the text the source by stating, for example, that Metzger wrote such and such in the March issue of his newspaper *Christkoenigsbote* that year, or that his friend Monsignor Baumeister remarked something particular about Metzger to me.

While researching the Freiburg chancery archives, I met Marianne Moehring, a member of the *Society of Christ the King*, founded by Metzger. She too was working on Metzger's life and work, as her doctoral dissertation. She was understandably anxious when she learned that another scholar was so far down the same path she was traveling—if substantially I "scooped" her, she would have to write a whole new dissertation. Fortunately, that did not happen. Although I was finished with my writing by the end of 1964, and the manuscript was accepted by Bruce Publishing Company for publication in 1965, before the manuscript got into print Bruce sold out to Macmillan and my book never came into existence—till now. In the meanwhile, Moehring completed her dissertation in the winter of 1966 and rushed the book into print that summer (*Täter des Wortes*, Meitingen: Kyrios-Verlag, 1966). It is a good book, complete with 673 footnotes and 146 pages of documentation, charts, appendices, and indices beyond the 157 pages of text. But in any case, it is quite a different book from mine, probably because of the dissertation format. We obviously covered most of the same archival material. I apparently found some early letters and garnered some information from interviews Moehring did not, but she found some things I did not. Hence, I took advantage of the publication of her book to add some half-dozen pages of this supplemental information to my presentation. For the rest I was pleased to find my factual research corroborated by Dr. Moehring's; I now reciprocate.

As one leafs through these pages it should become apparent why Max Josef Metzger's life elicits the writing of a biography. Many groups of twentieth-century reformers have ample reason to be thankful for the pioneering efforts of Metzger. He was a vigorous pioneer of the popular biblical and liturgical movements already in the 1920s. The same was also true of Catholic involvement in ecumenism and social ethical action and the restructuring of "religious orders" to deeply involve active laity, and the founding of what became the new category of "secular institutes." These later pioneering efforts began already in the second decade of this century, as did also Metzger's founding of the first effective Catholic world peace organization. But beyond that, Metzger was obviously a fascinating, magnetic personality who spellbound and inspired many, and enraged others; the former tended to be liberals and the latter conservatives.

In the end, Metzger showed not only a pioneering and prophetic spirit, but also extraordinary depth and staying power—to the fall of the axe. He became a martyr to the cause of peace and religious unity, for his ecumenical work was intimately bound up with his final peace effort, arrest, trial, imprisonment, and finally execution by beheading. In fact, one of the memorial trees along the road to Yad Vashem, the World Holocaust Remembrance Center in Israel dedicated to the Just Gentiles who gave their lives saving Jews from the Nazis, could well be dedicated to Metzger, for he was also smuggling Jews—though the Nazis never learned of it.

As will be seen, Metzger had his faults, but his gifts and responses to the overwhelming challenges thrown at him were so much greater that he became an authentic hero. His life and accomplishments deserve to be known beyond the German-reading world.

I want to express a brief word of special appreciation to my wife Arlene for the many weeks of researching alongside me. The burdens, the excitement, and the awe were shared day by day, giving us both a memorable summer. I also wish to note the gracious help given to me by Sister Gertrudis Reimann, the superior general of the Sisters of Christ the King in 1963 and at the time of Metzger's death, and Sister Maria Theresa at Graz, both close associates of Father Metzger. Special thanks are also due to John Heidbrink, who through the Fellowship of Reconciliation raised a small grant to help pay for the research costs.

Leonard Swidler

April 17, 1977,
the anniversary of Metzger's martyrdom,
and 2023

IN THE NAME OF THE GERMAN *VOLK*

In the criminal proceedings against the Catholic priest Dr. Max Josef Metzger of Berlin, born 3 February, 1887, in Schopfheim (Baden),

At present in police custody

Because of conspiracy to commit High Treason

The People's Court, First Senate, on the basis of the trial of 14 October, 1943, at which participants were as Judges:

President of the People's Court Dr. Freisler, Chairman . . . . Has justly recognized:

Max Josef Metzger, a Catholic diocesan priest, who, convinced of our defeat, in the fourth war year attempted to send a "Memorandum" to Sweden to prepare the way for an inimical pacifistic-democratic, federalistic "government," with the personal defamation of the National Socialists. As a traitor of the people, forever without honor, he will be punished with death.

Reasons:

Max Josef Metzger is a Catholic diocesan priest who already in 1917—in the midst of war!—worked in Austria in a World Peace organization (Just like Erzberger's behavior in Germany), helping to undermine our war front.

Furthermore, he could not let off with that now either. He says himself that he believes Germany will collapse. Therefore, so he declares, he had it in mind to write the Führer that he should step down, for he believed then a negotiated peace would be possible!! Of course he did not carry that out:

    1. because he believed his letter would not reach the Führer;

> 2. because he judged that in any case he would meet with no success in his request;
>
> 3. because he feared he would then be arrested.

Instead of that he composed a "Manifesto" and attempted to transmit it to the Protestant Bishop Eidem, whom he knew from Una Sancta work (efforts at the reunion of the Catholic and Protestant confessions). This was to be done through Mrs. Imgart from Giessen, a former Swede and present German citizen . . . . This Manifesto . . . is a sketch of a system of government for Germany which would subordinate it, in a democratic pacifistic defenseless condition, to a terror army of our enemies. It would not be a unified state, not even a confederation—hence the realization of the wildest dreams of our enemies! Metzger says he thought that upon a German collapse Archbishop Eidem, whom he considers a Germanophile, would propagate such lines of thought among our enemies so as to "save" Germany with such a government rather than an enemy government. A completely monstrous thought as only a complete defeatist could conceive it. An outrageously traitorous thought as only one who thoroughly hates our National Socialist Germany would be able to articulate. A thought of High Treason because it proceeds from and pursues as a goal the replacing of our own National Socialist way of life with long since surpassed "ideas" which are hostile to the Volk. First, however, whoever sets forth such a scheme in the world during a war—for any reasons whatsoever—if it falls into the hands of our enemies, weakens our power of resistance and strengthens our enemy. For the enemy would doubtless use such a document as propaganda. It would give the impression that there were forces in Germany that thought about defeat and which after the defeat would attach themselves to the enemy, forming a powerless German government in order to play a helping role within the structure of a system subordinated to our enemy . . . .

Even if Metzger were really convinced that this document could not fall into hands which would use it against Germany, such would not influence the judgment of the People's Court. For the whole manner of behavior of Metzger is so monstrous that it is irrelevant whether it can be juridically defined as High Treason (Metzger says he had never considered violence) or as favoring the enemy (Metzger says he had thought only of action at the moment of an effective collapse)—all that is beside the point. For every people's comrade knows that such stepping out of the battle front by a single German is a monstrous, damaging act, a betrayal of our Volk in its struggle for its life, and that such a betrayal is deserving of death. It is treason oriented toward High Treason, treason oriented toward defeatism, treason oriented toward favoring the enemy, a treason which our healthy Volk-sensitivity judges deserving of death (par. 2StGB) . . . .

His archbishop has declared him in a letter sent to the defense, and which was read, as not being a criminal, but rather he called him an idealist. But that is a completely different world, a world which we do not understand . . . .

Everyone must submit to being measured by the German National Socialist norm, and that norm clearly dictates that a man who so acts is a traitor of his own Volk.

Metzger, who through his behavior has forever lost his honor, must therefore be condemned to death.

Because he is condemned, Metzger must also pay the costs.

Dr. Freisler

"There was one fellow sufferer who, because of his upright bearing, his carefree look and his almost white hair, despite a youthful face, made a deep impression on me. One always tried to speak with those for whom one felt a spiritual kinship. The clothing of course made us all alike, and often it was weeks before one realized that in these walking rags there was a general. At first I judged the new fellow sufferer to be an actor, a great dramatic performer. He said to me, I am a Catholic priest, which made me happy. I soon learned his name; Father Max Metzger, born in Schopfheim . . . .

"I was asked who this tall man with the white hair was. We were all agreed that Father Metzger, although perhaps many did not know what he was, had a calming influence on all the fellow sufferers. I had often observed him walking and looked to see if I could not make out a halo. His picture in the book [the edition of the prison letters] and the way he really looked during the last months really are considerably different. His hair became whiter and his face grew thinner and from his eyes there came a light that was almost unearthly. In the picture in the book Father Metzger is a priest who was standing in the middle of life. In the last weeks he gave the impression of a man who stood above life, whose soul was transfigured, who indeed bodily

still lived on the earth, but whose spirit already stood before the blessed heavenly Father."

These are the recollections of one of the last men to see Max Metzger alive.

In the midst of all these scholars and pastors, one name kept appearing time and time again, the name of one whom many described as a "prophetic" voice; it was that of Fr. Max Josef Metzger. What these and others seemed to see in him was a dynamism to turn their thinking into action. His own experiences in World War I had shown him the weakness of a divided Christianity. He had met and mingled with active Christians from all backgrounds in the search for peace after the war and longed to see a reconciliation between them all. Unlike any other ecumenical writer or leader, he had been martyred for his beliefs.

BEGINNINGS

Max Josef Metzger was born on February 3, 1887, in the quiet little Black Forest village of Schopfheim. His father, Friedrich August Metzger, was a secondary school teacher devoted to his work. He taught history, Latin, and with a particular passion, French. He knew the literature well and spoke the language fluently—partly, no doubt, because the family lived so close to France and the French-speaking areas of Switzerland, and partly because he often went to France and traveled or enrolled in advanced studies. His efforts were, at least to some extent, recognized, for in 1887 he moved from Schopfheim to a post at the Meersburg Academy and then eventually to a teaching position at the pedagogical academy in Freiburg im Breisgau, from which he was finally pensioned.

First photo of Max Josef Metzger, 1887.

Despite these advancements the Metzger family had financial problems. Things were so bad in 1905, the daughter Maria recalls that her father planned to ration bread, milk, and meat in the family and just try to get used to hunger himself.

Nevertheless, the Metzger home was a cheerful one. Friedrich August Metzger, who had a reputation for being enigmatic, could espouse the most impossible thesis with a perfectly straight face; it was only in the middle of a heated dispute that a sly smile told you that you had been duped again by Metzger senior. Though the mother, Anna Gaenshirt Metzger, suffered from chronically poor health, most notably asthma, her children later remembered her as often singing about the house. In fact, music was a very important part of the cheerful Metzger household, as it was in many educated German families. The father played the piano and particularly the organ very well. Max apparently had a very pleasant voice and later enjoyed composing texts and melodies of all sorts. In the *Alleluja-Liederschatz*, a song book published by a religious society he founded, forty-one out of the ninety-one songs were written by Max. The music of the family life impressed itself on Max's whole life to the bitter end when he composed and sang an Easter Alleluia for the prison chaplain in Brandenburg a few days before his beheading.

The Metzger home was a strongly religious one; the children grew up in an atmosphere of simple, solid piety. Max was the only boy and the eldest of four children. (The fact that he had only sisters may have had something to do with Max's later having much greater success in founding a religious society of sisters than he did in founding an order of brothers.) His piety showed up in his enthusiasm for playing Mass; his sister remembered that he was very particular about her answering the prayers and performing the ministrations. Even in early childhood he often talked of becoming either a missionary or a doctor. Before he was eight years old, he wrote to his priest uncle, Father Gaenshirt, and his aunt:

> Dear Uncle and Aunt,
>
> Now Christmas is past and you will be wondering what the little Christ Child has brought me. Listen then and I will tell you. He brought me the following: 1) a wonderful little altar, which makes me most happy. And now I want to tell you thank you very very much for the altar, dear Uncle. You are really my most loved and best uncle because you always make me so happy with your wonderful presents. I promise always to be a good boy so that you will always be proud of me. Every day I'll pray for you and all my friends at my little altar.
>
> Also thank you very much for the knife that I wanted for so long.
>
> Mama will tell you about all the rest of the things I got.
>
> Happy New Year.
>
> Many greetings from your grateful nephew.
>
> Max
>
> Schopfheim, January 4, 1895

A little more than two years later he wrote Father Gaenshirt and promised to help him in the missions when he got big.

Max's piety was mixed with high spirits and a terrible tendency to tease. Instead of walking around horses on the street or waiting for them to pass, he would laughingly run underneath them. When he and his younger sisters visited Father Gaenshirt at Oberhausen during vacation times, the village would be in a mild state of uproar. This sense of humor, although it matured, never left Max, to the great discomfort of his many opponents throughout the rest of his life.

Little Max's self-awareness was greatly heightened in his early home life by three major factors. The first was that his father was determined to make Max a model young boy and was consequently most exacting in his demands. (Is the root of Max's later "free" attitude toward the letter of the law and authority partially to be found here, by the way of reaction?) Max soon began to expect first place performance from himself, to the point that a second place in a spelldown would result in tears. Max later wrote of his early boyhood that he was in general an obedient lad—naturally less out of insight into the meaning of obedience than from fear of his father's discipline, who "was a 'stern schoolmaster,' sternest of all with me, who he wished to raise as a model boy, although I had little talent or inclination thereto . . . . No king who was ever dethroned could be more crushed than I was. It was incomprehensible to me that I should have lost my first place."

Little Max was also made very conscious that he was a Catholic. Southwestern Germany was a very confessionally mixed area. Since the Reformation the religion of a German state followed that of the prince and because until the nineteenth century the political map of much of Germany looked like a multicolored jigsaw puzzle, Protestants and Catholics tended to live in contiguous but mutually exclusive ghettos. In Max's hometown of Schopfheim, there was no Catholic parish from 1557 until 1846, and then it was only a mission parish served by a priest living elsewhere until 1899. But in addition to the ghettoizing tendency promoted by the diaspora experience, the whole *Kulturkampf* atmosphere in the Germany of 1870 onwards reinforced the polarization of Catholics and Protestants. As a consequence, Max, who more and more wished to "run with the boys," was restricted to his home. His parents forbade him to visit the house of his schoolmate, who happened to be the son of a Protestant minister. Max later wrote, "In Schopfheim I clearly must have been so very carefully protected by my parents as the apple of their eye that outside of taking walks with my parents, I very seldom got out of the house, and particularly seldom onto the street." The religious tension was further intensified by the parish priest in Schopfheim, Dr. Arthur Steinam, who had a strong influence on the young Max. In his mature years Max wrote of him, "I cannot today sufficiently condemn it, but he had perhaps somewhat equated 'anti-Protestant' with 'Catholic.' Perhaps it was necessary to emphasize the differences in order to secure thereby the faith consciousness of a diaspora congregation."

The third factor that played a significant role in heightening the self-awareness of young Max was strangely, but not atypically for that time, connected with his being a Catholic in a predominantly Protestant Germany: a strongly developed German nationalism. Of course, it is true that the latter part of the nineteenth century witnessed an extraordinary buildup of nationalism in Europe, and in a very special way in Germany as a result of its unification in 1870. Also, this German nationalism was abetted at the turn of the century by a rising neoromanticism and the German youth movement. But an additional religious element was added for Catholics. German Catholics' Germanness was questioned by the dominant German Protestants—much as was the case for Catholics in America until recently. In fact, this was the whole point and basis of the *Kulturkampf*. The common response of German Catholics was twofold: they greatly stressed their Catholicism and their Germanness. They developed a minority's 110 percent allegiance attitude. Thus, Max later reported that in his very early years the children addressed their father as "Papa," a Latin-rooted word. Somewhat later, however, following a "wave of consciousness of their being German," the German *Vater* was insisted upon. Likewise, the parents forbade Max to play with Jewish children!

Beginning of school: Max Josef Metzger
with his little sister, 1893.

Despite restrictions, the outdoors was also part of Max's heritage. Friedrich August Metzger was an editor of a magazine devoted to beekeeping. Father Gaenshirt's house, where Max regularly spent his vacations, had an orchard and vegetable garden in the middle of a German *Bauerndorf*, which means there were plenty of farm animals around. All this was set in the midst of the Black Forest, one of the most beautifully scenic areas in all of Europe. Anyone growing up in these surroundings would almost have to be a bit romantic, as Max Metzger was.

Schooling

Max went to the grammar school in Schopfheim for three-and-a-half years instead of the usual four years. Then he studied at the secondary school *Realschule* in Schopfheim where his father taught. Max had his father as teacher in French and history classes during this time. He received no special treatment, except the especially hard treatment which is usually the fate of teachers' children; but nevertheless, in his spare time during those four years, Max also studied Latin privately with his father.

The *Progymnasium* at Donaueschingen—still in the heart of the Black Forest—was the next school Max attended. During his stay there he lived with another uncle, Herr Kamerrat Gaenshirt. While here he had an experience that was a real thrill to his thirteen-year-old boyish heart: the Emperor came for a visit.

> The whole city was bedecked in festive fashion and the street from the train station all the way to the castle was heavily laden with garlands, coats of arms, flags, etc. At the station a magnificent gate of honor was set up. The Kaiser was received at the station by the Fuerst and his guests, the mayor, etc. All along the way to the castle the various organizations, schools, farmers, groups, etc. lined the street. When the Kaiser passed by he was greeted by jubilant shouts. Afterwards all the massed groups walked past the castle to the train depot where they broke up. In the evening at 9:30 there was a torchlight parade in which the pupils of the Progymnasium also took part. All the participants gathered in front of the park gate: the boys of the seventh and eighth grades of the grammar school, the gymnasium students, the folk-dance groups, the clubs, the firemen, etc. All carried either pitch torches or Chinese lanterns, which lit everything up splendidly. At the castle we paraded by twice and then remained standing. The Kaiser, the Fuerst, the Fuerstin etc. were on the magnificently decorated veranda . . . . Never will I forget this day!

> On Sunday morning he [the Kaiser] again returned and at eleven o'clock he went to services in the Protestant church here. I saw him very well . . . . He drove out of the park by the train station but not, as was expected, around the bend toward Huefingen, but rather straight ahead because the curve was too sharp to make at that speed. The whole crowd raced after the carriage. I had gone over the railroad tracks and stood right next to the carriage. The Fuerst stepped out and called to me that I should clear a path for him among the people (the whole street was jammed) because he wanted to drive by way of Huefingen. You can imagine how proud I felt that he spoke to me! The Kaiser is supposed to have said in a telephone conversation with the Kaiserin that he was very pleased with his stay here. Also, it is said he really liked the local beer. It's rumored he sent several cases to Berlin . . . .
>
> A loving greeting and kiss from your grateful son,
>
> Max
>
> Donaueschingen, April 3, 1900

After one year at Donaueschingen, Max returned home (in his curriculum vitae he merely says "because of circumstances"—perhaps financial?) and commuted to the gymnasium at Lörrach on the German-Swiss border for his fifth and sixth years of secondary training. While at Lörrach Max's enthusiasm got him into trouble, a foretaste of the sort of thing that was to plague him all his life—and death. One evening when Max was riding home from Lörrach the train stopped at the village of Haagen as usual and as one of the schoolboys was getting off Max snatched his cap and threw it out the window onto the platform. The boy leaped out, grabbed his cap, and called Max a *lausbub* (rascal). Feeling his boy's honor was at stake Max jumped from the train and just as he was about to grab the other boy the conductor shouted, "Board!" Max gave the boy a shove and ran as fast as he could back onto the train. The boy fell and banged his knee and then was picked up by a trainman. Unfortunately for Max this incident was reported by the station master to the traffic inspection bureau in Basel and from there to the Lörrach gymnasium. Max received six hours of disciplinary detention.

In writing to Father Gaenshirt and his sister housekeeper about the incident, Frau Metzger commented, "If only this will be a good lesson for him. He promised high and low to be calmer and better behaved. According to the description from Haagen you would think he were a terribly impudent ruffian. But no one could really think that of him. Thoughtless, headstrong, that's the worst one can say of him."

In other respects, Max did well at the Lörrach gymnasium; his first year there he wrote Father Gaenshirt that he was the first in his class. However, in 1902 Friedrich August Metzger was appointed to the pedagogical academy in Meersburg. Max then decided to attend the gymnasium at Constance and stay at the *Konvikt*, St. Konradi Haus, a sort of minor seminary. The rector of the St. Konradi Haus at this time was Dr. Conrad Gröber, who later became Father Max Metzger's archbishop in Freiburg and was his archbishop at the time of his execution.

Max followed pretty much the usual course of study in "humanistic" gymnasium, with a strong emphasis on languages, particularly the ancient ones, and literature; he studied Hebrew, Greek, Latin, French, German, and apparently some English. He did very well in all his subjects, with the exception of Hebrew, in which he received a C. In all the rest he received As and Bs. For application he was given As but in deportment he seemed able to manage only a B. He applied himself with typical intensity to preparation for the grueling state examinations, the *Abitur*, at the end of the nine-year gymnasium period. He passed with the highest rating: *sehr gut* or "A." He still found leisure for his music, particularly piano and organ, and also stenography; in his final gymnasium year he passed a teacher's exam in shorthand with a *sehr gut*. He had learned this, as well as his music, from his father and put it to wide use up to his death.

Theological Studies

In 1905, Max began his theological studies for the archdiocese of Freiburg im Breisgau at the University in Freiburg. That was the year the financial situation in the Metzger family deteriorated so badly that Friedrich August Metzger was going to inaugurate rationing. Max's situation was equally bad; he wrote on November 12, 1905, that although he was enjoying theology the food was so bad that he was wasting away. Nevertheless, he stayed on and did very well in his studies.

Max, however, still had the old problem of being a bit headstrong. Dr. Conrad Gröber reported that Max's talent—even in music—was very good and his application and religious moral attitude quite good in general, but that in his entire character he was very ambitious, fickle, forward, and inclined toward particular friendships [a *terminus technicus* for what at one extreme is cliquishness, but which are often normal friendships in boarding schools]. Gröber felt that "this highly talented young man" might have a vocation to the priesthood, but that if he were to become a good priest it would behoove Freiburg to maintain a watchful eye and a firm hand which would "humble his high-flying spirit." He recommended that any eventual request to study at a university other than Freiburg should not be granted until Metzger's character had "clarified itself so that he seeks only God in the priesthood and not himself. From all appearances the parents did not spare the incense when it came to their only son, and if he is reproved and a warning is given, the defense of the son rings louder in one's ears than the well-intentioned voice of the superior in charge."

An undated report (*Skrutinialbericht*, probably from 1908) from the theological seminary said that Max tended to take a leading role in various matters—the writer assumed this stemmed from his family training—and that although he took admonitions all right, he had not as yet attained the desired humility. Max was never at any time in his life one to follow in step for its own sake. *Er tanzt aus der Reihe* (he danced out of line), as one of his colleagues later said.

In May 1908, Max asked for permission to continue his theological studies to a doctorate, since he would be below the canonical age for ordination by the time he finished the regular seminary course of studies. He hoped to do his further work at the University of Bonn. (It is still quite common for Catholic students for the priesthood in Germany to study at two different universities during their philosophical and theological studies.) The adviser at the *Konvikt* wrote to the chancery office at the same time supporting Max's request to study for a doctorate but suggested that Bonn would be unsatisfactory because Max would not be able to live in a religious house (*Konvikt*) while studying there—it was felt he needed the direction. Innsbruck was then mentioned. However, Max later submitted a request for Fribourg in Switzerland, partly because he wanted to improve his French. And this is where Max finally went for several semesters, after which he returned to Freiburg in Germany to complete his studies.

While at the University of Freiburg Metzger devoted a large portion of his time to church history studies under the direction of Professor Georg Pfeilschifter, who later published a small book entitled *Die kirchliche Wiedervereinigungsbestrebungen der Nachkriegszeit* (Reunion Efforts of the Churches in the Post-war Period). Max's lifelong friend and school comrade, Monsignor Wilhelm Baumeister, wrote that

> in connection with the Freiburg church historian Pfeilschifter, it should never be forgotten that he really understood how to introduce the young students in his church history seminar to serious, scholarly

research. Already in the first semester of theological studies [Metzger] produced, as a result of this discipline, scholarly lectures on St. Fridolin, the patron saint of Oberrhein.

It was under this same professor that Max finished his work for a doctorate in theology. For his prize-winning doctoral thesis he edited and compared the theological contents of two medieval pontificales. This is a concrete indication of Metzger's early interest in liturgical renewal. The responses to the 1914 publication of his dissertation were all positive, including, for example, the evaluation of Josef Braun in *Stimmen der Zeit*: "All in all the present book is a first-rate work and an admirable contribution to liturgical scholarship."

The young Metzger.

By the end of the summer semester of 1910, Max was finished with his theological course work and was able to take the examinations. He wrote to Father Gaenshirt that he was really happy to have his exams behind him, for he found working for deadlines not only exhausting but also incompatible, making it impossible for him ever to delve into individual questions and tracts which particularly interested him, at least not to the extent he wished. He felt one always had to hurry so as to get through everything, and in that regard he liked the examination system at Fribourg much more. There, one's whole attention could be limited to a restricted number of theses, which one could pick according to one's own taste—the purpose of the examination not being to prove that one knew relatively everything, but that one had learned a method, that is, knew the principal perspectives from which the individual questions of a discipline must be approached.

> I am just now beginning to realize the work was exhausting. Even though I fortunately don't have any discomfort or physical distress this year I nevertheless am very tired out now and feel a real need for a period of complete relaxation. Most of all I would like to go to the mountains for a short while and lie under the Black Forest pines, alone and still. But there doesn't seem to be any chance of that. I would be only too happy to go up to the Altglashuette for a week by myself—but it's taken!

This letter exhibits quite a mature attitude toward study—no longer the need to excel for its own sake or for praise. The same growing maturity was exhibited by another letter Max wrote December 29 to a group of his friends (a so-called *Freundesbund*). He said that his aim was not to become a scholar, or someday to obtain an honored and comfortable position, but rather to become a committed priest and pastor and

> to develop all my powers for the honor of God. In what area of work I shall be placed I gladly leave to divine Providence: *Deus providebit*. If I have often thought of a particular position it was not, believe me, you have my solemn assurance on this, because of egotistical concerns, but because, after much prayer, I believed, through God's enlightenment, myself to be directed that way, because I felt I could put my talents to work most fruitfully right there where I could develop enthusiasm for Christ and the Church in those circles on which so much depends. My efforts in my studies are not in order to attain a specific goal, but to develop me ascetically as well as in an all-around scholarly-practical way so that as a pastor I can accomplish the most useful tasks for the honor of God regardless to which post the divine plan will direct me.

While a student, Max drank beer and wine along with his comrades. It could hardly have been otherwise living amid some of the most beautiful wine country in the world; the Black Forest—*Weinstrasse*—runs right through Freiburg. His classmates relate that he never failed to empty the bottle of beer that he, along with the other theological students, received every day. But Max's habits in this regard changed radically during his stay in Fribourg, Switzerland. While there he first became acquainted with the problems of alcoholism. Along with other members of the student St. Vincent de Paul Society, he spent his Sundays working with children from the slum areas of the city. But he was soon impressed with the futility of bringing wholesome recreation to those children one day a week when the other six days would more than destroy all his efforts.

Temperance

One of the most pernicious of the forces of destruction, he felt, was alcoholism. What sense did it make to deliver coupons for bread, meat, coal, and such necessities when whatever money was earned went to the taverns? Max decided one had to attack not the symptoms but the root of so many of the social problems he saw. Since he could not ask anyone to do something he did not do, he pledged himself to total abstinence from alcohol. Metzger's decision was a purely practical one. He saw tremendous social misery all around him and saw alcohol figuring prominently in the midst of it. He joined with millions of others in Europe and America during this period—the movement reached its climax in America only in the Prohibition era of the twenties and early thirties—in combating alcoholism.

Max made further revealing remarks in the 1910 letter to his Freiburg group of friends (the *Freundesbund*—besides this small number of German friends Max also established the beginnings of many international friendships during his Swiss study days).

> It was just this [abstinence] that for my further moral development was of decisive significance. At that time, I for once acted in earnestness so that to the beautiful words of love I added a deed which cut into my own flesh. For the first time I recognized the moral significance of the spirit of sacrifice.

Metzger did not insist on complete abstinence for others, although he was often very persuasive. He himself embraced total abstinence because he thought this example was needed to draw the intemperate to temperance. Already before his ordination, Max had expressed these sentiments rather precisely in a letter to Father Gaenshirt.

> Of course, I would forbid no man his glass of wine. I see abstinence now as always only as the means—toward a general and ideal moderation. To the degree that I go to all lengths to win as many as possible over to abstinence, and thereby overcome the present-day problem of alcoholism, do I also reject any attempt to force anyone by external means to accept it. As much as I view it as a moral obligation for youth to offer up this sacrifice for the love of neighbor, I would never begrudge an older person's following his custom of drinking his glass in moderation—for him it would physically and morally be a much more difficult sacrifice than for us young ones. I believe you can accept and approve my position.

The concerns Max developed during his student days included more than the study of theology and liturgy and active involvement. Also, in the 1910 letter to the *Freundesbund* he outlined his aims, in addition to promoting the abstinence movement, from which he expected a "spiritual religious renewal" of the people (much as did many earnest temperance people in America). They included pastoral care among students and intellectuals, especially through the *Akademischen Bonifatius Verein*, social welfare work of all types, and the formation of a "Vita communis" of Reminded priests similar to the Oratorians—in other words, the expansion and eventual formalization of the *Freundesbund*. Max eventually undertook all of these projects.

Max spent the academic year 1910-11 at St. Peter's Seminary, a beautiful old Benedictine abbey that had been secularized in the Napoleonic period and returned to church authorities in the twentieth century; it stands high up in the Black Forest mountains just a forty-five-minute drive by car from Freiburg. It is here the last year of a seminarian's training is spent in order to fulfill the canonical prescription of one year's seminary training for students for the priesthood. In June of 1911, Max was ordained a priest. He celebrated his first Mass in his uncle's church in Oberhausen. His friend Father Baumeister, who, because he had not taken on any additional theological studies, had been ordained the year before, served as deacon, and a comrade of Max's from the Polish provinces of Prussia, Father Codes, was sub-deacon. Father Banholzer, who showed up later in Metzger's life as a rather vicious enemy, was invited by Max to take Baumeister's place in case he couldn't come at the last minute.

EARLY PASTORAL WORK

Father Metzger's first assignment after his ordination was to the large city parish of Sts. Peter and Paul in the industrial city of Karlsruhe. He arrived on August 31, 1911, and was transferred on October 11, 1912. In his months at Karlsruhe, young Father Metzger earned from his pastor a highly indignant report to the chancery office on the occasion of his transfer. Metzger was described as self-willed, self-confident, shunning advice, ambitious, and, worst of all, as having done some things without having informed the pastor. Oh, he was full of energy and very talented, particularly in music, but he was ruining his ability because he had become a fanatic on abstinence—he even wrote and composed all sorts of things for it. The pastor complained that Father Metzger had ruined a youth society by pushing abstinence too much; he even had those members from age ten on up writing essays on alcohol. The pastor also mentioned that Father Metzger had been active in the *Kreuzbündnis*, a Catholic temperance society, and that he had arranged for some religious speakers on temperance.

Monsignor Wilhelm Baumeister, who eventually became an important figure in the archdiocese social work and the national Caritas organization, also knew of Father Metzger's activities at the time and evaluated them somewhat differently. According to Baumeister, the archdiocese of Freiburg owed Metzger a debt of gratitude for his thorough organization of a widespread preaching tour by the prominent Franciscan, Father Elpidius from Cologne, which led to the founding of Catholic temperance organizations throughout the archdiocese. Father Metzger also published numerous articles and brochures on alcoholism during this period, continuing the work of his student days when, for example, in a letter from Fribourg to his aunt he included a rather long poem on Christian temperance which he had just published. In this first year of pastoral activity the work that achieved probably the greatest popularity was his re-editing of Neumann's *Mässigkeitskatechismus* (Catechism of Temperance); it went through seven editions and, as his friend Msgr. Baumeister remarked, "spread clear ideas on the foundation and goals of Catholic temperance work everywhere." Later when Cathedral Dean Simon Hirt wrote Metzger's necrology, he merely referred to this Karlsruhe report as describing Father Metzger as the most zealous of abstinence pioneers in the diocese.

Father Metzger was hardly finished with bad reports from his ecclesiastical superiors. From October 12, 1912, to January 27, 1914, Father Metzger served as parish assistant in Mannheim, another industrial city. Here he fortunately found a like-minded priest, Father Risch, as another assistant. But his second pastor was less pleased, for when he learned that Father Metzger was about to be transferred, he immediately wrote to the chancery office requesting that the replacement not be an anti-alcohol man, since he was still richly blessed in this regard with Father Risch. Apparently, there were a number of younger priests in the diocese who were interested in the temperance movement, since the pastor made a strong point of saying that he and his elder colleagues could not see the advisability of devoting much time to this movement.

It was only a little more than seven months later when the same pastor submitted a service report on Father Metzger in which the criticism of the first pastor's report was matched and even surpassed. Father Metzger was described as capable and efficient, but the pastor qualified this by adding that Metzger could accomplish still more if he were not over-involved in abstinence work. Then the Mannheim pastor shot out some scathing remarks of the sort that Father Metzger inspired time and again throughout his life.

> I even have the impression that he hoodwinked the gentlemen in Freiburg. Had they known him they would not have accepted him into the seminary. This is not meant as an accusation against the Konvikt administration; Metzger is very sly and at the right moment he can be very disarming. Apparently already as a young lad he was too far gone. *He lacks sincerity of character.*

Some fifty years later, Msgr. Baumeister, who never knew about this report, mentioned that Metzger's unusual power of convincing people of the reasonableness of what he was saying and doing probably won Metzger many enemies; people resent being talked into or out of something, if only subconsciously. People could be angry with Metzger before or after meeting him, but never while talking to him.

Msgr. Baumeister appears to have described perfectly the reaction of the pastor from Mannheim. He apparently had been persuaded to accept or condone things which he probably could not effectively gainsay while Father Metzger was talking to him, things that probably did not fit in with the pastor's old patterns of thinking and doing. Only after Metzger left the room did the pastor begin to realize what he had let himself in for. This no doubt happened time and again during Metzger's two years in Mannheim, and, given the seven months between Father Metzger's departure and the writing of the regular report, time during which the pastor could settle back into his old ways and realize how far he had been pulled along by Father Metzger, it is not at all surprising that he complained loudly that he, and anyone else who had not resisted Metzger, had been duped by him.

What is surprising though is the fact that both the pastors, the one from Karlsruhe and from Mannheim, simultaneously sent Metzger what purported to be copies of their reports on him to the chancery at Freiburg; one would not have recognized the priest spoken of in the copies as being the same. The copy Metzger received was positive, whereas the copy sent to the archbishop was, of course, very negative. One of many examples is the following. The Freiburg version read: "One can see no evidence of a solid scholarly education." The version sent to Metzger: "Scholarly education is very good." Such duplicity rather deeply undermines the confidence one can place in the evaluation these men made of Metzger.

Father Metzger spent the seven months following his transfer from Mannheim assisting his uncle in Oberhausen who had become quite ill with a cancer that eventually caused his death.

WORLD WAR I

August 3, 1914. Germany marched into France amid the enthusiasm of the German populace. National patriotism was at its peak in all European countries, and each felt it was justified in entering the war. Even though Germany was forced to sign the guilt clause after her defeat, most scholars have long since concluded that France, Russia, Austria, and others share equally or more in this guilt. Hence, it is not difficult to understand how each populace felt its cause was the just and noble one. It is also not difficult to understand how young Father Max Metzger, the same lad who had been so wildly enthusiastic about the Kaiser's visit some fourteen years before, could write to the archbishop asking permission to volunteer as a front-lines chaplain—on August 3, 1914. Father Metzger left no record of how much, if any, his motives were influenced by patriotism or how much by pastoral zeal to be where the need was most pressing. Probably both elements, along with others, were there.

Max Josef Metzger, Chaplain
in the First World War, 1914-15

Unfortunately, not very many of Father Metzger's letters from the front seem to be extant. Those few that are available were all written during the two months from the end of February to the beginning of May 1915. This was a relatively quiet period on the Western front, which may be why his letters reveal very little revulsion for the war. He mentioned that he was quite satisfied with his activity since he found a much more open-hearted response among the troops than at home. In rather soldier-like fashion he described being at a French castle near Cirez which had been owned by a former Bavarian officer who had fought against the French in 1870, and who had later become a naturalized French citizen. "He was shot during the battle because he had been directing the fight from the lookout—in favor of the French!" This same rather nonchalant attitude toward warfare showed itself again in a letter to his uncle on March 24, 1915. He wrote that things were going along in rather pedestrian fashion. "Everything, praise God, is well as usual." He then casually mentioned that his division's dragoons had been attacked yesterday and the day before and had lost nine killed and fifty wounded.

May 6, 1915, he was decorated with the Iron Cross for "self-sacrificing actions" and particularly for courageous work in the frontline trenches of the 42nd cavalry brigade. When writing to his archbishop the same day he added that note only in a postscript. In these letters there is nothing of the vigorous pacifist of the future. The experiences of the summer and fall of 1915 must have deeply changed Father Metzger, but we have no record of these experiences.

Still, in the spring of 1915 a decision was made by Father Metzger that shaped the whole of his subsequent life. As a result of his earlier abstinence activities, his reputation as an energetic and efficient organizer had traveled as far as Austria. In the first part of 1915, Professor Johann Ude, a Catholic priest, visited Metzger's home in Freiburg in an attempt to recruit him as general secretary of the Austrian *Kreuzbündnis* (League of the Cross). Since Father Metzger was at the front, he wrote him of his offer. Metzger did not even consider leaving the army to take up this offer. He, like most other Germans, expected the war to be over rather soon and fully expected to serve till its end. Moreover, he had some other rather specific plans for his post-war work.

In writing to his uncle, he said that although he would in many ways have liked to take on the organizational work that was waiting in Austria, he had almost completely rejected it from the beginning, for he had another plan. He hoped to return to the university to prepare himself for social and urban pastoral work; some members of the theological faculty and the chancery officials had encouraged him in this. Nevertheless, Father Metzger wrote to his archbishop and presented the two choices to him and asked for his advice in the matter. Father Metzger felt that the archbishop's answer showed a decided displeasure with him. The archbishop declared he could not and did not wish to decide the question, but if Metzger wanted to go, he would give him a leave of absence.

> My Freiburg plan he handled in an almost despising manner so I see that in this direction there will be at best no hope of encouragement from him. Past judgements of me by Gröber [Metzger's former *Konvikt* rector, and future archbishop] are always plaguing me and it appears that no effort on my part can change things. It is a bitter experience for me, but of course it does not make me turn bitter. But so much is certain for me now: in my own diocese for years to come I will have to reckon with receiving in my work not encouragement but rather restrictions and discouragements from above. Consequently, I have no prospect in the foreseeable future of receiving a responsible post in my own diocese in which I could be satisfied with the work. You know me and my abilities. To just sit quietly for years—I can't do it. That would be the death of my nature as God gave it to me. And I cannot, indeed may not allow exactly those talents with which I can contribute something simply to go to waste. On this everything depends, as far as I am concerned. So it is that the longer I think about it the more I come to the conclusion that perhaps the whole thing is a providential act of God. The task that awaits me in Austria is not a particularly esteemed one or one that is likely to bring me great honor, but it is one that is doubtless full of blessings. Whereas the Freiburg plan had perhaps attracted me more because the fruitful work also promised an externally very attractive position. Perhaps God wishes to lead me in this manner along the more thorny path? I don't know.
>
> . . . So, I really don't know what to do or what I should decide . . . . I pray and seek to recognize God's holy will and ask you to do the same and also ask your opinion, which certainly will weigh in the balance of the final decision. (March 24, 1915)

By the sixth of May 1915, Father Metzger made his decision to accept the invitation to go to Graz, Austria, as general secretary of the *Kreuzbündnis* and head of the *Priests' Abstinence League* after the end of the war. In his letter to the archbishop informing him of his decision, Father Metzger included a brief paragraph in which he very carefully and politely told the archbishop he was aware of his position in the Freiburg diocese. "Although on one hand the decision weighed very heavily on me, I nevertheless believed I had to grasp the opportunity because in this position, at least under the present conditions at any rate, I can best serve the salvation of souls."

The consummation of Father Metzger's decision did not have to wait until 1918. In the fall of 1915, he developed a severe case of lung inflammation and was discharged from the Army. He was free to take up his new post, and that October he left for Graz.

SOCIAL AND APOSTOLIC WORK

The nineteenth century in general spawned all sorts of reforms, and the disastrous advent of World War I merely reinforced many of these reform movements, including the temperance movement. In the United States the prohibitionists were able to gather the necessary support for a constitutional amendment; in the beginning of the 1920s the vast majority of the American people, if not actively in favor of prohibition, were willing to go along with it for the sake of the common good. It should also be recalled that because of various circumstances the deleterious effects of alcohol were probably much more widespread a half-century ago than today. For example, it was almost impossible to buy a nonalcoholic drink in German restaurants; they simply did not sell soft drinks or fruit juices in those days. In any case, temperance work around the time of World War I was not the work of just a lunatic fringe. Max Metzger stood in the midst of the mainstream of reform. He was concerned with complete renewal of society, and, as will be seen, founded an organization which he hoped would serve as a many-edged instrument that would help bring it about. Like many others, Metzger thought temperance was one of the essential cutting edges.

Graz Temperance Work

Upon his arrival in Graz, Father Metzger took over the position of general secretary of the Catholic League of the Cross of Austria (*Katholische Kreuzbündnis Oesterreich*), successor to the Catholic League of the Cross against Alcoholism for Austria (*Katholische Kreuzbündnis gegen Alkoholismus für Oesterreich*). The *Kreuzbündnis* was a nonpolitical society whose purpose was "to combat alcoholism through natural and supernatural means which are both curative and preventive, and to cooperate in building the health, commercial, social, moral, and religious aspects of life on foundations of sobriety." Besides a personal example of temperance by the members, and publicizing of the problem and its solution, the society promoted effective legislation, supported establishments for the cure of alcoholism, and provided alcohol-free education of youth. Connected with this general temperance league was the Priests' Abstinence League of Salzburg of which Father Metzger was also general secretary. The whole program seems to have had wholehearted episcopal support. Metzger himself quoted from the local bishop's statement of June 19, 1916: "The Ordinary wishes that the *Katholische Kreuzbündnis* in its noble and extremely important efforts to combat alcoholism ... be most energetically supported and fostered by the reverend clergy."

Much of the work consisted of writing and editing. On December 9, 1915, he was elected head of publications for the *Katholische Kreuzbündnis*, which had as its headquarters the *Volksheilzentrale* in Graz, Austria—the building included a large alcohol-free restaurant. The movement had two organs, one aimed at adults and one at youth, the *Oesterreichs Kreuzzug* (Austria's Crusade) and the *Oesterreichs Kinderkreuzzug* (Austria's Children's Crusade). Metzger handled the adult magazine himself and delegated the work of the second, though still retaining responsibility for both. But already in 1916, the demands on his time were so great that he asked for additional help in his editorial work. Besides this magazine work and the directing of the Volksheil Publishing Company, Metzger also wrote fifteen brochures and booklets for the *Volksheil Verlag* between 1917 and 1920.

Yet he found time for a demanding lecture schedule. During 1916 alone he delivered 119 lectures and talks on alcoholism from Graz and Linz in Austria to Freiburg and Berlin in Germany. Although his audiences were of a varied sort, he had a particularly close and personal relationship with the German *Kreuzbündnis* and the German *Quickborn* youth organization, (a German Catholic youth group, begun about the time of the First World War, which brought the idealism and commitment of youth to the renewal of the Church; under the leadership of Romano Guardini it was strongly influenced by the liturgical revival). So great was Metzger's enthusiasm for the *Quickborn* movement at this time that he gave lectures in Vienna, St. Poelten, Linz, Salzburg, and Innsbruck to promote the movement in Austria.

On October 15, 1916, the *Kreuzbündnis* held a conference in Graz; 1,200 representatives from all parts of the Austro-Hungarian Empire were present. On the opening day it was declared that

> although out on all fronts cannons are still roaring and battlefields greedily drink up the blood of Christian peoples of Europe, the Catholic *Kreuzbündnis* of Austria calls all of its individual members and groups and the whole public to a large peace conference .... All forces should be gathered for the defeat of the 'most dangerous internal enemy of our people.'

This most dangerous internal enemy was, of course, alcoholism. This conference, to which both the Austrian and German emperors sent telegrams, thus brought together two matters which so intimately concerned Max Metzger throughout his life: the causes of temperance and of peace.

In the courtyard of the Johannesheim with distribution of work for those recovering from alcoholism.

Renewal of Society Through Religion

Although Father Metzger saw alcohol as a critical problem in the life of society, he felt that society's ills demanded reform in many other areas as well, that there was a whole circle of evil that ringed Western humanity which had to be broken at every point. But Metzger believed this reform should be inspired by a religious spirit. It was not sufficient to merely establish another organization or two in nineteenth-century fashion. Renewal was needed not only in society but also in the Church, and the renewal of each depended in large measure on both learning to care about the other.

Effectively renewing the Church and society had long been a central concern for Father Metzger. Even during his student days in Fribourg, Switzerland, he had begun to lay the groundwork for the many organizations he later founded, with the *Mission Society of the White Cross*—later called the *Society of Christ the King*—as their dynamic center. While at Fribourg he formed his international "friendship league" with a number of his fellow seminarians, young priests, and a little later, lay people. This league was one of the first two roots of the future Society.

The second root was provided by Father Wilhelm Impekovin, a member of the Steyler Congregation. The two men met at a conference of the German Catholic *Kreuzbund* in 1911, the year Metzger was ordained. At one of the meetings Metzger spoke with youthful vigor, and afterwards Father Impekovin, later known as Brother Gottwills, came up to him, shook his hand and said, "We two belong together." The two men discussed their plans and exchanged ideas.

> He [Br. Gottwills] came more from the 'religious' side and I more from the 'social.' However, as we discussed our thoughts together we found that they matched amazingly well. For I could conceive of effective social action, far-reaching relief for the social needs of the day only through the renewal of the parched wellsprings of [the] power of Christianity. And Brother Gottwills was too much a friend of all the poor and too much a 'Christian' with the deepest bonds with his Master to be able to imagine 'religiosity' without its working out in everyday life, or in a Christianity of deeds without far-reaching social charity. And so, overwhelmed by the moment, we shook hands with the idealism of youth and promised that with God's grace we would join forces in the future.

Founding of the White Cross

In 1912, Brother Gottwills started his "World League of the White Cross" by simply drawing up a set of aims and constitution for his organization and getting signatures—he started with three. (The name comes from the white cross that is normally impressed on the Mass host and reflects the revival of the devotion to the Eucharist.) Brother Gottwills gathered commitments and signatures wherever he found a sympathetic hearing. Although the project moved ahead very slowly, on Good Friday 1913, Brother Gottwills decided to celebrate the public founding of his world league during the convention of a Catholic society held in Merzig, Germany.

But the events of August 1914 canceled all plans for several years. Brother Gottwills became a chaplain on the Western front and developed what then apparently was a new technique with his *Kapellenauto* (chapel car). At first the vehicle was to serve simply to bring a Mass altar to the front. But each succeeding truck became larger and took on new functions such as serving as a mobile library and a medical aid station.

In the meanwhile, Father Metzger's work progressed in Graz. Yet he continued to move toward the founding of his own organization that would provide the enduring inner vitalizing elan to the various institutions and groups with which he was involved. A further step was taken in this direction by the founding of the "World Peace League," an international peace organization of Catholics, in 1916. That same year, Brother Gottwills visited Metzger in Graz and mentioned that he had changed the name of his "World League of the White Cross" to "World Peace League of the White Cross." Consequently, when in the following summer Brother Gottwills came to Graz to permanently join Metzger, they decided to merge what there was of their organizations and give the new body the name "World Peace Work of the White Cross." That summer they both worked on the details of the organization that was slowly being molded.

Graz, Austria: Metzger with his first co-workers, 1917.

Within the next two years the organization took rather definite shape and settled on names that would be stable for a number of years. The broad, generic organization was given the simple title of "White Cross (Catholic Inner Mission)," and the smaller central group was named the "Mission Society of the White Cross." This latter was to be a "whole order with the openness and mobility of laity," consisting of men and women, married and single, lay and clerical. There were to be three groups within this "Catholic Salvation Army," as Metzger sometimes referred to it. The first was to consist of those who had a vocation to the common life with the observance of the three religious vows; these were to be neither public nor permanent but renewed every year on the feast of the Sacred Heart. This group was to be the nucleus or inspirational force for the other two groups. The second section was to consist of free members (*Freiregulierte*) who, although they often lived in a community, were not necessarily to remain celibate and therefore could live outside the community as assistants in ordinary or extraordinary pastoral work; they were expected to go where a religious community (*Regulierte Gemeinschaft*) could not penetrate. The members of the third group were to remain in their individual jobs and carry on the work of Christianizing their milieu, not unlike members of a Third Order.

The Mission Society of the White Cross (*Missionsgesellschaft vom Weissen Kreuz*), whose name was changed for the last time in 1925 to "Society of Christ the King" (*Gesellschaft Christi des Königs*), had no specific apostolate, but rather provided a common spirit and rules to live by; work would be decided upon as the needs in society appeared. The society did not wish to undertake tasks already handled by other orders; it wanted to fill gaps caused by a rapidly changing social environment.

> They envisaged works of all kinds . . . pastoral work, spiritual work, works of mercy, the winning of lay apostles, work for peace and for the unity of the Church, efforts to promote wholesome and simple living, and to provide help for those suffering under the un-Christian economic order of the day.

Already early in 1917, Brother Gottwills insisted that if the new society was to grow at all it needed a house. Metzger agreed but was skeptical about getting the necessary money. Brother Gottwills maintained that "God will provide." So he and Metzger agreed that they would select a suitable house, take an option on it, and if the necessary money was not available by the time the option ran out they would abandon the project. Brother Gottwills chose a huge, several-story house which cost 200,000 Friedenskronen. They took an option which ran until Christmas 1917. Brother Gottwills solicited the countryside for the money and by that fall was able to collect only 12,000 Kronen. Matters suddenly improved, however. One of the occupants of the house, a well-to-do gentleman, was anxious about losing his fifteen-room apartment when he heard the house was to be sold. He approached Metzger and Gottwills and they reached an agreement; the man would buy the house in the name of the White Cross and he would have the right to live in his apartment for the rest of his life—he lived there for another twenty years.

In 1918, when Brother Gottwills gave a lecture at the Catholic seminary of Salzburg on the consecration of the family to the Sacred Heart, Edward Hasenbichler, a young priest in his year of pastoral training, was in the audience. He was so impressed by Brother Gottwills and by what he had to say about the White Cross Movement that he arranged to visit Graz later that year. He immediately felt content there, with the people and the work, and soon joined the society permanently, taking the name Brother Franz.

Max Josef Metzger with brothers of the Christkoenig community in Meitingen before the building was expanded.

These three, Brothers Paulus (Metzger), Gottwills, and Franz, seemed destined to be the heart of the White Cross. But events soon took another turn. Brother Gottwills, who had been in rather poor health for a long time, died. Brother Franz lived another five years in the Society and then his health, which also had always been precarious, also failed. He contracted tuberculosis and in September of 1923 he too died, leaving Brother Paulus to lead his growing community alone.

Support from Rome—Not from Home

Though Metzger and his society were often discouraged at the episcopal level, they received warm encouragement from the Vatican. As early as 1917 Metzger wrote to Pope Benedict XV about the founding of the World Peace League of the White Cross and received a most sympathetic reply from Cardinal Gasparri, the Secretary of State, on June 27 of that year.

> The Holy Father has taken notice of the program of this "Institution" which your Reverence and your colleagues humbly sent him with the letter dated February 20.

> The Supreme Pontiff, Vicar on Earth of the King of Peace, blesses your ardent desire to see peace restored quickly among nations, and prays that the full and precise observance in individual and social life of the principles of justice and charity preached by the Divine Master may forever protect the people from the horrors of war.
>
> I very gladly take advantage of this contact to reaffirm that I have a profound esteem of your Reverence and am ready affectionately to serve you,
>
> Cardinal Gasparri[1]

As difficulties seemed to multiply within the diocese, encouragement from the Vatican and the Pope himself increased. In the first two weeks of October 1920, Father Metzger went to Rome.

> I found a very friendly reception from his eminence, Cardinal Secretary of State Gasparri. His eminence was already well instructed about us and promised to make favorable arrangements concerning the matter of the Catholic International. I had the privilege of a longer private audience with the Holy Father, whom Cardinal Gasparri had already informed about us, and gave him a detailed report on the White Cross and the Catholic International. The Holy Father received me very graciously and was very interested in our work. As I spoke of the program of the whole apostolic work of the Holy Father he interrupted me with a meaningful gesture and the simple word 'Caritas.' This was my entire impression: the Holy Father lives entirely for the idea of spreading the Christian love of neighbor more among Christians and thereby also serving social peace. Since this is exactly

---

[1] Il Santo Padre ha preso conoscenza del programma di cotesta "Opera", che la S.V. Illma ed i suoi Colleghi Gli umiliavano con la lettera in data del 20 Febbraio u.s.

L. Augusto Pontefice, Vicario in Terra del Re Pacifico benedice il Loro ardente desiderio de vedere presto ristabilita la. pace tra le Nazioni, e fa voti che la piena ed esatta osservanza, nella vita individuale e sociale, di principii di giustizia e di carita predicati dal Divin Maestro, allontani per sempre dai popoli gli orrori della guerra.

Profitto ben volentieri dell' incontro per raffermarmi con sensi di distinta stima.

di V.S. Illma
Affmo per servirla
Card. Gasparri

the program of the White Cross the Holy Father understandably rejoiced in it and encouraged me in further work. The Holy Father indicated the possibility of a written recommendation of our work.

I found particular support in his eminence Cardinal Fruehwirt, who immediately became a member of the White Cross and enthusiastically promised to enter into our work. Full of enthusiasm he said: 'You Hungarian morning star and you Jewish morning star! You all will pale before the morning star which comes up from Graz.'

I found so much understanding in Rome and so little in this diocese. Yesterday I visited the 'Chancellor' of the diocese. As I reported to him about our work he said to me: "Listen, our attitude is that if a priest prays his breviary and says his Mass correctly and correctly prepares himself for preaching and catechetics, that is absolutely enough. There is absolutely no need for an organization besides this pastoral care!"

One of the earliest sources of Metzger's difficulties with the diocesan officials and many of the clergy in Graz was his involvement in a public debate in 1916 about the moral obligation of total abstinence in the contemporary social circumstances. The debate was carried on in articles and pamphlets between Metzger and Karl Weiss, professor of moral theology at the University of Graz. The discussion grew very heated and polemical and, in the end, earned Metzger the continuing ill will of the Austrian episcopacy in general and that of Graz in particular, despite Metzger's public apology.

Farewelling of apostolic workers, Meitingen, 1934.

At about the same time Metzger ran into difficulties within the *Kreuzbündnis*, the consequences of which were to plague him the rest of his years in Austria. A serious difference of opinion developed between Professor Ude, the president of the *Kreuzbündnis* and the leadership of the Vienna wing of the organization. Metzger attempted to avoid a permanent split by acting as a mediator; he suggested a new presidential election and suggested two compromise candidates. Ude rejected, and resented, this intervention, with the result that Ude, who was soon relatively reconciled with his opponent in Vienna, turned his anger, and that of all his followers, on Metzger, who he thought was maneuvering to become president himself. Ude soon attempted by vote, and other means, to have Metzger ousted from the executive committee of the *Kreuzbündnis*—but to no avail. Ude himself then withdrew, but not his followers. They sent in, as Metzger later wrote, "petitions against me to the governorship, to the bishop, to the ministry . . . . I was denounced to the state attorney, the Christian-Social party was incited, etc. All these machinations were to no avail." However, in some instances they very nearly did succeed. For example, in 1920 a very serious effort was made to have Metzger deported. The red herring was dragged out—Metzger once provided refuge to a communist fleeing from Germany. At the last moment, however, Metzger's Austrian citizenship papers came through. For the next few years resentment against Metzger seemed quiescent.

Growth of the White Cross

Despite its problems the White Cross grew, and by Easter of 1922, Brother Franz could report that there were about fifty members of the Mission Society of the White Cross—the inner group—about half of them sisters and half priests and brothers. Although the next four years were particularly difficult for the White Cross and Metzger, the sisters in the society were able to expand their work in some areas. They reported in 1926 that there were twenty-two *regulierte* sisters, three novices and two postulants, and also eight *freiregulierte* and *freie* sisters who labored full-time in mission work and twenty-eight *freie* sisters who worked part time. The men's group had shrunk considerably, having eight *regulierte* brothers, including novices and postulants, plus seventeen *freiregulierte* and *freie* brothers.

At the same time the White Cross also reported having houses and/or members in and near Graz, Vienna, Lausanne, Bruenn in Czechoslovakia, Pettau in Hungary, London, and Frankfurt. Besides these mission stations the White Cross had small groups or individual members in Yugoslavia, Italy, Belgium,

Holland, France, Denmark, and the Union of South Africa. The work was various, including assisting in pastoral work, social work, care for families and children, homes for the aged, retreat houses, alcohol-free restaurants, street preaching, recreation work, promotion of the liturgy, Bible study, abstinence, peace work, and instruction in Esperanto. Members published a number of books and pamphlets and also a series of monthly newspapers: *Friedensruf, Friedensherold, Neue Zeit* (discontinued in 1921), *Katholika Mondo* (in Esperanto), *Katholischer Missionsruf* (9,000 subscribers), *Ruf zu Wahrheit, Gerechtigkeit und Liebe* (17,000 subscribers), *Frohe Jugend* (10,000 subscribers), *Heimatmission und Laienapostolat (pro Domo)*, and *Christoenigsbote*. In later years the society continued to expand and develop in the area of social work.[2]

At the time of Metzger's death in 1944, the society was still engaged in an extraordinary variety of social work, even though the Nazis and the war restricted activity greatly. By then the establishment at Meitingen, a small village about a dozen miles from Augsburg, had become the mother house.[3]

---

[2] For the year 1937, for example, they reported:
Care for:
        68 people living in poverty for 1,515 days
        25 people addicted to alcohol for 3,079 days
        25 people with mental health conditions for 7,282 days
Distribution of:
        10,003 meals to people living in poverty
        12,406 meals to children
        806 items of material assistance, like clothes
Services rendered:
        853 days of care for sick people
        280 nights of care (note: this is besides a full day's work!)
        15,717 nights of lodging for women and girls
        2,180 sewing hours for people living in poverty
        1,500 families and children cared for on Christmas Eve
Spiritual services:
        10 retreats - 202 participants
        40 days of recollection - 1,949 participants
        4 apostolic vacation weeks - 89 participants
Distribution of literature:
        58,777 items of a general sort
        10,670 mission letters
        3,593 brochures, etc. free to people living in poverty

[3] Here they conducted a home for sober living, which was later converted into a home for the aged, a home for transients, and another for incapacitated persons. At the end of 1936 the direction of this last was turned over to the Sisters of the Holy Family from Munich. In Augsburg an alcohol-free restaurant and refreshment place serving only

For many years Metzger found it impossible to obtain ecclesiastical approbation of the statutes of the society, which naturally made it much more difficult to attract vocations and to move into new dioceses. However, after many tedious and painful attempts, approval was finally obtained from the bishop of Bruenn, Czechoslovakia, on April 22, 1929. The society, by now named the Society of Christ the King, was canonically described as an international pius union. The three types of membership were reduced to two, the *regulierte* who made yearly promises of poverty, chastity, and obedience, and the *freie* who lived in the spirit of the rule "in the world." The spirit and structure of the society was much like that of the present secular institutes—they had no existence in canon law then—which is what the Society of Christ the King is today. This aim of having committed religious individuals in the world even manifested itself in the matter of dress. Today the secular institute members wear no habit, but a few years ago such an innovation would have been considered a revolution. Instead, Metzger insisted that the *regulierte* sisters' garb be simple and neat and as unclerical in appearance as possible. The habit looked much like that worn by the nurses of the twenties and thirties in Germany.

The "Time of Troubles"

The year 1924 proved to be a bad one for Metzger and the White Cross. Central Europe was in the depths of disastrous inflation, and this was one of the roots of Metzger's legal troubles. Shortly after the war, Metzger, with two other men, had founded a consumers' cooperative *Wirtschaft Gemeinschaft*, *Wige*, which prospered until 1924. Disastrous economic circumstances led to a run on the *Wige* by the stockholders and then to bankruptcy. Since Metzger

---

non-alcoholic drinks was begun. The society took on assistant pastoral and sacristan work and the care of convalescents in Berlin-Aldershof while maintaining in Berlin itself the "Piusstift," which included a kindergarten and a combination home and hospital for poor people. Some members of the society were employed in a social work secretariat in Bruenn where the Sisters also conducted a home for unmarried girls and women. At Buchenlust they operated a home for people with epilepsy and a home for the elderly and persons with disabilities until the Nazis confiscated both in 1940. The Nazis also confiscated a home for young girls in Graz and a nursery in Untertanowitz. In Friedrichshafen on Lake Constance in Graz, and in Soemmerda in Thuringia, members took over assistant pastoral work; in Lobberich in the Rhineland and at Pforzheim they performed family help and social work; in Gleiwitz they maintained an alcohol-free restaurant and home for working girls. In addition to these "official" foundations there was also the work done by the members of the third section of the society, those remaining at their various professions.

held an important position on the board of directors, he was involved in the litigation. Moreover, it was a common misconception that the *Wige* and the White Cross were one and in order to clarify this matter, Metzger had to go to court.

But this was only the beginning of Metzger's legal difficulties. For the next five or six years he was involved in a series of court cases, all of them generated by one man, a Brother Bonaventure Baser of the third order of St. Francis. Baser seems to have lived on a righteous sort of hate—he had earlier been dropped from religious life because of his constant troublemaking and pathological tendencies. Baser took it upon himself to champion everyone who had some sort of grievance against Metzger. A few examples will suffice.

An alcohol-free restaurant was started in Graz just before the war by a *Kreuzbündnis* organization, the predecessor to the one Metzger became secretary of in 1915; it was taken over by this successor *Kreuzbündnis* organization. After the war, this restaurant, along with some other activities, were absorbed by the White Cross since support for the *Kreuzbündnis* was declining and it could no longer adequately handle the work. The running of the restaurant was put in the hands of Elizabeth Bayer who quickly made it solvent as well as a great benefit to the public. (The restaurant provided healthful meals for less than 15 cents and seated 1,000 persons.) In 1923, Bayer decided she did not want to continue her formal association with the society—everything remained amicable, however—and so it was decided that she would buy the restaurant and thereby ensure its efficient continuation, which was all that Metzger and the White Cross were interested in. Baser, a former member of the *Kreuzbündnis*, saw fraud here and went to court to claim that the restaurant was not legally the White Cross's to sell. Despite many efforts, he was never able to make good his claim.

In January of 1924, a Mr. Heller was invited on a trial basis from Cologne to take over the running of the *Paulusverlag*, the Society's publishing company. After only a few weeks it was decided he was not capable of the job—he was hard of hearing and stuttered, among other things. Heller was very unhappy and wrote some rather ridiculous letters to Metzger and the Freiburg chancery, which was very cold in its response; the letters complained about everything including the vegetables he had to eat and his cold room. Baser eventually dragged him and Metzger to court.

There had been some trouble with Ernst Burkard, the cashier for the alcohol-free restaurant; when he refused to show the books to the board of directors, the police were called by Metzger. Everything proved to be in order, but Burkard from then on sought revenge on Metzger. He had also vainly sought the hand of Metzger's sister who was working in Graz at the time. Baser also dragged him into court against Metzger.

Baser also quickly fastened on a Fraeulein Binzegger who had joined the society for a while and then left; she was obviously emotionally quite unstable. Baser encouraged her to advance a money grievance.

Baser became wilder and began referring to Elizabeth Bayer as Metzger's "former mistress." The Freiburg chancery advised Metzger to bring a libel suit against Baser, which he did, but it took several attempts before he could get a conviction. In the meanwhile, because of the libel suits, he became involved in litigation against the local newspaper and other individuals. Metzger's personal files at the Freiburg diocese contain at least two volumes of letters and documents on the court cases and difficulties of these few years—probably a third of the letters are written by Baser. After a time, the chancery refused to answer Baser's letters, but he continued sending them for months, even after his conviction for libel.

In the early 1920s Metzger seriously contemplated moving into academic life. He probably did not intend to abandon the White Cross, but rather would have used his professorship as a shield to protect it. In Europe, university professorships are vastly fewer in number than in America and carry with them a prestige that is the antithesis of the American notion of the "egghead." One wag said that in Europe, Germanic Europe anyway, the professor is the fourth person of the Blessed Trinity! Also, in Germanic countries, a doctor's degree is not sufficient as an entrée into the professorial world. An additional major piece of research must be submitted in order to receive the degree of Doctor habilitation, which would then allow the holder to seek a university position.

It was in order to fulfill this requirement that Metzger intended to approach Professor Kuenstle, professor of liturgics at the University of Freiburg; he hoped to write his habilitation dissertation in the area of liturgics under Kuenstle. When Metzger went to the university to see Kuenstle he attended one of Kuenstle's lectures, expecting to speak to him afterwards. It happened that during this lecture, Kuenstle spoke of the temperance movement and referred to Metzger, being unaware of his presence, as a "crazy fellow." A number of the students did, however, know Metzger and Metzger himself had to do all he could do to keep from laughing out loud. Nevertheless, although Metzger was able to enjoy a laugh at his own expense—this trait was one of his most friend-winning and enemy-making characteristics—he realized he would never be able to take a doctor's habilitation under Kuenstle and apparently serious concern for an academic career went no further.

Besides some rash errors and some obvious bad luck, particularly in having such an insatiable, pathological foe, Metzger's difficulties stemmed largely from his incredibly poor judgment of people. He seemed almost incapable of realizing that all people were not as good, innocent, and open as he. This was, in fact, the tragic flaw in a noble character.

Because of these difficulties and others, and because the Graz diocese did not want any innovators, the diocese of Freiburg was pressured to recall Father Metzger in 1926. Metzger fought the action as well as he could, but because the lawsuits were not effectively settled until the end of 1929, the best he could obtain was a six months' delay to make the necessary arrangements. He of course asked that he not be forced to relinquish his leadership of the Society. In fact, he even offered to return to the Freiburg diocese with his society. The Freiburg chancery caustically rejected that suggestion but gave him permission to continue his work elsewhere—outside of the Graz and the Freiburg diocese. Fortunately, an opportunity arose in 1927 to take over a rehab center in Meitingen by Augsburg. Metzger accepted this offer from the Caritas Society of Augsburg and transferred the mother house of the White Cross there, where it has remained.

The Institute buildings in Meitingen, still used today.

Metzger had some of the usual inevitable minor difficulties with some Augsburg chancery officials, but the "time of troubles" seemed to pass and the society prospered and expanded. About this time the name of the society was changed to Society of Christ the King although the name Mission Society of the White Cross also continued to appear for a while as a subtitle on letterheads.

Priests and South America

In the thirties, Metzger was able not only to expand membership at the mother house in Meitingen and establish other small foundations, but also to seriously recruit and train seminarians for the society. By 1936 Metzger was looking for a major seminary to which he could send several seminarians that had joined the society. The diocesan seminary of Eichstaett agreed to accept them, and during the period from 1936 to 1940, nine seminarians for the society studied there. The number reflected the society's overall success during this time; it expanded considerably and by 1936 had 61 male members, with 38 living in community, and 176 sisters, with 97 living in community. Metzger's spiritual dynamism continued to attract followers, so much so that his seminarians were noted for their great admiration for Metzger, and even their imitation of his mannerisms.

Metzger apparently greatly upset the rector and other seminary officials by not adhering closely to canonical technicalities, such as those dealing with the official letters of commission (*litterae dimissoriales*) for the ordination of each of the seminarians. Metzger apparently thought he, as religious superior, could issue the letters. His religious position, however, did not empower him to do this. This problem helped lead him into another venture.

In the summer of 1938, a year before World War II broke out in Europe, Metzger's good friend Father Wilhelm Baumeister arranged to serve as a chaplain on the Cap Arcona, which was going to South America. Father Metzger talked Baumeister into letting him take his place. So, from June to August of 1938, Metzger sailed to South America and back. He spent one day in Brazil and twenty days in Argentina. During this time, he made a series of contacts, particularly with bishops, partly with a view to obtaining *litterae dimissoriales* (dimissorial letters) for his seminarians, especially those who did not have the state diploma (*Abitur*). He was received very well by Cardinal Copello of Buenos Aires, the Apostolic Nuncio, Pietta, and several other bishops.

Among these bishops was José María Carlo Rodríguez, the archbishop of La Serena, Chile. Metzger came home with a signed agreement from him. The archbishop promised to send *litterae dimissoriales* for the society's seminarians and they in turn would go to his diocese after ordination to do parochial work, particularly among the workers' areas of large cities where the inroads of the socialists and communists were heaviest. Everything was to be done to help the society's priests to live in community.

A similar arrangement was also made with the capitular vicar of the archdiocese of La Plata, Argentina, but its necessary ratification was not forthcoming. Nevertheless, a sizable sum of money was anonymously deposited for the financial support of the society in Argentina. Metzger also had an offer from a large landowner in Brazil of an orphanage with a great amount of land attached, and the promise of continued upkeep of the property; but, afraid of splintering his efforts, he felt he had to decline this last offer.

Several seminarians were actually incardinated into the La Serena diocese and were ordained, but only one Society of Christ the King priest, Father Bartholomaeus Holzhauser, ever arrived. The archbishop visited Meitingen on July 14, 1939, and Father Holzhauser sailed to South America that summer, but World War II ended all travel in September 1939. The war also stopped the influx of seminarians; it ended many other things, too, including Father Metzger's life. The tie with South America, however, was not completely broken. In 1963, the Christ the King Sisters sent over the first of what they hoped would be a growing stream of sisters to work in Chile—in Father Holzhauser's parish.

Thus, we can see how Father Metzger, through the work of the *Kreuzbündnis* and its offshoots, through the founding and development of the White Cross, and its successor, the Society of Christ the King, was at the forefront of many movements of that time, some of which are really coming into their own only now. Perhaps three words can summarize that aspect of his life: *diakonia*, or service, community, and laity.

From the middle of the nineteenth century onward, a Christian concern for social problems developed ever more intensely. Christian socialism grew in England, while in America the social gospel was preached with growing vigor as the twentieth century approached. In France many Catholic organizations concerned with social problems were founded, culminating in a way in *Le Sillon* under the leadership of Marc Sangnier at the beginning of this century. Bishop von Ketteler and Father Kolping led the way in mid-nineteenth century Germany in Catholic concern with social problems. Pope Leo XIII with his encyclical *Rerum novarum* in 1891 brought the prestige of the papacy to bear on the need for Christian concern and action in the sphere of social problems. But although the list of organizations and heroic Catholics and Protestants involved in social renewal could be extended to a great length, the resistance to social involvement by Christians on all levels of authority and the simultaneous geometric growth of social misery made the efforts of the Christian churches seem very meager in face of the magnitude of the problems. By the middle of the twentieth century, for example, it was stated openly by French Catholic clergy and lay intellectuals that the working classes were lost to the church. The situation was not a great deal better in Germany. Far too often the clergy thought of themselves as a sort of aristocracy, set apart—and above— the people. It was only with Vatican II and John XXIII that the notion of "service" again, as in the primitive church, became the key characterization of the clergy, and the Christian in general—at least in theory. Metzger was a priest who realized that "service" was at the heart of the Christian life, and doubly so at the heart of the priesthood. His years were passionately spent in social service.

Metzger's passion for service to men and women was to them as individual persons, one by one. But he also saw that this could truly be done only by reknitting the shredded skeins of human community, or even building new communities where modern forces had so disrupted the lives of men and women. Hence, he was greatly concerned with attempting to find solutions to problems by forming societies of one kind or another out of the people who had the problems, as for example the consumers' cooperative. He also realized that the most effective way to influence a society suffering from disrupted and decaying communities on so many levels was to build vital communities that had both the necessary inner cohesiveness and elasticity to adapt to contemporary needs; these communities would then not only be able to vigorously attack the problems they were designed to meet, but also exercise a very important, if indirect, influence in society merely by their presence as dynamic, but open, human communities.

Ever since the growing dislocations of the semi-medieval society structures under the impact of industrialization, Western men and women have been in sore need of a sense of community. Marx and others saw this in the nineteenth century and were vastly more effective than the Christian churches in supplying the needed sense of community—twentieth-century Fascism and Nazism as well as Communism are monumental evidence of this gnawing need and the Christian churches' failures in meeting it. Metzger strove valiantly to rebuild the human community within a renewed Christian framework; he tried to bring the "Church in the Modern World," and was practically concerned about "secular Christianity" long before it became the popular phenomenon of the sixties.

Metzger's great concern with human community led him radically away from the centuries-old stress on clericalism. From the very beginning he built the organizations and communities he founded or worked with in such a way that laypeople in all levels of society would be as actively involved in societal work as their circumstances permitted. The White Cross was a perfect example; there were many levels of lay participation, and even the central communal group was supposed to "have all the mobility of laity," and since they had to have a habit (in the tight ecclesiastical system that only now is beginning to loosen up it would have been impossible for Metzger's society to operate within a Catholic framework without having ecclesiastical approbation, and the concomitant regulation; as it was he was always skating the edge of disaster in this regard). He insisted it be as little clerical in appearance as possible. Metzger's leadership in active lay participation in the liturgy and his enthusiasm for the burgeoning youth groups are further indications of his broad and early concern to stress the importance of the laity in the Church. In this too he preceded, and thereby helped bring about, Vatican II.

Metzger's concern for new forms and a new spirit in the Church's mission to the world went beyond what he was able to accomplish in his own organizations to joining forces with others of like mind to plan strategy on how to influence the whole Church. In 1930 he attended a meeting at Salzburg of members of different religious communities. He reported that there was a great variety of types of communities represented, including those which were oriented toward the past and those searching for new external forms which would allow greater mobility and possibilities for development of each individual and for apostolic work. Metzger, however, thought that the latter, though important, was not sufficient.

> What the times are crying for are not old men in new clothes, but rather new men who are as deeply gripped by the needs of the world around us as Christ was, and who are as absolutely unequivocally involved in the powerful apostolates of our day—being simultaneously filled with eternity and immersed in time—as was He.

Along with the later well-known pastor of St. Alban in Lyon, Father Remillioux, Metzger stressed the need of a new spirit of *penitence* and *service*.

> All individual efforts are useless unless we penetrate much more deeply than we have in the past with our spirit, unless we vividly realize that the old, everyday spirit was and is not strong and vigorous enough to conquer the world for Christ, unless, especially among us, a new spirit of authentic penitence and deep humility that is ready to serve seizes a prominent place all our apostolic activity can attain no profound or lasting success.

The Salzburg meeting provided the first contact for Metzger and others with kindred concerns. Metzger worked to bring these concerns before Rome, and to this end met with Father Remillioux, Msgr. Kornilowicz of Warsaw, and Father A. Genelli, O.F.M., then rector of the Catholic University of Milan and also founder of the "Missionaries for Christ the King" in 1937 at Milan. Genelli and Metzger then issued an invitation to all "religious communities whose members wished to devote themselves entirely to an apostolic life in the spirit of the evangelical counsels" to come to a conference held May 21–22, 1938 under the protectorate of the bishop of St. Gall. The purpose of the conference, which drew representatives of fifteen communities from eight countries, was to prepare a petition to Rome for a new canonically recognized form of religious community. Another meeting was planned for 1939 but was prevented by the war. Nevertheless, it is certain that the ideas conceived and discussed in these conferences were forwarded to Rome and found their expression in the Apostolic Constitution *Provida Mater* of 1947, which approved and outlined the founding of secular institutes, that is, religious communities which fulfilled the aims of Metzger, Genelli, and the others. Today Metzger's Society of Christ the King is a secular institute.

WORLD PEACE

One of the causes to which Father Metzger devoted so much of his energies, and later his life itself, was world peace. In the May 1929 issue of his newspaper *Ruf zu Wahrheit-Gerechtigkeit und Liebe* Metzger described something of the beginning of his Catholic world peace organization. He recalled that on the last Sunday of January 1917, he entered the pulpit of the church in Graz, Austria:

> In the anguish and misery of a war which divides the peoples and nations in two, the peoples of Europe lift their blood stained hands to heaven, weary with the gruesome murder of brothers, outraged by the misery that this frightful war has brought upon humanity, ashamed of the decline that it means for the once culturally proud Europe. It is as if the dumb crosses on all of the hundreds of thousands of mass graves were come alive; it is as if the graves opened up and as if the hundreds of thousands of wooden crosses marched at the head of the procession of death of the numberless flowering youthful lives which were cut down so early, as if all of the millions of the suffering widows and orphans joined this tragic procession . . . .
>
> Thus, did I speak. And I asked, 'Why is there no peace? Is there no possibility for understanding?' . . . .
>
> And again I said: 'Peace! How humanity hungers to enjoy the blessings of peace! There is no land in which there is not the same longing for the cessation of this frightful pouring out of blood, for the return of joyous peace. Indeed, it is like a single outcry from the depths of all men and women's hearts, a cry for the peacemaker, a Savior!' You heavens rain down the just one! You clouds pour him forth! . . .
>
> And then I developed a program in which all Catholics of all lands can and must unite themselves, the International Catholic World Peace program.
>
> "We demand an end to the useless pouring out of blood on the battlefields and at the same time an end to a politics which seems to overcome the world problems of the co-existence of the nations by power and thereby condemns humanity to a constant series of wars . . . .

"We demand a renunciation of the senseless arms race of the nations on both land and sea and the concentration of their energies on positive cultural goals...

"We demand the renunciation of race and nationality struggles and all attempts to overcome one portion of a nation by another, and a recognition of the right [for each national group] to possess the facilities to develop its own language and culture within the framework of the entire state...

"We demand the overcoming of the class struggle which, along with the spirit of the naked *Machtpolitik* in the life of the individual nations and their relations with each other, caused the world war; it should be overcome by the spirit of social compensation, of the will to social justice and a reconciling of Christian love of neighbor...

"We demand a re-orientation of the education of youth which will avoid all chauvinism, all fostering of the spirit of war, which will awaken the awareness of social obligations, truthfulness, honesty, selflessness, justice, fraternal love, readiness to help others and social responsibility...

"We demand the return of all nations and states and of all their individual members to lived Christianity, an unlimited and unrestricted acknowledgment and application of the Divine Moral Laws with their demands of justice and love of neighbor, and see the guarantee of the success of all peace efforts, the irresistible source of power of the spirit of peace in the spiritual and real communication of all nations and their neighbors with the King of Peace: 'Christ, yesterday and today and forever.'"

The peace program of the White Cross was the first peace program sent into the world by Catholics. Into the 'world'? That was not simple. For the borders were blocked by censors fearful of every expression of peace as the fostering of defeatism.

Still it was possible to publish the peace program in various countries beyond our border. In Germany and Austria it was sent to all Catholic leaders and Catholic organizations as well as to the international press. Of course, it had the noteworthy result pointed out by the Protestant pastor T. Vogl in *Die evangelische Kirche und der Weltkrieg*: "this peace program, which the Catholics should be proud of, unfortunately could be learned of only in the social democratic press...."

The Holy See was also sent a copy of the Peace program. On June 27, 1917, Dr. Metzger received the communication from Cardinal Secretary of State Gasparri in which he said:

> The Holy Father has taken notice of the program of this 'Institution' which your Reverence and your colleagues humbly sent him with the letter dated February 20. The Supreme Pontiff, Vicar on Earth of the King of Peace, blesses your ardent desire to see peace quickly restored among nations, and prays that the full and precise observance in individual and social life of the principles of justice and charity preached by the Divine Master may forever protect the people from the horrors of war . . . .[1]

Metzger wrote later,

> A few weeks after this encouraging letter there appeared the famous peace encyclical of the Holy Father on August 1, 1917, in which many points of the thoughts of our Catholic peace program were unmistakably echoed. And today we know how during the months of August and September the Holy Father had his diplomats vigorously working in the service of a peace arbitration. Unfortunately, in vain! Those in military control in Wilhelmine, Germany, could not be brought to the point of allowing their hunger for power to be overcome in favor of a declaration by Germany concerning the desire for justice on the part of Belgium, which was necessary for the declaration of peace. And all the Catholics in all other countries were also hard of hearing and cowardly . . . . Not Christianity but rather Christendom underwent bankruptcy . . . .

The Role of the World Peace League of the White Cross

By 1916, Father Metzger had, at least in an initial way, founded the World Peace League of the White Cross. This international organization of Catholics, in cooperation with non-Catholics from the beginning, sought

> the creation of a genuine league of nations built on a democratic recognition of all states and nations which will be conducted with the basic Christian principles of mutual justice and trust, filled with the spirit of truthfulness and honesty, unrestricted faithfulness to treaties,

---

[1] See note 1.

> solidarity and general preparedness to help, which thereby will only be the external expression of the inner community of nations.

It became even more specific when it declared in its statutes that it stood for "construction and expansion of an international law of nations and states which in particular internationally guaranteed the protection of national and religious minorities, freedom of conscience and freedom of religious practice."

The statutes stated further that it advocated

> the cooperation of all states in the international solution of the burning social problems through an international code of law, the cooperation of the free organizations of all nations for the realization of social and cultural progress, the elimination of all power politics from the entire social and political life of the nations and a substitution of an unrestrictedly Christian politics of justice.

One general statement of purpose established a means of reconciling peoples and accomplishing the other specific goals: the establishment and promotion of a Catholic International. This International, which was actually founded soon after the war, was to be the crowning point of a pyramid of Catholic organizations. In the meanwhile, the function of the World Peace League of the White Cross was to join together all the local and national Catholic peace organizations.

Metzger soon helped populate his organization with Father Magnus Jocham and Father Franziskus Stratmann, O.P. In 1918 Metzger founded the Peace League of German Catholics (*Friedensbund deutscher Katholiken*). Its main center was originally in Munich. In the early years, Jocham was responsible for South Germany, Stratmann for North Germany, and Metzger for Austria. The official statutes of the *Friedensbund* stated that it would operate according to the statutes of the World Peace League of the White Cross and was in fact a branch organization of it.[2] In the July 1919 *Friedensherold*, Metzger reported a "local group" (*Ortsgruppe*) of the World Peace League of over 150 members in Berlin with *Geheim Rat* Fassbender and Pater Stratmann at its head. At this early stage the *Friedensbund* was so closely allied to the World Peace League that its closing statute declared that in the case of the dissolution of the *Friedensbund* all property and effects would go to the World Peace

---

[2] "Sätzungen des Friedensbundes deutscher Katholiken," Der katholische Völkerbund Blätter für die katholische Friedensbewegung (Berlin-Graz-München). Nr. 1 (1920), p. 3.

League of the White Cross. By 1924, however, the two organizations had become quite separated.

The influence of the *Friedensbund* grew considerably until the Nazi period. When the Nazis took power in 1933 there were six archbishops, fourteen bishops, nine auxiliary bishops, and 250 priests among its membership, which reached 40,000 at one point; it enjoyed considerable influence. But it was one of the first organizations to be crushed by Hitler. The official end came on July 1, 1933. The tragedy of its collapse during the Nazi era is told by Gordon Zahn in *German Catholics and Hitler's Wars*. Metzger was one member, however, who died for his principles of peace.

Already in the nineteenth century various elements of the modern peace movement began to develop. However, the Catholic Church did not become involved, perhaps because it was associated with liberalism, Pius IX's archenemy. The first attempt at forming a Catholic peace organization was led by Alfred Vanderpol of *Le Sillon* at the beginning of this century. He founded the *Société Gratry* in 1906, named after a French thinker whose social and pacifist ideas greatly influenced *Le Sillon* and its leader Marc Sangnier. Sangnier was a member of the executive committee of the *Société Gratry*, and through his initiative, peace groups sprang up in Belgium, Holland, and England, which in 1911 banded together in Brussels into the *Ligue Internationale des Sociétés Catholique pour la Paix*. However, this Catholic peace effort apparently attained no significance, and completely evaporated before the advance of the war. It is against this background of the almost complete absence of Catholics from the modern peace movement that Metzger's work must be seen.

Even before the founding of the *Friedensbund*, Metzger and his World Peace League of the White Cross had been energetically working for the cause of peace. In November 1917, the World Peace League represented Catholics at a peace conference held at Bern, Switzerland. In the same city two years later, Metzger again represented the World Peace League of the White Cross at the International League of Nations Conference. He complained in the April 1919 issue of his newspaper, the *Friedensherold*, that there were only a very few Catholic delegates present "since Catholics have until now concerned themselves far too little with the momentously important question of peace—and of the *League of Nations*." Because of this lacuna in Catholic life Metzger voiced his determination to make his World Peace League of the White Cross into an organization "which would bring the Catholics together in a work serving the reconciliation of the nations and join them together into a powerful Catholic International."

Already at Bern in 1917 Father Metzger met many representatives from neutral and "enemy" nations who showed an extremely great interest in the White Cross and its efforts. Metzger ended his report on the conference with the plea, "God grant that the 'Catholic League of Nations' be born soon; it is the foundation and prerequisite of the political league of nations which the powers wish to form with one another!" Then Metzger immediately set out to lecture from Vienna to Breslau, Berlin, and Amsterdam on "The League of Nations and the Catholic International." In less than a year his plan began to be fulfilled.

The World Peace League of the White Cross took a strong position in favor of peace at a time when it was not particularly popular to do so. In May of 1918, the armies of the central powers were supremely confident of final victory. They were triumphant from the Volga and the Black Sea to the Marne and the English Channel. The Russians had accepted the disastrous treaty of Brest-Litovsk; the Austrians were poised for a huge offensive against the Italians, and the Germans had already been on the march in the West since March. Still, when a new Austrian Foreign Minister was appointed—Baron Burián—Metzger's *Die Neue Zeit* published an open letter to him signed by the World Peace League of the White Cross. It was a long and forceful letter urging Baron Burián to do everything possible to attain peace according to Pope Benedict XV's plan.

Disaster overtook the Teutonic forces a few months after that letter was published. But an even greater catastrophe threatened humanity immediately afterwards: the structuring of a peace treaty that would only be the seedbed of a more titanic, suicidal struggle. In the January 1919 issue of *Friedensherold*, Metzger reported the sending of a letter by the World Peace League of the White Cross to all of the bishops of the Entente countries and to the Pope. The letter said that the German people had thought they were fighting for their existence, they had only too late learned that they had been duped by militarists and self-seekers. They were now humble. But they were also fearful for there were rumors that the peace demands would not be made in justice, as had been promised by the Allies—an obvious reference to Wilson's Fourteen Points. The bishops were asked to publicly use their influence to obtain a lasting peace, one with no annexations or reparations and with a League of Nations where all were equal. No significant public help was forthcoming from the bishops.

Metzger's League received a warmer reception from the Central Powers bishops—understandably so. In June 1917, in a letter addressed to the bishop of

Augsburg explaining the League, Metzger mentioned that "a great many bishops in Germany, Austria, Hungary and also even abroad" have greeted it warmly. The Cardinal Archbishop Skrbenský, Primate of Hungary, forwarded a recommendation of the League to the Holy Father. By 1917 Metzger's plans and results were already laid before the Holy Father; the response was the letter of approbation and blessing. Two years later, on September 15, 1919, the Holy See addressed another letter to Father Metzger, again giving the Holy Father's full support to Metzger's peace work:

> As I already mentioned to your Reverence in my letter of 27 June 1917, the Holy Father is happy to see that the Catholic people, under the leadership of their clergy and following the teaching of the Gospel, wish to work to foster the reconciliation and education for peace of the nations in the love of Jesus Christ and hopes that in the name of the divine Master they will successfully tear down the hate and enmity which today has divided such a large part of humanity.

In the early fall of 1920, Father Metzger went to Rome and personally described the work of the League to the Cardinal Secretary of State, Gasparri, and the Holy Father himself, Benedict XV; the reception was most encouraging.

During this period Metzger also began to work with Protestant Christians, particularly in his peace work. He was especially involved in the International Fellowship of Reconciliation, "a movement uniting Christians, both Catholic and Protestant, in work for peace." In 1920 he attended one of the early council meetings, "a young Roman Catholic priest who had heard of this movement and felt it to be something after his own heart . . . . For some eight or ten years we had the benefit of close contact with him on our council." Father Metzger even invited the IFOR to send a delegate to a conference of his *Weltfriedensbund* at Constance in 1923. This representative, Lilian Stevenson, was the only non-Catholic present; she referred to her experience as a "memorable week." Metzger remained active in the Fellowship at least until 1927 when he took part in a Fellowship-sponsored youth conference at Vaumarcus, Switzerland, centering around the seven-hundredth anniversary of St. Francis of Assisi. The Fellowship's songbook, *Eirene*, contains a peace song written and set to music by Father Metzger during this period.

The liturgical and Biblical movements, both of which did much to prepare the environment in which Metzger later founded the Una Sancta Movement, began to flourish in the Catholic Church between the wars. Metzger himself and through him his Society of Christ the King were deeply influenced by these currents. Already the organization of the *Missions-gesellschaft vom Weissen*

Kreuz in the early 1920s included the *Benediktus-Diakonat* devoted to the fostering of the liturgical movement and the *Hieronymus-Diakonat* to encourage the reading of the Bible movement. Writing from his prison cell in 1943, Metzger questioned himself about the society. "Was it capable of becoming a movement, both Biblical and liturgical . . . . And finally, through it all, the realization of an 'Una Sancta' as the Lord would have it and as the world needs it?"

A visit to Meitingen today would no doubt produce an affirmative answer to the first part of Metzger's question, just as Metzger thought it would in the thirties and early forties. In a small pamphlet he invited Protestant ministers to visit Meitingen and take part in the daily liturgical celebration, feeling confident that they, like many other Protestant ministers before them, would be surprised at what misconceptions abounded. He then described the manner of celebrating Mass: a lector read the instructional parts of the Mass aloud in German and the whole congregation answered the prayers and either recited or sang the Gloria, Credo, etc., one day in German and another day in Latin; at the offertory the people brought in procession the hosts which the priest later consecrated and distributed. "Nothing there is 'insincere' or 'pure ceremony'; the whole community celebration breathes the spirit and letter of the primitive church." The practices Metzger also preached in numerous liturgical conferences in parishes. All of this obviously was strongly in the spirit and letter of the liturgical movement and anticipated the liturgical reforms of Vatican II by some thirty years.

Sister Gertrudis Reimann, Metzger's long-time coworker, recalled that the New Testament was a "rule of life" for him and that he was a "herald and prime mover of the liturgical and Biblical movements." Metzger not only early structured the work of the Bible Movement into his Mission Society of the White Cross, but also stressed the Bible and its daily reading in his lectures, conferences, retreats, and writings. His newspaper articles and booklets are full of the idea.

In the Protestant journal (edited by Friedrich Heiler) *Eine Heilige Kirche* Paula Schaefer wrote in 1934 of Metzger's major contribution to the burgeoning Catholic Bible Movement:

> Also, the Christ the King Society of the White Cross in Meitingen bei Augsburg has recently placed itself vigorously in the service of the Bible Movement. In felicitously composed articles in its magazine Christkoenigsbote, Bible reading is stressed time and again and introductions to and explanations of general biblical matters are provided.

In that same year Metzger began editing a series of some nineteen booklets (the last one appeared in 1940) entitled "Life School of Holy Scriptures." The series, praised by both Protestants and Catholics, was designed to spread the reading, understanding, and application of the Bible among the masses of the Catholic laity.

Metzger explicitly expressed those goals to his Meitingen community in a letter from Zakopane, Poland, in July 1937:

> How much do I wish that all of you would think nothing more important, no devotional exercise more primary, than the daily absorption of God's word speaking to us in the Holy Scriptures! Of course, it is not being 'hearers' or readers,' but rather 'doers' that counts! But the daily living with the word of God, the submission to his Spirit accomplishes of itself in the grace of God that 'doing'! Then will 'saints,' as the world awaits them, appear—and women of the grace of God who again will reconcile heaven and earth.

Portrait photo of Metzger for
his 50th birthday, 1937.

Internationale Katholische Liga "Ika"

By 1919 Father Metzger had decided to progress beyond the World Peace League of the White Cross, apparently because the response to the founding of the League was only relatively modest, and because he saw the need for a Catholic world organization broader than just the peace movement, one that would be built on existing Catholic organizations. It was because of this second aspect that Metzger found even the international plans of the White Cross too narrow. As we have seen, from the beginning Metzger had envisioned as one of the main aims of the World Peace League of the White Cross the founding and developing of a Catholic International, that is, a supra-national Catholic organization that would parallel the League of Nations and coordinate on the international level all of the more particular interests and organizations on the national and local levels.

When in 1920 a congress of Catholic Advocates of Esperanto met in the Hague, Father Metzger was present. Through his initiative the Congress voted to become a branch organization of a Catholic international organization which was then formed—it was called the *Internationale Katholische Liga* (Catholic International), or "*Ika*."

Metzger brought his great energy to the organization of the *Ika*. The White Cross center in Graz became its center and several of the most efficient members of his society devoted themselves to its work. The following year, from August 10 to 14, 1921, the Catholic International held its first conference in Graz. There were five major sections of the conference: meetings on the Catholic peace movement, on the Catholic youth movement, on Catholic missions, the general assembly of the World League of Catholic Esperantists, and the general assembly of the Catholic International. About 200 participants from 19 different countries were present, from England, Belgium, Algeria, France, Italy, Yugoslavia, Holland, Poland, Rumania, Lithuania, Germany, Czechoslavakia, Hungary, Switzerland, Austria, and also Danzig, the Saar, and Upper Silesia, among others. Declarations of support came from over twenty-five Cardinals, Apostolic Nuncios, and bishops from many of the above countries and also from Spain, Canada, and the West Indies. Telegrams arrived from all over Europe, including ones from the Italian People's Party in Rome (the forerunner to the Christian Democrats, founded by Don Luigi Sturzo), and the Czech People's Party in Prague.

Father Metzger, the secretary general of the *Ika*, greeted the assembly on the opening evening in Esperanto. Following this was some choral and solo singing in Esperanto—with Metzger accompanying on the harmonium. Three presidents were then elected: Prelate Dr. Giesswein from Hungary, Director Phillippe from Belgium, and Professor Arnold from Switzerland. Metzger was named representative of the presidents at the Center and a Mr. Ce from Romania general secretary. Later, national directors were elected for thirty different countries. The delegates from Switzerland declared that all of its Catholic societies and youth organizations had joined the *Ika*; similar declarations were made by other areas and organizations.

The next several days there were lectures and discussions in the various areas. The discussions on the peace movement were apparently quite exciting and ended with a resolution to expand the membership of the international Catholic peace organizations, which out of a true love of the Fatherland would help to build a Christian world order. The section of the *Ika* conference where Metzger's influence can be seen most of all was the conference on the Catholic youth movement. More than a year before the Graz *Ika* conference, Father Metzger, along with the help of his Mission Society of the White Cross, had founded a Catholic World Youth League, the "*Moka*" (*Mondjunularo Katolika*). One of the members of the Society, a gymnasium teacher named Mielert, started the *Moka* by a loose association of students belonging to the two dynamic Catholic youth groups "*Hochland*" and "*Quickborn*." By 1921 it had over a hundred delegates in fifteen different countries, including some non-European ones, who sent reports and information into Graz, and had started a circular letter in several languages and a letter exchange system among the youth of the world. By that same year *Moka* had been joined by a large number of organizations in eight countries. The general secretary of *Moka* was Hans Sappl, a member of the Mission Society of the White Cross. The president was Father Metzger himself. Among other things the *Moka* in its general assembly within the *Ika* conference resolved to become a member organization of the *Ika* while maintaining its own independent existence, and to promote the *Katolika Mondo*, the Esperanto language organ of the *Ika*.

The Graz conference of *Ika* was a success, as was also the one in Luxemburg the following year, 1922. It likewise was largely organized by Father Metzger and the White Cross. The 1923 conference in Constance was perhaps the most successful of all the *Ika* gatherings and also the last one that Metzger and the White Cross were so centrally involved in. Over three hundred persons attended the August 10 to 15, 1923 conference, which met under the honorary chairmanship of Bishop Colbrie of Kaschau. The theme was "Practical Work for Peace in the Kingdom of Christ." As at Graz, sections of the conference were devoted to youth and to mission work. In the section under the sub-theme "We Catholics and the Papal Peace Program," Metzger gave an address, as did Conrad Gröber, among others. It is interesting to note this in light of

Gröber's later attitude toward Hitler's wars and his statements to the Nazi prosecutor concerning Metzger's crimes.

It was also the Constance conference that saw, as was later reported in 3. Internationaler Kongress (Graz, n.d.),

> the blending of the *World Peace League of the White Cross* with the *Catholic International* in such a manner that now the Catholic International worked expressly as an international peace organization on the basis of the papal peace program and through a special international Catholic committee for the peace movement, made up of the foremost promoters of the Catholic peace movement in all countries.

Pope Pius XI and sixty bishops sent their well wishes and blessings to the 1923 conference. Even before the conference took place the Apostolic Nuncio to Germany, Eugenio Pacelli, wrote on January 13, 1923:

> From my heart I wish the conference the good fortune of having behind it a small cohesive group that is bound together for common practical action and animated by courage and decisiveness and which shrinks from no difficulties. I gladly express the desire that the Catholic International yearly come significantly closer to its ideal goals (which are built on the solid foundation of Catholic principles) of promoting harmony and social peace, and that the Catholic brethren of all lands may again find each other on the basis of a common work for the kingdom of God.

The *Ika* continued to prosper, holding yearly conferences at least until 1927. Although the White Cross was in a way the mother organization of the *Ika*, Metzger was always careful to keep the two separate. Partly for this reason, by the end of 1924, the *Ika* center was moved from Graz to Zug in Switzerland. Switzerland, with its tradition of neutrality, seemed to be the best location for an international organization. Also, the personal attacks Metzger was suffering led him to step into the background of the *Ika* so as not to bring it any additional problems.

The World Congress of Christ the King

Metzger's part in bringing worldwide organizations into being, however, was not quite finished. Although the *Ika* flourished throughout the twenties and into the beginning of the great depression, it seemed to lose momentum after that. A new organization was founded, probably in 1931, through the initiative of "Consistorial Advisor" Kalan of Yugoslavia. The organization was called the World Congress of Christ the King. Inspired by Pius XI's encyclical *Quas primas* on Christ the King and the motto "the peace of Christ through the reign of Christ," its purpose was to give annual public, solemn witness to the idea of Christ the King throughout the world and to support Catholic Action in all countries by the exchange of ideas and experiences. In its statutes a very specific statement was made about abstaining from all state and party politics.

Members of the Christ the King Institute in Meitingen.

Just exactly when Father Metzger became actively involved in the World Congresses of Christ the King is not clear, but it was certainly before 1934 when the White Cross was energetically promoting them. In 1937, when the Congress was under the protection of Cardinal Hlond, Primate of Poland and Archbishop of Posen (the Congress was held in Posen that year), Archbishop Innitzer of Vienna, and Archbishop Verdier of Paris, Metzger was appointed the Secretary General. Internal and international developments, however, soon stopped further activity along this line.

The Esperanto Movement

One of the reasons for Father Metzger's success in his international work was his ability with languages. But even though he was an unusually able linguist, he worked energetically for the spread of Esperanto as a universal language, which he considered an aid to better world understanding and peace. The official international language of the World Peace League of the White Cross was Esperanto, and its organ, *Blanka Kruco*, in the beginning was published in Esperanto and German; after 1920 the organ was solely Esperanto and was named *Katolika Mondo*. Even the song book of the White Cross, *Alleluja Liederschatz des Weissen Kreuzes*, contained nine songs in Esperanto. The Society's *Paulusverlag* also published a number of books promoting Esperanto, including an Esperanto instruction book and an Esperanto prayer book. One of the many working divisions in the Society, the *Hildegardis-Diakonat*, devoted itself solely to the promotion of Esperanto. In Graz, the Society was able to help start a Catholic Esperanto group, and on the international level it sent delegates to Esperanto congresses. Herr Mielert, the member of the Mission Society of the White Cross who was so important in starting *Moka*, also established among the students of his pioneering organization the practice of communicating with each other in Esperanto.

Naturally Metzger did not limit himself to his own White Cross in the promotion of Esperanto. He spread his message in whatever way he could by writing and speaking at conferences. In a lengthy and strong article in his own *Neue Zeit* (Berlin-Graz-Munich) of December 1920, Metzger called upon Catholics to further Esperanto; he pleaded that all Catholic organizations, schools, seminaries, etc. should immediately start courses in it. He referred to it as a Catholic language and insisted that not only the socialists should have an "international." Catholics ought also to have such an organization, but to be effective it needed an international language—Esperanto.

At the annual conference of Catholic Esperantists held in Breslau in 1919, Father Metzger attempted to bring about the merging of the causes of the Esperanto movement and the peace movement. He was unsuccessful that year, but matters improved the following year at the Hague. This was the beginning of the *Ika*, which had its first conference in Graz in 1921. Not only did Metzger address this latter conference in Esperanto—as he did in many other assemblies—but so did many of the other delegates. During the conference the *Ika* requested an International Catholic newspaper—in Esperanto. Thus, there was founded the monthly *Katolika Mondo* which was adopted as the official organ of the *Ika*, the *Moka*, and the World Peace Society of the White Cross. It was at this same *Ika* conference that the ratification of the new International Catholic Esperanto league took place. Through the initiative of *Ika*, and with the support of the Italian Catholic Congress in Bologna in October 1920, all the existing Catholic Esperanto organizations joined in the founding of an international league in the spring of 1921. It took as a name that of a similar former organization, *IKUE* (*Internacio Katolika Unnuigo Esperantista*). Two men of the three-man presidium elected were members of the White Cross, Mielert and Sappl. At the general assembly in Graz, August 1921, Father Metzger suggested as a resolution, which was accepted unanimously, that the *IKUE* become a member organization of the *Ika*.

International Peace Conferences

Besides the *Ika* conferences, Metzger attended almost all of the international peace conferences held in Europe during the twenties. He attended the peace conference in Bern in 1917, lectured at the German Pacifist Congress in Berlin in June of 1919, made a lecture tour of Holland in 1920, attended peace conferences in the Hague, Breslau, Bologna, Prague, Rome, Düsseldorf, Essen, Leutesdorf, Graz, Paris, Luxemburg, and Constance by 1923, and later again at the Hague in 1928 and 1929 when he delivered major lectures.

His experience at the Paris conference in 1921 was perhaps his most electrifying. This was the first international congress to which representatives from Germany (one was the philosopher and writer Dietrich von Hildebrand) and Austria were invited after the war. The congress was led by Marc Sangnier, the French leader in social and peace affairs and the founder of the dynamic French Catholic organization devoted to social causes, *Le Sillon*. A large crowd assembled at the Pantheon and cheered the speeches on peace. Some with more nationalistic feelings shouted to Sangnier, "What do the Germans have to say?" Sangnier then turned to Metzger and asked him to reply that he was the first German to speak in Paris after the war. He was greeted with a tumultuous applause, and as he spoke in French almost every sentence was punctuated by cheers and applause.

> I stand before you as a citizen of my Fatherland. I love this Fatherland of mine and I work for its cause. And I believe that you yourselves would despise me if I did any differently. But I would view it as a false patriotism if I believed that to love my Fatherland meant to fight against the Fatherland of another. No, I believe that whoever loves his Fatherland must want to live with others in peace and harmony, for all nations are ordered toward a cooperation within a great community of peoples. Men have artificially torn the peoples apart and have baited them, have set up divisive walls which in reality do not exist.
>
> Men have tried to convince the nations that they are by nature mutual enemies and they all have one thing in common: war. But there is

> something else that all have in common because it brings good fortune to all nations in like fashion: peace. I stand before you at the same time as a citizen of a larger Fatherland which is common to us all and I greet you as fellow citizens of this larger Fatherland of ours; I as a priest of my Church greet you as citizens of the kingdom of God, as children of God, as brothers of the Son of God—and therefore as brothers! I have often raised the question, how is it even possible that nineteen centuries after the death of the master of love men can still murder each other in hatred and enmity? And I have always found only one answer: Because men everywhere have forsaken the fundamental laws of God which alone can assure peace among men—justice, truthfulness, and love.
>
> When self-seeking and deeds of violence dominate the world instead of justice, when the statesmen pledge their allegiance to *sacro egoism*—and I must confess that the statesmen of all nations, without exception, subscribe to this corrupting principle!—when the diplomats use language only to conceal their thoughts rather than to express them, when untruthfulness, hypocrisy, and dishonesty is trump in the world, peace cannot endure. Only the realization of what is the dream of us all can bring peace: a true league of nations, a coalition of all nations in a genuine Christian family of nations worthy of man.

On December 12, 1921, the newspaper *Ere Nouvelle* reported the speech as "an historic event." Another paper, the *Jeune République*, stated on December 18, 1921:

> A salvo of applause greeted Dr. Metzger, whose declaration was then listened to with a passionate attention in absolute silence. "You know one Germany and Austria—the one the newspapers describe. There is another one, and that is the one that has sent me." . . . Enemies as well as friends were struck dumb by the solemnity of the hour. Even more significant than the words spoken was the event itself; for the first time in Paris after the war a German spoke at a public gathering and the Parisian crowd applauded his fraternal and pacific discourse. This is an event that will cause a stir in the world.

Although Metzger by no means withdrew from peace movement activities in the middle 1920s, most of his energies were absorbed in the development of the Mission Society of the White Cross and also in extricating himself from the thicket of legal and other entanglements that ensnared him during this period. But as the "time of troubles" passed he again played a more prominent role on the public peace platform. On August 2, 1928, Father Metzger spoke at the International Day of Peace at the Hague. His lecture, entitled "Peace in the Kingdom of Christ," is one that could, and should, be delivered from pulpits today.

> ... Is there a man who has witnessed the horror of war, who has seen mangled bodies lying in shell holes, twitching limbs hanging from barbed wire entanglements; is there a man with human feelings in his heart who does not turn away from murderous war, who does not wish peace for humanity?
>
> Is there a statesman with a sense of responsibility who in the face of the threatening horror of a future war in which a few gas bombs would transform entire metropolises into cemeteries, I ask, is there a statesman with a sense of responsibility who in the face of such a sheerly incredible, gruesome, and yet near, catastrophe could view any other task as more important and more pressing than the avoidance of war, the insurance of peace?
>
> What is the reason that despite all the peace conferences in all countries, especially the conferences of the diplomats in their peace pacts, the fearful specter of war does not disappear, indeed, appears as an ever-present *Mene mene teklphares* on all the walls?
>
> *Justitia et pax osculatae sunt.* Justice and peace are inwardly bound sisters. These words of the psalmists give the answer to this question, in which the psalmists like the prophets and like Christ himself used the word just in a comprehensive sense as a synonym for the *Kingdom of God. There is no assurance of peace without the realization of the Kingdom of God. This, shortly and essentially stated, is the fundamental truth of the whole Christian peace movement,* which all those interested in peace and those responsible for peace cannot have drummed into their ears often enough.
>
> There has been war in the past because *the realization of the Kingdom of God on earth has been lacking.* And we may not be certain of a peace for the future if the *Kingdom of God* on earth is not more deeply rooted than it has been in the past.
>
> The Kingdom of God however is *truth, justice,* and love.
>
> ### War - Lies!
>
> War owes its existence in the world to the father of lies. War itself is a lie; it comes from lies. Only through lies can it become possible

today. Greedy mammonism, shameless imperialism, arrogant nationalism, cynical Machiavellianism, these lying brothers stand at the side of its cradle. Untruthful diplomacy has built a chasm of mistrust between all peoples so abysmally deep that the difficulty of overcoming this mistrust is the reason why statesmen always conclude nonaggression pacts and immediately sharpen the dagger which they have hidden in the folds of their garments.

Si vis pacem, para bellum. (If you want peace then prepare yourself for war.) This arch-pagan principle is still deeply imbedded in all of us, even the allegedly 'Christian' statesmen.

Otherwise war preparations would not take over in the period of nonaggression pacts! And when the moment comes, after having been induced by the lies of *sacro egoismo* of its leading statesmen, to take up arms, the refined, well-oiled organization of the deception of the people by a mendacious and venal press would be as little assistance as it was in past wars . . . .

You people of Europe! Once and for all *have done with this system of lies in politics! Veritas liberabit vos!* The truth will make you free. It alone! All lies, including the lies of politics, have short legs!

You statesmen! For you too the words of Christ are valid! Let your speech be: Yes, yes, no, no! What is beyond this is of evil! Unrestricted truth without a double level secret diplomacy will create *the trust* which more than anything else lays the foundation for the mutual undertaking of the nations, for the agreement of nations in peace.

And Justice!

Justitia fundamentum regnorum. Thus it is written on a city gate of Vienna. Unfortunately, it is only on dead stone, not on the living consciences of the responsible guides of the history of nations. Justice is the foundation of all human community, most of all, of course, a community of nations and therefore of peace.

Justice is the contradictory of all Machiavellianism, which pursues the naked egoism of the individual nation or state as the highest standard of all politics, thereby only calling forth in the neighboring nations a similar unscrupulousness in its own politics, a similar attempt to make raw power prevail. Can anyone be in doubt that in politics between states in the past naked paganism was trump? Or was there a single statesman who in his policy placed before himself even once the Christian question of conscience: is what I am now attempting to attain for my state also reconcilable with the life interests of the neighboring states? Can anyone but a naive person be in doubt that only through the renunciation of these raw power politics will it be possible to reach a genuine surety of peace?

However, and this is the decisive point, one cannot expect that justice will become a basic law of activity in international life when in intranational life, in economics, in party politics, in social intercourse, an unscrupulous power politics is dominant.

You nations and states of Europe! *Either! Or!* "I have laid before you war or peace! Now Choose!" Thus, speaks the Lord. Untruthfulness, injustice, self-seeking, in short, the Kingdom of Belial, the Kingdom of Satan, *these mean war! The Kingdom of God means peace!* Now choose!

You wish to choose peace? That means you must begin to sacrifice your ego with its preying tendencies—with beasts of prey no state and no community of nations can be built! It also means you must cease your idealization of the state, to which, until now, the living man with his conscience has been sacrificed, so that the state, and the class that had control over it, could dispose of other men as material—"man power" was the euphemistic term used in the war!—where men were forced into war service and the murder of men against their consciences. *Respect for living men* and for *human life is demanded* by true Christian justice.

If you wish peace it means that in the place of the lordship of men you must put Christianity, in the place of naked *power politics* in intrastate and interstate activity *understanding and social equality* on the basis of justice and equity must be established. Then it means that you must above all make a radical break with the system of murderous capitalism whose one sin which applies to everyone is the holding back of earned wages and hard-won fruit of labor and thereby is the source of indignation in the ravaged individual men and nations. It means that you must substitute for this a Christian economy in which man is no longer a means and tool of economy and its law of profit, but rather the economy is a means and tool of man and his community....

> *The Kingdom of God means peace.*
> *Peace means the Kingdom of God.*

Therefore, you statesmen and diplomats! If you wish to undertake the foremost and most pressing task of all politics in earnestness and uprightness, you will become preparers of the Kingdom of God—repairers of the Kingdom of God in personal as well as national life! There is only one law that holds for the community as well as the individual. *Every double standard of morality is a lie and corruption*! Become first of all yourselves men of the Kingdom of God who realize *truth, justice*, and *love*! Then will you also automatically become workers of the Kingdom of God . . . .

There is no assurance of peace without the realization of the Kingdom of God! This is what we must say to all those responsible for peace, statesmen and politicians. This is what we must say to all those men of all nations who for their lives' sake are interested in peace.

And the Church?

. . . would not the Church become a scandal for numerous people, would it not be untrue to its most sublime mission in the world, would it not default on its life-infusing and constructing powers in society and earn the rejection of itself by all living men, indeed a *rejection by Christ*, its King, if it did not step forward, with all its powers of persuasion, inopportunely and opportunely, as the apostle admonished, in favor of truth, justice, and love all along the line, in national and international life as well as individual life and thereby in favor of the peace of Christ in the Kingdom of Christ? *Amica mihi patria—amicior veritas, justitia, caritas, pax.* The fatherland is dear to me, however even more dear is truth, justice, love, peace!

The Cross of Peace

It was in South America. For a half a century there was an uninterrupted feud between Argentina and Chile because of the drawing of their border. Conclusions of peace were, as they usually are, only armistices to give the defeated time to rearm for the next conflict and to overcome the enemy. Toward the end of the last century a new armed conflict stood in the offing for which both of the republics with the greatest sacrifices had been arming themselves for years. Then it was that the bishop Benavente, who burned with a Christian love of peace, found the courage to strike a blow for true Christian peace.

On Easter Sunday in the year of 1900, in Buenos Aires, the capital city of Argentina, he gave an enflaming sermon on peace and the reconciliation of the two nations, and then he began to climb into pulpit after pulpit in his diocese in order to promote this Christian idea in contrast to the patriotism that was rife in the land. On the other side of the border a Christian bishop began to preach a similar crusade from place to place. At first only pious women and priests came to hear the preachers but soon the circle of those who were gripped by the desire for peace gradually became ever larger. Thousands of petitions were sent to the parliaments of both nations demanding the cessation of hostilities. And indeed, the governments saw that they were forced to give in. Both nations accepted an arbitration decision by the King of England and since this time all shedding of blood has ended. All fortifications were razed. The warships were sold or transformed into trade ships. The unused military expenditures were eliminated; this saving made possible introduction of social welfare activities. Today a rail line runs across the Andes connecting the capital cities of the two nations.

Up above, however, from the top of the Andes, at the height of over 12,000 feet, there stands today a gigantic statue of the King of Peace, poured from the metal of formerly death-dealing cannons blessing people of both lands, who now enjoy in a noble peace pact the blessing of the peace-of-the-Kingdom-of-God.

May we see the day in which all the workers of the Kingdom of God preach the peace of Christ in the Kingdom of Christ from all the pulpits of the whole world with a similar power of persuasion and apostolic intention as did the two bishops of South America. Then we will also see the day when the instruments of murder of the so-called Christian states of Europe will be transformed into the instruments of life and culture and when Christ as King will bless from on high the league of the Kingdom of God, the true *peace league of the nations of the world*.

Christian Pacifism and Parallels to Communist Ideals

The following year, 1929, Metzger was again invited to address a peace conference in the Hague, a congress of Those Opposed to Military Service (*Kriegdienstgegner*). The topic of his lecture was "Men of All Nations Unite!" It was obviously so structured as to form a parallel to the appeal of the Communist International. Metzger strongly supported conscientious objection and even maintained that in requiring universal peacetime military service the state laid an unlimited claim to power which overreached the natural law basis of the state; hence, citizens should refuse to serve. It should be recalled that in a situation where the two "natural" enemies were the "Christian" nations of Germany and France an *effective international* appeal for conscientious objection on a Christian basis could have been a devastatingly practical preventive of the outbreak of war. Consequently, Metzger supplied the Christian motivation for pacifism—Christ the King of Peace. But beyond Christ, Metzger held up Francis of Assisi as a herald of peace. One can also see in Metzger's words, as well as his choice of a model, the attempt to steal the Communists' thunder: "It is understandable how this man of God, who had nothing before his eye but the interests of the Kingdom of God on earth, placed himself in the bloody battle between the haves and have-nots, decisively on the side of the *minores*—in modern terminology we could almost say, the proletariat and significantly call the brothers of his new order *fratres minores*—dare we say 'proletariat brothers?'"

Metzger closed his address with a statement of radical Christian pacifism: "The Peace movement must make this radical activism its own with a holy conviction of conscience as Francis of Assisi, with a holy reverence for God-created life which was withdrawn from the grasp of man by the unqualified "Thou shalt not kill," with the conviction of the divine power of a holy nonviolence in the service of the Kingdom of God; with the holy determination to realize this Kingdom of God all along the line. This is what will bring peace, this spirit of the ultimate personal self-offering even at the cost of one's own life, as Christ paid it on the cross, the self-offering for truth, justice, love, peace, for the Kingdom of God on Earth." [Metzger would one day back these words up with *The Deed*.]

This Christian radicalness won Metzger not only many friends, but also many new enemies, largely because he was not content to deliver the speech once. As a result of his lectures at the Hague peace conferences in 1928 and 1929 Father Metzger was invited to speak in a number of other localities in Holland, including Eindhoven, in the Catholic diocese of 's-Hertogenbosch, on May 23, 1929, where he gave the same lecture he had just delivered at the Hague: "Men of All Nations Unite!" He delivered it in German, and it was translated into Dutch by a Protestant clergyman, Dr. van Peursem. There was apparently no particular excitement that evening although a number of Communists were handing out propaganda leaflets, but five days later the Catholic bishop of 's-Hertogenbosch addressed a handwritten letter to Karl Fritz, Archbishop of Freiburg. Among other things he referred to van Peursem as a Communistic clergyman (*communistisches Dominée*). His letter was to inform Metzger's bishop of his activity in Eindhoven with the suggestion that it be investigated. He included a newspaper clipping from one of the two local Catholic newspapers that reported Metzger's lecture. It is important to note that he sent only one of the two Catholic newspaper reports; the other was much more sympathetic to Metzger and the peace movement.

The bishop's newspaper clipping reported the meeting as being largely a Socialist and Communist gathering of about two-hundred persons. "The Catholics of Eindhoven, not allowing themselves to be led by the nose, for the most part remained away. Only around ten came, among whom were one or two curious women who were as shady characters as Professor Metzger was." The paper also complained that it was painful to see the sorrowful figure of this Catholic priest in the midst

> of the arch-enemy of the social order and the Catholic Church—whose head, the Pope in Rome, he gave one to believe, approved and encouraged his action . . . . Above all, propaganda was made by the Communists through the distribution of pamphlets like 'The Free Socialist,' 'Under the Red Searchlight,' 'The Conscientious Objector,' 'Murder of the Conscientious Objectors in Prison,' etc., while on the walls here and there Communist slogans were plastered, such as, 'Every Kaserne is a Murder Hole,' and the like.

The writer seemed unaware that if the meeting was made up of 95% Socialists and Communists, the propaganda efforts were almost entirely wasted; if it were not, then a Catholic priest's articulate presence could serve as an effective counterbalance.

Such, also, was Metzger's explanation of the matter to the Freiburg chancery when questioned about the bishop's letter. He wrote that he received an invitation from a neutral Dutch committee of the peace movement to speak at the Congress of Those Opposed to Military Service in the Hague and then also in several other local areas. He accepted the invitation because he believed he should not let the opportunity pass for a Catholic priest to outline the thoughts and aims of the Catholic peace movement before a large number of non-Catholics. At the same time, he privately received from conservative Catholics—apparently also from Eindhoven—an urgent message not to accept the invitation. He replied to them, however, that although he would welcome any Catholic initiative against the threatening danger of war, if, unfortunately, such initiative did not come from the Catholic side, he nevertheless felt he was acting according to the intention of the Holy Father when he worked for peace.

Father Metzger also pointed out that the other Catholic newspaper reported the meeting in almost the opposite fashion and ended by lauding the gathering, although the paper regretted that the Communists used the meeting for propaganda purposes

> even though this was disapproved by the association's leaders. In a neutral gathering this was very difficult to avoid; the Catholics naturally had the same right as the opponents to distribute their literature. To cast an aspersion on me on this account and to describe me as a Catholic priest in the manner that this [the former] 'Catholic' paper loves to do is indeed a sad symptom of the low level of this press.

And there the matter ended.

Writings on World Peace

Besides his lecturing, Metzger also wrote a great deal on the cause of peace. His first effort along this line was an essay entitled *Friedensruf an die Völker* (A Peace Plea to the Nations), which he wrote soon after his discharge from the army in 1915. The essay, which was proscribed by military censorship, was published shortly afterward in Graz under the title *Rassenhass oder Völkerfriede* (Race-hatred or Peace of Nations). In the same year, 1916, Metzger published another essay in booklet form, *Der Feind und die Zukunft Oesterreichs* (The Enemy and the Future of Austria), in which he maintained that the fact that Christians were fighting each other in such bloody and senseless fashion was a sign that Christianity was bankrupt or nearly so; therefore, he called for immediate peace which would be based on justice, truthfulness, and love. "To be without Christ means war. Christ means justice and love, Christ means peace. The triumph of Christianity!"

The following year another essay came from Metzger's pen, *Klassenkampf und Völkerfriede* (Class Struggle and the Peace of Nations). Metzger saw no possibility of lasting international peace unless it was based on a renewal of the social order. He rejected secular socialism as a possible answer to the social problem, for although it too sought the welfare of all the people, its means, class hate, and class struggle, would not attain them. He accused the capitalist of not being concerned about his workers' welfare, but at the same time warned the workers that they were guilty of the same greed and hate; they were just as unfair in their statements as the capitalist in his—if they were in the capitalist's position, they would act the same way! Only if attitudes and actions changed on both sides could there be internal and external peace.

In 1917 Metzger also wrote *Waffenstillstand oder Völkerfriede* (Armistice or Peace of Nations). He wrote of how, on a beautiful spring day in May, he climbed to the top of one of the Styer mountains in southern Austria and stood gazing at the beauty around him.

> As I stood there in quiet, meditative stillness I suddenly heard far in the distance a horrible dull rumble as if the whole of nature shuddered within itself. And then another rumble, and another, and another. And down the valley—yes, there they were—there moved train after train in the direction of this horrible rumble, filled to capacity with men in the prime of their power. And there were other trains dragging cannons, machine guns, and trucks and other munitions, all in the direction of those mountains which stood in the distance with their snow-covered peaks like venerable gray heads whose hair the years had bleached.
>
> It cut into my soul like a sharp knife. This contrast! This undisturbed virgin beauty of the nature of God in which men rejoiced, in which they all could be happy with one another—and there beyond is war!! There in the distance in those mountains, on its virgin white snow, there flowed day after day blood, red warm human blood . . . .
>
> Then there entered my mind images from the time when I stood among these poor men who found themselves in the desperate situation of being forced to shoot and stab one another. In spirit I looked over the battlefield sown with the grisly dead and twitching wounded who screamed for water. I saw the mass graves before me in which there were thrown so incredibly many irreplaceable men in the flower of youth (once there were 330 of my countrymen and as many of the enemy thrown into a single grave); I saw in spirit the land which the war had made a desert of, shelled cities and villages, still burning houses, ruined fields and all around cross upon cross on the numberless graves—a huge cemetery of modern man . . . . !

Metzger continued, saying that all the men in all the armies were tired of the senseless bloodshed; they wanted peace. But they could not speak to each other. The diplomats, statesmen, kings, emperors, and presidents could speak to each other. Why then was there no peace? They too were all in favor of peace, but they said they wanted a lasting peace, and the prerequisites for it were not present: for one side they include the dismemberment of the evil giant, Russia, the humbling of Italy and France and war reparations; for the other, the dismemberment of the multinational state, Austria, along national lines, the overthrow of the imperialistic Hohenzollern dynasty, a warm-water port, Constantinople, for Russia, and war reparations. Obviously, all these prerequisites for peace would never be forthcoming.

However, there was another group that spoke out for immediate peace without annexations or reparations. The typical reaction to this position was that it was completely unacceptable because the other side was the one responsible for starting the war. Metzger argued that the problem of war guilt was very complicated—neither one side nor the other could claim complete innocence; both contributed to the circumstances that made the war inevitable. (This 1917 view of Metzger's was amazingly like the balanced one of objective scholars many years later.) Paramount in these contributory circumstances were militarism and Marinism, including munitions-making (obviously Krupp, etc.), practiced by all the major nations, which produced an atmosphere of distrust, perfectly designed to end sooner or later in war.

> Here lies the key point to the whole problem of peace. A lasting peace, as all Europe yearns for it, is only possible if it is a peace which in fact creates relationships with which every nation can be satisfied, in which every nation can develop itself undisturbed—a peace therefore which will give to each nation its just due in the future. And it must be a peace in which the constant threat and danger to the harmony of the nation, fostered in the past by arms races, will be once and for all eliminated.
>
> Such a peace however will be possible only when every nation without exception not only outwardly, forced through conditions, but rather inwardly, convinced by the irresistible logic of this war, makes its stand on the foundation of justice, fraternal love, and truth . . . .
>
> Truthfulness in the life of the individual and in the life of the nations! It alone is able to overcome gradually the confirmed mistrust of the past and create a relationship of friendly trust which alone can calm the fears of the nations of the earth about each other's peace. Without the most general disarmament possible there will be no lasting peace. But this is impossible, indeed it would look almost like a crime for a statesman to move in this direction, so long as he cannot rid himself of the conviction that his neighbor has a firm purpose in the most secret part of his soul to fall upon him at the next favorable opportunity. The first step to peace therefore is the open declaration of all the nations of the earth and their statesmen that the unchristian maxim of diplomacy accepted until now, that the end justifies the means, bears the burden of a major guilt for the war, and to proclaim loudly

the decision to re-establish in the future the law of truthfulness to its rightful place.

In justice, as it is demanded by Christianity, lies the second real guarantee for peace. *Suum cuique*, to each his due, this is the demand of justice not only in individual life but also in the life of nations. Justice in the life of nations demands an honest testing of the rights and claims of the neighboring states; it requires that everything necessary for their existence and their healthy, vigorous development be given them in the same measure one would claim for one's self. It will not be easy to work out in complex competing interests. However, with good will in the end it will be possible in all cases to find a solution that both parties can accept. Of course, it is presumed that the upright and honest will of all nations will include the recognition of the right of the neighbor to claim that which one sees as justified for oneself. Russia, for example, a nation of such huge expanse, is without any doubt faced with the need of finding an outlet to the sea which will enable it to carry on world trade even in the winter. The fulfillment of this wish, in itself obviously justified, has appeared until now to Russia to be possible only through the possession of Constantinople, which since the time of Peter the Great has been the great Russian aspiration. Naturally such a solution immediately conflicts with the vital needs of Turkey which as well as Russia can make a claim that it should not be injured in its most vital concerns. Must there therefore be war? No! If one investigates the demands on both sides that are made in justice, it will immediately appear that a solution must and can be found which will assure Russia free access to the sea through Constantinople without robbing Turkey of its capital city. Such a solution is without question possible when the move is made not by power but rather by the will of both sides to seek justice. This must penetrate into all of the relationships of the human society. It must also lead to the guarantee of natural rights of the individual nationalities which are divided among the different states, which of course includes the development of their own culture. Thereby many of the sources of irritation among the nations today will of themselves be eliminated. The demand of the Entente that Austria must be broken up into its national parts loses every appearance of justification just as soon as all nations renounce the absorption of individual parts into one nationalism.

Metzger's suggestion of an international arrangement for the passage of Russian ships through the Bosporus not only showed an unusual sympathy for an "enemy" country, but also made eminently good political sense, which has since been put into concrete form. Political good sense shows even more clearly in his espousal both of the causes of the individual nationalities within the Austro-Hungarian Empire (a bold position to espouse in Austria when the war was far from lost) and that of continuing the supranational structure of Austria. If this could have been accomplished creatively the Balkans would have prospered economically, socially, and politically and would not have fallen prey to Nazi Germany and Communist Russia. The alternative was the "Balkanization" of the Austrian Empire. The consequences provided part of the tinder for World War II.

A rapprochement between France and Germany was of particular concern to Metzger. To this end he tried such things as starting a "Peace Sunday" when the Germans and the French would pray for one another. In 1930 he published articles suggesting that French priests spend their vacation in Germany; the Society of Christ the King would put them up cheaply.

In the decade and a half between the end of the war and the rise of Hitler, Metzger not only established the first effective Catholic peace organization, but also attempted to further Catholic forces working for an international Catholic league that would match the efforts of the League of Nations. Not that he advocated Catholics absenting themselves from the work of the League, but he felt there were additional forces and motivations available in the Catholic Church which needed to be thrown into the struggle. He also took the same approach in his speeches to mixed groups like Sangnier's Democratic Congresses and conscientious objection organizations. From those movements and organizations that followed the "signs of the times," but which Catholics could not in good conscience join, such as Marxist socialism and the *Comintern,* Metzger drew what good he could and advocated matching their appeal by placing these positive goods within a Christian framework. Thus, he promoted Christian socialism, based on justice and cooperation rather than class warfare as Marxism was, and a Catholic International, based on Christian doctrine and practice rather than Marxist doctrine and practice as the Communist International was. However, in the early 1930s Metzger's peace work was radically deflected, as was everyone else's.

From 1930 onward the catastrophic Great Depression spread from the United States to Europe and the rest of the world. In Germany, unemployment and social dislocation was followed by political confusion and chaos. With the increase of unemployment there came a corresponding rise in the Communist party—which was viewed by the Catholic Church as the archenemy. Largely in reaction to this Communist strength, the anti-Communist National Socialist party also grew tremendously.

In 1930, the Catholic Church vigorously opposed the Nazi party on theological and moral grounds. But by January of 1933, when Hitler took power, not a few Catholic priests and prelates had joined the Nazi party. Metzger's bishop, Conrad Gröber, strongly supported the party, and was later even referred to as "the brown bishop." Although he, like many other bishops, later publicly opposed the government on a number of issues, he never did so on the question of war and the murder of the Jews.

Metzger, however, was not among those Catholics who reversed their attitude toward the Nazis in 1933. In May 1933, when it was highly dangerous but still possible to voice criticism of the party, Metzger's *Christkoenigsbote* published a full-page, front-page editorial on the new government. He stated in clear and detailed terms his past, and obviously present, objections to the party.[3]

> We openly acknowledge that we have been convinced opponents of the movement which in the meantime has seized the rudder of state for itself. What led us to such basic opposition was certainly not partisan interest—we have never subscribed to a particular party—but, in the final analysis, our evangelical conscience. We sensed in the young National Socialistic movement a natural force which as yet had not been baptized by the Holy Spirit, which appeared to destroy with rage and recklessness, without respect and consideration which alone promises a fruitful construction. We did not agree with a critique of the present and the past which quite obviously was not always reconcilable with truth and justice. We could not sanction a pagan power principle standing in opposition to the Christian point of view, even when it promised to protect Christian interests. We could only say no to a power principle which one-sidedly builds upon blood and race alone and appears to rob the spirit of its divine image. We heard too much pathos and too little reasonable reflection; we saw too much propaganda and suggestive demagogy and found too little objective

---

[3] As clear as this public opposition to Hitler was stated, it was, necessarily, considerably more restrained than an earlier expression of Metzger's attitude in a private letter dated February 11, 1933. "Yesterday evening we heard Hitler on the radio. My worst fears were surpassed. He is a completely hysterical maniac or a thug of the worst sort. After the lecture I said I would have no qualms about shooting him if I could thereby save the lives of the thousands of men who will have to die because of him. Even if I were torn apart in the process . . . . I have a very pessimistic view of the future for Germany. Hitler is obviously determined not to relinquish power if he does not receive a majority in the election but will stage a strike against the state.

> power of persuasion, and feared therefore a decline of that which is most worthwhile in the German heritage. We were anxious about a Germany which wantonly brought upon itself a world of enemies instead of finding its task in world history in the great mission of spiritual and intellectual leadership. That was the basis for our opposition.

Metzger then turned to the positive elements in the party's program, obviously hoping by this to do his small bit in directing the party's energy along these lines.

> Never before has a man in Germany received into his hands such power as Adolf Hitler. We are not among those blind admirers of the new *Führer* of Germany. But we acknowledge his courage and his power of decision. We gladly believe in the sincerity of his character, in the genuineness of his love for the German people. And we gladly affirm everything he does to serve the people. If and when he daringly undertakes to solve the titanic tasks such as freeing the Germans from the fearful popular pestilences of alcoholism, tuberculosis, venereal disease, etc.; when he breaks the chains of economic exploitation and sets up a genuine community of the people in the economic arena; when he strives to make every German once again economically independent on his own plot of ground and lead him to a modest prosperity through magnanimous land settlements; when he eradicates what has always been moral decay and corruption and helps to renew the roots of the power of the German people; when he protects the Christian faith and morals and promotes a genuine evangelical Christianity; when he assures the German people of its place in a peaceful competition among the nations [all aims publicly proclaimed by the Nazis]—in short, wherever he strives and works for the true national welfare of the German people—he will find us there as prepared and active helpers.

Metzger then took a position that was obviously incumbent upon him as a law-abiding citizen. He pledged his loyalty to the new legal state and looked to Hitler to prove his worth in his future actions.

> Out of a love for truth and justice, and at the same time out of a love for the German people, we stand in complete loyalty to the new state. We realize that in the battle for political victory some things must take place which in more peaceful times a sober insight and reflection would reject. We would regard it as unfair to tag the movement itself with the irresponsible statements of individuals. It is not the words of individual self-appointees, but rather the deeds of the responsible

leader [*Führer*] that must decide the historical worth of the national revolution.

But Metzger's concluding statement retained the autonomy of the individual conscience. He pledged his willingness to die for principles greater than the Fatherland. He was to keep that pledge someday.

> We know also that in the new state there will be struggles and, when it is necessary, suffering. It is honorable to die for a 'Fatherland,' but even more so for truth and justice. And we repeat again today what we said before, that the Fatherland is dear, but even more dear is truth, justice, and Christian conviction.

In the center of this large article, in a heavy black frame, there was in large print a prayer for the German nation and its *Führer*. In its closing phrases Metzger once again expressed his burning concern for peace.

> Let us pray for the German people and its *Führer* . . . . Let it be one in mutual respect and mutual service in genuine national community and true love of peace! Lord, in your eternal mercy grant it and all nations the peace of Christ in the Kingdom of Christ!

Metzger made one last overt plea for peace. On March 7, 1935, Hitler announced Germany's repudiation of the Treaty of Versailles and the Locarno mutual-guarantee treaty and simultaneously sent twenty thousand German troops into the Rhineland—which had been demilitarized by the Treaty of Versailles. On March 16, Hitler proclaimed the rearmament of Germany; the Reich would at once reintroduce compulsory military service and would increase the peacetime size of her army to more than half a million men. This same month Metzger ran a front-page picture and article in the *Christkoenigsbote*, which was entitled, "Give us peace Lord in our days!" Within a matter of days, the *Christkoenigsbote* was suppressed by the Nazis.

ECUMENISM

Although Father Metzger was one of the first Catholics on the scene of the current ecumenical movement, it must be remembered that the Catholic Church, and hence Catholics in general, were latecomers to the movement. Before the situation would be apt for the Catholic Church's entrance into the ecumenical dialogue a number of historical developments were necessary.

Protestant theology underwent a radical change at the time of the First World War. During the nineteenth century the strongest school in Protestant theology was "liberal theology," in which the Scriptures were treated as just another set of human documents, and the Christian religion was analyzed as merely the latest and highest evolutionary expression of humanity's religious drive. But in the pessimism following the First World War, Protestant theologians turned away from its former presuppositions and methods, and, particularly under the leadership of Karl Barth, again saw the Bible primarily as the word of God spoken to humanity. Theology became much more God-centered than humanity-centered; the various critical methods were made strictly ancillary to the search for God's message to humanity. Moreover, Barth and others insisted that theology not be wedded to any particular set of philosophical categories, but that it speak the language of the Scriptures, and that the preaching of the word of God was incumbent upon the Church.

Such changes in Protestant theology helped to make it much more concerned about the disunity of the Church and also made it a more apt partner for a dialogue with Catholic theology, which had been a stubborn opponent of the "liberal theology."

The extraordinary change in Catholic Reformation scholarship that took place in the twentieth century, particularly in Germany, on the Catholic side helped to clear the way for a fruitful conversation.

Ever since the time of the Reformation, Catholic and Protestant scholarship was poisoned by polemics that made it impossible for scholars, and the laity following them, to present any sort of objective analysis of events and persons. It was again really only after World War I that Catholic writing on the Reformation began to ascribe some guilt and evil to the Catholic Church and some righteousness and goodness to Luther and the other Reformers. The best example of objective and irenic scholarship by a Catholic in the area of Reformation studies is the monumental *Die Reformation in Deutschland* published by Joseph Lortz in 1939 and 1940. Here Catholic faults were objectively described and acknowledged, and the many legitimate desires and great talents of Martin Luther were outlined and recognized.

This scholarly revolution helped to make it possible for Catholics and Protestants to begin to speak to each other rather than to straw men.[1]

Ever since the time of the Reformation with its motto "sola scriptura," the Protestant churches placed a strong accent on the Scriptures both on the scholarly, ecclesiastical level and on the level of the individual Christian's use. In reaction to this stress, the Catholic Church—in much the same manner that it unfortunately froze on a Latin liturgy in recoiling from the Protestant adoption of a vernacular communal worship—placed great restrictions on the use of the Bible—again, doubtless to its own disadvantage. This anti-scriptural attitude pretty well prevailed till the time of Pope Leo XIII (1878-1903), who did much to encourage both Catholic Scripture scholarship and the spread of the Bible among the faithful. Although Catholic Scripture scholarship, along with Catholic scholarship in general, received a serious setback with the loss of the Modernist heresy hunt during the first decades of this century, it gathered momentum after the First World War. Catholic scholars began to absorb the results of the critical research done by Protestants more and more and to approach them in an apologetic fashion less and less. By 1943 the scholarly climate had so changed that Pius XII could write his encyclical *Divino afflante Spiritu*, which was the Catholic Scripture scholar's *Magna Carta*. But even before this, much was being done to promote the use of the Scriptures among the masses of the people—very particularly in Germany. By the early 1930s, a Bible movement was underway in Germany. The impact of this Catholic Biblical revival in the area of ecumenism was, of course, immense. Bishop Besson of Lausanne once remarked that whereas the Bible had been the source of division to our forefathers, it would now become the means to reunion.

Another Reformation pillar was the notion of the priesthood of all believers. Although this concept has been put into practice in varying degrees by different Protestant Churches, it has nevertheless been characteristic of Protestantism in general to stress the importance of the laity within the structure. The opposite has been true of the Catholic Church even before the Reformation.

---

[1] See Leonard Swidler, "Catholic Reformation Scholarship in Germany," *Journal of Ecumenical Studies*, 11, 2 (Spring, 1965), 189-204.

In fact, the extreme growth of clericalism throughout the Middle Ages no doubt contributed considerably to the coming of the Reformation. Of course, after the sixteenth-century upheaval the Catholic Church reverted even more strongly to a clerical emphasis in the Church; tome upon tome was written in apology for the hierarchical structure. Great stress was placed on the position of the clergy apart and above the laity, who were pretty well relegated to a passive and at best a very ancillary role. But with ever-growing insistence, the lay person in the Catholic Church was encouraged to take a more active part in the life of the Church. The response to this call was increasingly vigorous, manifesting itself not only in the layperson's involvement in the liturgical and Biblical movements, but also in a myriad of lay organizations and enterprises and the rather dramatic growth of professionally trained and articulate lay theologians—although the lay theologian is nothing new in the history of Christianity. What this raising of the layperson's position in the Catholic Church has done in preparation for a possible rapprochement between Protestants and Catholics is no doubt obvious.

Beginnings of a Liturgical and Ecumenical Movement

In the first part of this century, both the Catholic and Protestant Churches in Germany began to experience the beginnings of a liturgical movement. The commonness of the experience and the mutual influence across the confessional line already provided an impetus toward rapprochement. But, in addition to that, many of the reforms advocated, and eventually attained in the Catholic Church, such as congregational singing, use of the vernacular language, and more emphasis on preaching, had long been thought of as characteristically Protestant. The converse ensued in the Protestant churches; stress was placed on the Eucharist, the sacraments, and a richer worship life in general—all things thought to be characteristic of Catholicism.

One other major historical development served as a sort of precondition necessary to the Catholic Church's involvement in ecumenism in Germany: the growth of the "ecumenical movement" in the particular sense of the "Faith and Order" and "Life and Work" movements, which culminated in the World Council of Churches. The centrifugal forces inherent in the theological and historical structure of Protestantism worked for almost four hundred years with very little opposition. It is only with the rather sudden surge of the missionary movement within Protestantism in the last century that the ground was laid for a counterbalancing drive toward unity. In preaching Christ—a divided

Christ—to the non-Christian world, the Protestant missionaries became painfully aware of the sin of disunity they were bearing and perpetuating. It was then in Edinburgh in 1910, at the World Missionary Conference, that these feelings found mutual support and gave birth to the plan for the world Christian movement of Faith and Order. Shortly afterward a parallel movement, for Life and Work, was launched—based on the fear that Christians could put off working together until unity in the difficult areas of creed and church structure had been reached. After the initial world meetings, the former in 1927 and the latter in 1925, a need for uniting forces was mutually recognized. A proposal was put to the two bodies at their separate meetings in 1935 and approved. The completion of the union, which was delayed because of the outbreak of the Second World War, took place with the founding of the World Council of Churches in 1948 at Amsterdam.

The phenomenal growth of the ecumenical movement was partially the result of, but also in turn largely the cause of, a profound concern and search for unity among many Christians. Until recently the World Council of Churches, like its parent organizations, was almost exclusively Protestant in its membership; of late more Orthodox Churches have joined. From the very beginning, strenuous efforts were made to include all Christians, but Rome—usually politely, but always firmly—turned the invitations down. Nevertheless, ecumenism was in the air.

Even before World War I ended, German Protestantism had given birth to a High Church Movement (*Hochkirchliche Vereinigung*). In addition to its strongly liturgical orientation, it had a vigorous ecumenical wing which in the middle 1920s broke off from the original group over the very question of confessionalism versus ecumenism. The new group formed its own High Church-Ecumenical League (*Hochkirchlich-Oekumenischer Bund*) which published its own periodical, *Una Sancta*, from 1926 to 1928. It was at this point that German Catholics began to become involved; some of them joined the League in auxiliary fashion, began publishing in the *Una Sancta*, and eventually were placed on its editorial board.

However, in 1928 Catholic ecumenism suffered a serious setback. The first two world ecumenical conferences had just taken place; the Catholic-Anglican discussions under the leadership of Cardinal Mercier—the so-called Malines Conversations—had also just ended with the death of the Cardinal. A very misleading report about Catholic participation in what was described as an apostate inspired and inspiring organization, High Church-Ecumenical League was sent to Rome by a German Jesuit. These events helped precipitate the writing of the encyclical *Mortalium animos* by Pius XI in 1928. In the encyclical, he forbade Catholic participation in the world ecumenical organizations. In addition, a statement was issued by the Curia prohibiting Catholic membership in the League and any connection with its publication.

In the meanwhile, the League had rejoined the parent organization, which accepted ecumenism as a plank in its platform. The result of the curial statement, however, was the cessation of the publication of the *Una Sancta* and widespread disillusionment and disappointment. Nevertheless, a successor magazine, with no connection to the *Vereinigung* and with a different editor (Protestant, of course), the *Religioese Besinnung*, was founded. This periodical was not exclusively ecumenical or even theological in its orientation, but it did contain articles in that vein. In 1934 it was suppressed by the Nazis; its last issue carried an amazing challenge by its editor, Karl Thieme.

> Here, then, is the question which we now put to the Roman Catholic Church. There are German Evangelical Christians, there are Christian families, there are also probably whole believing congregations with their shepherds, all of whom are forced by their consciences to ask for admittance into the one eternal Church. But they are compelled by those same consciences, by their understanding of the welfare of the Church, and by the anxiety with which their brethren watch the course they are now taking, to insist upon conditions already accorded Slavic Christians—to request that under the guidance of their own shepherds they may, in their own beloved language, render God service and worship according to the ordinances of the Catholic Church. Will this plea be granted or repudiated?

The Contributions of Father Metzger

Several years before *Hochkirchlich-Oekumenischer Bund* began to publish contributions by Catholics in its organ *Una Sancta* where Father Metzger was publicly involved in discussions with Protestants. In fact, already as a student, Metzger kept a file of bibliography and notes entitled "Reconciliation of the Christian Confessions"—perhaps he was also stimulated in this direction by his dissertation professor, Georg Pfeilschifter, who published *The Ecclesiastical Reunion Efforts of the Post-war Period* in 1923. From 1919 on, Metzger took an active part in the conference of the International Fellowship of Reconciliation where he met and worked with many like-minded Protestants. In 1923, along with Father Hermann Hoffmann, Metzger attended the IFOR conference in Nyborg, Sweden. Hoffmann reported in 1963: "Thus we dared something unheard of at Nyborg in 1923. It seems to me that the idea came from Brother Paulus. That Wednesday was free of any activities. We suggested holding a meeting of the clergy of all confessions in the afternoon. It happened. There were the two of us Catholic priests, but there was a large number of Protestant ministers, especially from the Nordic countries. We suggested first that a president be elected, namely, Professor Geismar of the theological faculty in Copenhagen, the biographer of Kirkegaard and editor of his works. It was the first ecumenical world conference. The discussion was lively. Brother Paulus again proved himself skilled and open in discussion."

In 1924, when ecumenism was hardly a fad, Father Metzger delivered the major address at a meeting in Graz sponsored by the Graz Mission League of the White Cross under the title, "The Protestants and Us." The jammed hall was overfilled with clerics and laypeople, about half Catholic and half Protestant, who listened very attentively to Dr. Metzger's two-hour lecture, which was followed up by another evening of discussion. Even at this early date, Metzger espoused ideas that became avant-garde positions to Catholic thinkers and scholars only years later. He insisted on the unity of the Church being Christ's will—nothing new for a Catholic—but also insisted that convert-making was not the answer, and that although no one could imagine how final unity could overcome the present obstacles, every Christian had an obligation to take those steps toward unity that were possible; both sides should foster mutual understanding and fraternal charity—rather strange words in the mouth of a Catholic priest at a time not too far removed from the *Kulturkampf* and in the heart of the land of the Counter-Reformation. Metzger even anticipated Joseph Lortz's epoch-making work on the Reformation by some fifteen years when he maintained that by the beginning of the sixteenth century a "Reformation" had become historically necessary.

The discussion evening turned out to be a very exciting affair. For an hour and a half, several Protestants held forth in rebuttal of several of Father Metzger's positions and of the Catholic Church in general. The waves of the *Kulturkampf* rose rather high. One Protestant pastor maintained very vigorously the old Bismarckian line that the papacy was anti-German and that on the other hand Protestantism, Christianity, and *Deutschtum* were identical. There was one comic point when the young Protestant Pastor Pohl von Stainz attacked Catholics in the sharpest tone, particularly for their lack of the spirit of irenicism and reconciliation. In an attempt to document his position, he accused Catholics of having gone to the first evening when their position was presented, but not to this discussion evening when it was being refuted; when he asked for a show of hands of Catholics present, at least half of those present went up. But the high point of tension was reached when, during a response, Father Metzger mentioned that General Ludendorff had rejected Pope Benedict's offer of peace mediation. A number of the "Protestants" present were Nazis (*Hakenkreuzler*) who, as soon as Ludendorff's name was mentioned, screamed "He's insulting Ludendorff!" "Let's not insult Ludendorff!" But the challenges of the discussion were really Metzger's meat. His utter sincerity and goodwill, his brilliant speaking talents, and his amazing persuasive power were a match for the situation. He carefully answered each of the accusations and ended with a moving appeal "that Catholics and Protestants pray with and for one another that God . . . grant unity in faith again to Christendom and particularly the German people."

The influence of these early ecumenical meetings manifested itself in the formation of the religious groups set up by Metzger. In the 1924 guidelines for the members of the White Cross, all members were urged to help all men "whoever they may be, therefore even persons of other faiths, nations, parties, races . . . ." The work of the *Petrus Diakonat* section of the White Cross, which focused on peace work, was described as follows: "The truth of the unity of all humanity in one heavenly father, in one divine savior and in one Holy Spirit should be more and more emphatically preached everywhere, more and more clearly recognized by Catholics of every land. The unity willed by God of all Christians in a Catholic community that breaches all borders should, particularly in all Catholic Christians, become vitally conscious and practically lived out in them." Metzger also gave the successor of the White Cross, The Society of Christ the King, the task of working for Christian unity. Already in 1927, the statutes of the society listed the "cooperation with religious social movements like that for the reunion of the confessions and churches that are separated from the church" as one of its purposes. The 1932 revision of the statutes emphasized this task even more.

For the next few years, the "time of troubles," Metzger's energies were drawn off in other directions. But in 1927, the first world meeting of the Movement for Faith and Order prompted him to renew his efforts to promote Christian Unity. The August/September 1927 issue of his *Katholischer Missionsruf* published an article, probably written by Metzger, on the meaning of ecumenical. The position of the article was very strong for its time. After defining ecumenical as universal it continued:

> The problematical and difficult point however is how to understand the ecumenical, universal Christendom. If one were to mean by this a characterless syncretic *Mischmasch*, a church-political or dogmatic compromise among the various confessions, it would be fundamentally false, and we Catholics could never participate . . . . Ecumenicity is what true universality is: the transforming of multiplicity into a

> unity full of life; this is possible only in the power and fullness of living truth . . . . Whoever thinks therefore that he must reject ecumenical efforts in the interest of maintaining the purity or composure of the 'Catholic' truth does not know what ecumenical means, or he is not at all concerned about the full, living truth. What today is found in such a proud 'rejection' is in fact not a living faith . . . but rather a total system which simply sits in judgement on everything which does not have its stamp of approval. That amounts to setting up a self-made image as god before which all should bow down.

Elsewhere in the same number, Dr. Metzger told his readers that the *Missionsruf* should serve not only the causes of peace and social reform but also of the unity of Christians.

> Above all it is necessary to arouse the spirit of penance, to renounce the blind lack of self-criticism and the pharisaical self-justification of one's own side; to bring love into our thinking, our thinking about those who believe other and think other than we do, about everything 'other' in general. In this sense we hope this paper has made and will continue to make its modest preparatory service for this most necessary work of the Kingdom of God at this time, that all may be one, 'one shepherd and one flock.'

That same August, Father Metzger was visiting the Marienheim house of the White Cross in Lausanne, Switzerland, at the same time the Faith and Order meeting was taking place there. Taking advantage of this opportunity, Father Metzger asked Marius Besson, the Catholic bishop of the area, for permission to attend. The right to grant such permissions to Catholic theologians had been extended to him by the Vatican; Bishop Besson, who most fortunately showed a deep understanding and sympathy for ecumenical endeavors, even at that early date granted permission to at least two and perhaps as many as seventeen theologians. Happily, Father Metzger had for some time been in contact with Bishop Besson through the establishment of the White Cross sisters; as a result of this contact and the sisters' excellent work he received permission to act as an observer. Metzger daily attended the conferences and held long discussions with many of the leading Protestant theologians, including Friedrich Siegmund-Schultze. It was he whom Metzger and his friend from the pacifist movement, Father Hermann Hoffmann,[2] approached to help obtain permission of the conference leaders to make a report of the proceedings to the Holy

---

[2] Dr. Marianne Moehring believes Metzger and Hoffmann were the only Catholic priests at the conference. Marianne Moehring, Taeter des Wortes (Meitingen: Kyrios-Verlang, 1966) p. 103.

Father. Siegmund-Schultze led them both to the president of the conference, Episcopal Bishop Charles Brent of the Philippines, who gladly gave approval and a note of recommendation. Both men set out immediately for Rome; however, the Curia did not permit the delivery of their report. Metzger nevertheless did briefly report the events of the conference in the October issue of the *Missionsruf*; he also complained vigorously about the misreporting of the conference by the Catholic newspapers.

While still at the conference, Father Metzger composed a new melody for the so-called "Stockholm Song," *O Saliga Dag* by Natanael Beskow, which had been sung a great deal at the World Conference for Life and Work at Stockholm in 1925. He showed the composition to Siegmund-Schultze who immediately took him to Archbishop Soederblom, the prime mover of the Life and Work Movement. Soederblom graciously accepted the gift and hummed through the notes. He then commented:

> It would be very nice if we would be able to use this composition from a Catholic brother in our song book. However, first of all it would not fit the character of the poet or the song to have this hope for the unity and peace of the Church in a minor key . . . . And second—he added smilingly—the melody we are now using comes from my predecessor in Upsala, whose work I could not eliminate from our songbook.

Ecumenical Writings

From this time on, articles of various sorts on ecumenical topics appeared with increasing frequency in the *Missionsruf*. Most often they were written by Father Metzger himself. The articles continued to be irenic in tone, sometimes taking the form of an open letter to Protestants on such controversial problems as Marian devotion and the saints. They consisted neither of apologetics nor capitulation of all Catholic traditions. They were quite avant-garde for the time, though of course they were nothing like the work of Rahner, Küng, and others later who were able to speak the truth much more freely. Metzger took several occasions to recommend the ecumenical books of men like the Protestant Joseph Lortzing and the ecumenical endeavors of the Protestant periodical *Religioese Besinnung*. His articles were in turn quoted by Protestant journals. In 1933, he ran a letter from a Protestant minister on Protestant/Catholic union problems and invited replies. He received many—all very favorable—and published some of them. All of this was rather daring at this time; it was not too long after *Mortalium animos*, and the Nazis had just come to power, complicating matters.

In the latter part of 1934, Father Metzger devoted almost an entire issue of his paper *Christkoenigsbote* to ecumenism. The headline across the top of the front page read *Evangelisch-Katholisch*. Metzger asked in what direction the solution to the division between Protestant (or "Evangelical" as they are usually referred to in Germany) and Roman Catholic Christians lay; should Catholics become Evangelical or Evangelicals become Catholic? He answered: both.

> Catholic brothers in faith, become evangelical! Not that you should leave the Catholic Church, but that you should fulfill its real and ultimate calling. Evangelical renewal, a thorough Christianization (*Durchchristlichung*) of the Church, is the essential prerequisite so that the serious Christian of the Evangelical Church may recognize that here is Christ and his Gospel pure and unfalsified, in full, unbroken vital power. [John XXIII's call to the Second Vatican Council a quarter of a century ahead of time!]
>
> 'Evangelical' brothers, become catholic! Free yourselves from negative protestation, from pre-judgement, from all narrowness of national and racist attachment! Take up again where your forefathers left off! Make their demands your own—the genuine evangelical renewal of the Church. It will not be accomplished by holding oneself aloof from the life springs of the Church, but rather by living from them and by working together with all earnestly striving Christians to build up the "communion of saints, in the one, holy, catholic and apostolic Church."
>
> Catholics, become evangelical! Evangelicals, become catholic!
>
> When will there be the *una sancta*, the one holy Church for which we jointly strive and pray?

Those in the forefront of the ecumenical movement today, nearly a century later, could make these words of Father Metzger's their own.

Ecumenism in Germany

About this time ecumenical activity in Germany was beginning to expand rapidly. The anti-Christian pressure of the Nazis served as a sort of catalyst to the Protestant/Catholic contact that had already been slowly increasing as a result of such forces as the liturgical, Biblical, and lay movements. In Pentecost week of 1934, an extraordinary meeting took place at the seminary of Hermsdorf near Berlin, the result of the late Archbishop Soederblom's wish and with the sponsorship of the Catholic bishop of Berlin, Nikolaus Bares. The Protestant participants were members of the *Hochkirchliche Vereinigung* or like-minded theologians; they included Staehlin, Ritter, Heiler, and Nygren. Even Anglicans and Swedish Lutherans took part. The men from the Catholic side, theologians of equal note, included Pietryga, Pribilla, and Guardini.

The themes of the conference were grace and justification, grace and church, grace and sacraments. One participant reported that the conference

> clearly showed that there existed between the representatives of the *Hochkirchliche Vereinigung* and the Catholic theologians no point of dispute, and that there was a surprisingly far-reaching agreement even between the representatives of other Protestant schools of theology and the Catholic theologians; therefore, a continuation of this discussion should take place in smaller circles so as to gradually attain complete agreement with Catholic dogma.

The unidentified author (probably Friedrich Heiler) went on to say that for those Protestants close to the Catholic Church the obstacles to reunion were not so much matters of dogma as of discipline and liturgy. He asked whether the Holy See could not grant the *Hochkirchliche Vereinigung* the following five requests: 1) The use of the mother tongue in the celebration of Mass; 2) the basic retention of the centuries-old Lutheran form of the liturgy with adjustments and enlargements being made to correspond to dogma; 3) the use of a simplified ceremonial for at least a transitional period; 4) the reception of Communion under both forms; 5) the retention of a married clergy at least for converted Protestant clergy. The author felt that if these simple requests were granted, it would give a concrete example to other Protestants that joining the Catholic Church would not entail giving up their worthwhile traditions and customs, but rather would mean their preservation and completion. The writer even gave detailed suggestions as to how this might actually be accomplished and believed that the reception of groups and congregations of such Protestants into the Catholic Church would prepare the way for the complete reunion of the two Churches. This appeal actually sounded quite similar to the ones made by the Protestant scholars Karl Thieme and J. Lortzing in 1933; later, in 1947, the Catholic theologian Karl Adam strongly suggested that most of these concessions could and should be made.

It appears that this Berlin meeting was the spark that started the flame throughout the rest of a very combustible Germany. Friedrich Heiler, who was present, said the discussion was continued in circles in individual cities, particularly Berlin, Paderborn, Kassel, and Munich; there were reports of monthly meetings between Catholic and Protestant pastors in central Germany in Bornstedt, Sangerhausen, Eisleben, Nordhausen, and Erfurt. Apparently, the circle at Kassel quickly took a leading position, attaining a membership of two to three hundred in a short time, and it in turn gave impetus to the founding of more circles in other cities; still other circles arose independently. Even a partial list of the cities and towns in which there existed such circles of Protestant and Catholic laity and clergy is impressively long: Bielefeld, Berlin, Mainz, Frankfurt, Kassel, Hanover, Hamm, Leipzig, Hamburg, Munich, Stuttgart, Jena, Krefeld, Naumburg, Erfurt, Bornstedt, Sangerhausen, Eisleben, Paderborn, Passau, Bamberg, Alpirsbach, Niederalteich, Metten, Beuron, and Weingarten.

Even earlier, the "Einsiedeln prayer league for the reunion in the faith in Switzerland" was founded in 1929. It numbered around seventy-thousand members by the middle 1930s; it called forth a parallel group on the Protestant side in Switzerland. A much smaller prayer group was started by Father Pius Parsch in Klosterneuburg near Vienna; it pledged itself to daily prayer for unity and by 1940 included about six-hundred laity and clergy. It was called the "Brotherhood of the Praying Church."

Father Metzger, who was always at least up to the tempo of the times, likewise became more involved in ecumenical activities. But the newspapers he edited were one by one closed down by the Nazis, starting with the *Christkoenigsbote* in 1935. This merely meant that Metzger channeled more of his energies into personal contacts and lectures. In fact, in Father Metzger's case, the growing Nazi oppression helped to create more time for ecumenical work. He traveled throughout Germany and, through his many acquaintances on both sides of the confessional line, started many interconfessional study groups; many, of course, had started independently of him, but these too he contacted. He attempted to bring a little more structure to a movement that had sprung up spontaneously in many different places. To this end he founded the Una Sancta Brotherhood in 1938.

The Una Sancta Brotherhood

The purpose of the "Ecumenical Meeting-Circle," or "Una Sancta Circles," as they were soon called, was to promote a rapprochement and mutual understanding between believing Christians of different confessions in fulfillment of "the last wish of the common Lord, 'that all may be one!'" In a mimeographed circular Metzger suggested three different forms of such interconfessional meetings. The first was merely a mutual exchange of visits on the basis of friendship, with discussions on themes of common religious interest—a situation where two clergymen of different confessions lived near each other would be considered particularly apt for this type of Una Sancta contact. The second form was a public lecture series. These, he thought, would be best held in neutral locations, but alternation between halls belonging to the different confessions might also be successful. The series ought to consist of talks by members of both churches on the same questions and should take place regularly, about every month.

Material on a suggested series of themes covering Christian doctrine systematically, or material only on controversial questions, was available through the Una Sancta Brotherhood center at Meitingen. Metzger admonished those interested in this form of ecumenical work that they should not open lectures to an unlimited audience since it was all too easy for argumentative persons to slip in and ruin everything; the same was even more true in the case of the lecturers, "who should be, as far as possible, men who both know their subject well and are irenically inclined, who combine an earnest seeking of truth and a preparedness for understanding."

The third form of Una Sancta Circles was what Metzger considered possibly the most effective of the three types. This was a discussion group of carefully chosen mature people of different confessions. The number should not exceed thirty so as not to destroy the intimacy of discussion. He insisted that the choice of location for discussions was important, that it should be psychologically conducive to a friendly exchange of opinion, and that parliamentary forms be eliminated. He thought there should be two short, simple talks by persons of different churches of twenty to forty minutes in toto on a theme to be discussed at some length afterwards by everyone. He highly recommended that the meetings be opened and closed with a common prayer or reading from Scripture: prayers such as the Apostles Creed and the Our Father were obvious choices, as "Catholics ought to not shy away from praying the ancient ecclesiastical doxology at the end" of the Lord's Prayer.

In addition, meetings with common prayer were urged, especially during the Church Unity week from January 18–25 and the time between the Ascension and the Pentecost; members should carry on ecumenical correspondence, write in ecumenical-minded publications, and cooperate in social projects. Finally, he advised that organization be kept to a minimum, partly to preserve a free spirit in the group and partly to avoid police observation as much as possible. And Una Sancta work should be absolutely free from any effort at convert-making.

By the end of 1939, Metzger joined with the Protestant Superintendent Ungnad of Berlin in a more concerted effort to spread a concern for Christian unity among the masses of Christians. The focus of this effort was to renew Church Unity Week, which was not taken very seriously by many churches and in others had fallen into disuse in recent years. The two men drew up a public invitation to all Christians to engage in this prayer for unity and also to all churches to officially establish Church Unity Week and had it published. About eighty Catholics and Protestants of significance signed it, including Georg Boss (Prot.), the former editor of the interconfessional periodical *Religiöse Besinnung*; the well-known theologian Otto Urbach (Prot.), Alfred von Martin (Prot.); the former editor of the interconfessional periodical Una Sancta; Dom Odo Casel (Cath.), the liturgy scholar; Karl Adam (Cath.), the famous theologian from the University of Tübingen; Konrad Algermissen (Cath.), the author of the encyclopedic *Konfessionskunde*; and Otto Karrer (Cath.), the well-known Swiss theologian.

With the growing success of the Una Sancta Movement by Christmas of 1940, Metzger reported in a letter to Archbishop Gröber that the time had come to set up a theological ecumenical commission which would assume some responsibility for the entire movement. He did not wish to carry such a responsibility alone, but also realized that the Church could not yet take it over directly; therefore, he wished to set up the supra-diocesan commission (in addition to diocesan committees) which was to include Pater Arnold, S.J., Prior Emmanuel Heufelder of Niederaltaich abbey, Dr. Casper and Metzger on the Catholic side with Domprobst Simon of Paderborn as chairman (who chaired the important ecumenical meeting at Hermsdorf near Berlin in 1934) and Bishop Dietrich, Superintendent Ungnad, Pastors Schildge and Minker and probably Professor Hans Asmussen on the Protestant side. Whether or not the commission actually was ever formed is not clear; the growing persecution of the Christian church by the Nazis may very well have postponed its activity. It is interesting to note, however, that the ecumenical theological group that was started in 1947 and composed of theologians from all over Germany was very similar to Metzger's proposal, as was also the much later Bishop's Commission for Ecumenical Affairs in the United States after Vatican II, except that by this time the Church was officially committed to ecumenism. Even his idea of diocesan ecumenical committees has been implemented today.

In 1941, Father Metzger published an extraordinary article entitled "Breakthrough to Una Sancta," which put forth the program of the Una Sancta Brotherhood and its theological basis. He wrote that the blind apologetics of the past, which saw everything as either black or white, makes one ashamed of oneself today. But we are at only the beginning of a really spiritual meeting in genuine Christian freedom. (Hans Küng was to make this notion popular twenty-some years later.) He asked whether this meeting would be fruitful for both sides. He felt it certainly would, with certain presuppositions. First, both sides must be prepared under all circumstances to search out the truth of Christ and to honor it when found, whether it fitted into a pre-existing schema or not. Secondly, both sides must attempt to find within the errors (real or supposed) the kernel of truth that St. Augustine says is in every error. Thirdly, each must with brotherly love try to understand the demands the other believes he must make on the basis of the gospel; and, going beyond that, each must extend himself to grapple with the language and terminology of the other so as to understand him and to be able to judge him on his own terms. An interconfessional study of languages is not the least presupposition of a fruitful meeting.

In Metzger's own words:

> First, many differences are actually not very deep-seated; often they are only apparent contradictions brought about by the different terminologies of the two camps. As soon as an earnest attempt is made to present clearly the whole truth to the other side in their own language, it often turns out that the second side's thinking on fundamentals is not essentially different from that of the first side. Secondly, many differences are not of an exclusive character, but rather . . . arise from an emphasis (often one-sided and overdone) of one truth, with which, however, the apparently opposing truth is perfectly compatible in a higher unity. A genuinely Christian statement here will lead on both sides to the envisioning of the Christian truth, not in the attitude of 'I protest' (Reformation and Counter-Reformation!), but rather in 'catholic' fullness.

It was in just this open, mutual exchange of declarations and explanation of one's own position that Father Metzger saw the most fruitful means of interconfessional meeting. If carried out sincerely it would lead to a clearness about the religious beliefs of the other and thereby eliminate divisive misunderstanding and prejudices. By emphasizing the commonly held Christian truths of faith and teachings, a consciousness of unity and community would be fostered. The exchange should also bring each to scrutinize the differing convictions and attitudes to see whether and to what extent they could be looked upon as complementing viewpoints and united in a higher truth. In those questions, which seem to resolve into an either/or situation, it should lead to a joint striving to expound the truth most especially on the basis of the Holy Scriptures under the guidance of primitive Tradition. Differences which, despite all mutual honest efforts to arrive at the truth jointly, still remain should be carried in joint prayer before God who in the power of his Holy Spirit may bring about unity where human efforts failed.

In the same article, Father Metzger described the Una Sancta Brotherhood. He pointed out that the Una Sancta Brotherhood was not an organization, at least not in the sense of an artificial human-made project; it was much more something that happened as the result of God's grace. It had no "president" other than the common Lord, no statutes other than the common gospel of Christ, no membership obligations other than justice and unrestrained truthfulness, which God grants as a fruit of the Spirit (Eph 5:9).

Metzger further stated that the Una Sancta Brotherhood was neither Catholic nor Evangelical, that it was attached to no church community. The Brotherhood expected to find both an "evangelical" and "catholic" mind in its members: evangelical through an unrestricted recognition of the entire Gospel of Jesus Christ in both belief and life; catholic through an affirmation of the unity of all Christians, which comes from the "one baptism" (Eph 4:5), in "one flock" under Christ, the "one shepherd" (John 10:16).

For Father Metzger, the individual conscience was something very precious; it must not under any circumstances be violated or deprecated. He insisted that the members of the Una Sancta Brotherhood could serve the Una Sancta by fostering mutual contact of the separated brethren without any compromise in the conscientious loyalty of each individual toward his church. They serve both truth and love by overcoming all differences between the churches that flow from prejudice and misunderstanding, by respecting the conscience of the other.

> How should the unity of Christendom be realized? The Una Sancta Brotherhood deliberately does not propose a concrete program. It believes the one Church of Christ must simultaneously develop 'unity in multiplicity' and 'multiplicity within unity.' The 'how?' it leaves with complete trust to the leading of the Spirit of God. The more everyone, as a disciple of the Lord, will be prepared to place his own personal views and wishes in the background and simply look to the Lord and his will, the more they are of one mind and constantly pray in such a frame of mind to 'Our Father' that 'Thy kingdom come!,' the quicker the Holy Ghost will open the way which will lead to one flock under the one shepherd.

Father Metzger asked whether the goal of the Una Sancta Brotherhood is a utopia. It would be blasphemy, he said, to name what is obviously the will of the Lord. What was already realized in the primitive Church—that the faithful were "of one heart and of one soul" (Acts 4:32), that the heathens pointed with their fingers to the Christians and said, "See how they love one another!"—what for over a thousand years proved itself fruitful for the spreading of the Kingdom of God on earth, can again become real. What is beyond the wit and strength of humans, what remains missing by those of little faith will be granted by God in his own hour to those who have the faith to move mountains (Mat 17:20) and those who persevere in prayer (I Thess 5:17).

Resistance to the Una Sancta Brotherhood Activities

This extremely open and irenic article by Father Metzger, written a generation before its time, had severe repercussions. Father Metzger was called in before Msgr. Lichtenberger and Cardinal Preysing of Berlin—where Metzger was living at the time—and subjected to an inquisition on the orthodoxy of his faith. His utter sincerity, erudition, able intellect, and persuasive speaking power all stood him in good stead. He was not hindered in his work, although the Berlin chancery (and especially Msgr. Lichtenberger) did not particularly care for ecumenical activity at this time. However, Father Metzger had for some time sheltered Jews and continued to do so until the end at the risk of his own life. And it was the same Msgr. Lichtenberger who so strongly opposed the persecution of the Jews that he insisted on offering himself to the SS as an accompanying victim with the Jews going to the death camps; he felt that Christ must in the person of one of his priests accompany the Chosen People on the way to their crucifixion. It was he who inspired the character of Pater Ricardo in Rolf Hochhuth's *Der Stellvertreter*. In this matter Metzger and Lichtenberger were one; perhaps this oneness influenced Lichtenberger's tolerance of Father Metzger's Una Sancta activity. In any case it is obvious that not all opposition to ecumenism came from those of bad will and timidity. Nevertheless, Metzger was somewhat later forbidden to lecture on the Una Sancta in his home diocese, Freiburg, by Archbishop Gröber, and in the Breslau diocese by Cardinal Bertram. If there were further restrictions the Nazis and the war destroyed any evidence of them.

Advent of 1939 found Father Metzger in a Nazi prison. While there, he wrote a letter to the Pope concerning the divisions within Christianity and some suggestions about how to overcome them. Today the letter seems not only daring but also prophetic. In one sense it may well have helped to make the truth, since it was reported to have been carried over the border and there safely mailed to Rome; it was also given by Metzger to the Apostolic Nuncio

Orsenigo, who promised to forward it to Rome. Unfortunately, it will be almost another half century before the Vatican files of this period will be open to scholars. Metzger may have been influenced to write such a letter at that time not only because of the world situation—there was then a lull between the fall of Poland and further Nazi *blitzkriegs*—but also because Pius XII, the "angelic Pope," from whom much was expected and who had spent many years in Germany as Papal Nuncio, had come to the papal throne only a few months before.

Metzger began his letter by speaking of the urgent need for peace and described the impotence of a disunited Christianity in avoiding the disaster of war: but the fault for these divisions in Christianity "has not been on one side only"—almost the same words Pope John XXIII, and following him Vatican II, later used.

> Holy Father! The need of our day . . . imperatively demands the utmost effort to heal the dismemberment of the Christian Church . . . . I know that your Holiness grieves especially over the disunity of the Body of Christ . . . [and that] much has already been attempted in this direction during recent years. But the results have as yet been so meager. Why?

Metzger went on to say that too much was at stake for both Church and humanity to reject, without a fair trial, the suggestions of one even so insignificant as him. Besides, as a priest and Doctor of Theology, he offered his wide personal acquaintance with many clergymen of the Anglican, Old Catholic, and German, Swiss, Danish, Swedish and Dutch Reformed, and Lutheran churches, as well as his work in the ecumenical movement and his founding of the Una Sancta Brotherhood, as reasons for allowing his ideas on this problem a hearing.

In Metzger's opinion, difficulties of a spiritual nature were much more important in preventing a closer approach of other confessions to Rome than differences in dogma:

> The opinion of the most favorably inclined among non-Catholic Christians is that a certain proud self-righteousness on our side prevents our acknowledging the faults and failings within our own Church, the sins and errors through which we share in the guilt of these divisions; it prevents that readiness to repent which, they say, we always exact from others. They deduce from this that the Holy Spirit is not the soul of the Church because instead of putting her own house in order, she practices a too rigorous condemnation (1 Cor 11:

31) only finally to be delivered by the Lord. They do not believe that our leader is utterly prepared to serve as the Master did in all humility (John 13:14, Mat 18:4, 20-26) but see in the claim to authority (which they consider inconsistent with evangelical simplicity) a thirst for power and an all too human spirit of self-assertion. They consider that the exercise of his holy office in the Church is often incompatible with the apostolic exhortation in 1 Peter 5:3, and therefore distrust the office itself. They believe that in discussions with heretics there is more desire for a victory for dogmatic and narrow orthodoxy than holy zeal for the truth of God, and are convinced that they have experienced among many, even among leading representatives of the Church, an overbearing spirit and a merciless severity.

Metzger hastened to add (with irony?) that he didn't agree with these criticisms, but they had to be met seriously and dealt with.

More specifically Father Metzger suggested that although to some the time might seem ill-suited to increase efforts toward a reunion of Christianity, he believed that the immense suffering of war would open people's minds to such suggestions. In the 1520s the last Germanic Pope, Hadrian VI, attempted to arrange for an ecumenical council to which the Protestants would be invited. "Unfortunately, this great plan, which undoubtedly would have achieved the best results, was not carried out. People's minds were still too heated . . . . But has not the time come today to repeat this experiment?"

The description of how Metzger believed this experiment could be effectively carried out deserves special attention because it was prophetic in so many ways. He thought an ecumenical council would not be possible without extensive preparation, but that on the other hand it ought not be postponed. Twelve outstanding theologians drawn from countries where divisions exist most strongly could be commissioned to contact a similar number of outstanding persons in the other Christian churches to arrange a series of confidential conversations. A report would then be submitted to a pontifical commission to be studied with a view to preparing for a general council. Metzger then questioned:

> Is all this which I lay before Your Holiness too daring? I know that it goes far beyond what can be counted on to succeed. But it seems to me that only a great venture of faith, humility, and love can solve the problem of the fate of Christendom. Church history and world history alike will raise a memorial to that wearer of the triple crown who begins this work on a generous scale [John XXIII!], and to the one who may perhaps finish it later.

Post-war events have proved Metzger's suggestions to be practicable for, since 1947, fourteen leading Catholic theologians under the leadership of Archbishop Jaeger of Paderborn and a like number of leading Protestant theologians under the leadership of Bishop Wilhelm Stählin of Oldenburg have been meeting annually, and in 1959 Pope John XXIII called the Second Vatican Council and appointed men like Archbishop Jäger to a newly formed Secretariat for Christian Unity, which worked closely with Protestant theologians before and during the Council.

Una Sancta Conferences and Gatherings

In the spring of 1939, Father Metzger wrote a letter to all Protestant ministers in Germany stating that the Church of Christ was meant by the Lord to be one and that because the divisions come from men, it is the duty of all believing Christians to desire and work for the oneness of the Church, which is exactly the purpose of the Una Sancta Brotherhood. At the end of the letter—its tone gives the reader the impression of straightforward sincerity and genuineness, as do all of Metzger's letters—he asked for an answer. "A manifold echo came back. With only one exception the answers indicated on the part of the Evangelical brethren a strong concern and a readiness to cooperate in making unity in Christ a more visible and powerful witness before the world than it is today."[3]

Partly on the strength of these favorable reactions, Metzger held the first Una Sancta Conference at Meitingen during Pentecost week of 1939 (May 29 to 31). The conference, which lasted three days, was attended by sixty Catholic and Protestant clergy and laypeople. It was a careful groping toward one another. Father Metzger hoped it would bring out a mutual willingness to serve the truth unwaveringly and to act in charity at any price—even in relationship

---

[3] According to the *Schönere Zukunft* Metzger received 150 answers. At present at least sixty-two letters are extant; two of them reject the idea of a unifold visible church outright and ten are critical of one aspect or another of Metzger's letter. Five of the answers came from purported "German-Christians," Nazi-inspired racist persons who strongly infiltrated the Protestant churches. Metzger's letter, they said, "accidentally" found its way into their hands. Since from the very beginning of their movement these individuals expended every effort to form a unified Protestant Church in Germany so as to bring it more easily under the control of the state, these German Christians saw in the Una Sancta a way of accomplishing their goal on an even grander scale. Perhaps this concern had something to do with the presence of the Gestapo at the two Meitingen Una Sancta conferences and the infiltration of the Una Sancta by them that led to Metzger's downfall.

with the separated brethren. This would be enough to build on in the future. He was not disappointed. Both sides felt the conference was successful. As a sign of the stage the movement for unity had reached and as an aid to furthering it, it was decided to designate Thursday, the day of the Last Supper, as a day of common prayer for unity. The conference was unfortunately disturbed by Gestapo surveillance and confiscation of files from the convent.

For the next year and a quarter, Father Metzger spent much of his time and energy, when he was not in prison, organizing and inspiring local Una Sancta groups. But he had not forgotten about larger nationwide conferences. He prepared very thoroughly for a second Una Sancta Conference at Meitingen to be held in August 1940. Fourteen lectures were arranged for the period from August 4 to 9; they were evenly divided between Catholics and Protestants. Just the correspondence between Father Metzger and the various lecturers must have been a burden, judging from the extant letters. The theme chosen was also quite bold in the circumstances; it was "the Church." The specific lecture topics ranged from "The Church in the Perspective of Catholic Theology (Protestant Theology)" to "The Church and Reform" and "The *Ecclesia* in the New Testament." After each of the lectures a discussion period followed.

Among the fifty participants that came from beyond the local area, fourteen were Catholic priests and eight were Protestant clergymen, including an official delegate of the Berneuchener Circle (a Protestant liturgical reform group). More would have attended, particularly Protestant pastors, but were prevented by being called to military service. As a consequence, the conference received many letters of greetings and encouragement, including one from a Protestant Landesbischof.

On the Catholic side, there were university professors and pastors who came from the Society of Christ the King, Augustinians, Benedictines, Jesuits, and Carmelites. That the attendance was relatively small, and also that this was the last Meitingen conference, was partly due to the ominous presence of the Gestapo; there were at least two agents at the conference, including one disguised as a priest.

The conference was more than just an intellectual discussion and exchange. The whole meeting took place in the spirit of prayer. Every morning the Catholic Mass was celebrated in various communally participated forms—an all-Latin dialogue Mass, a mostly German dialogue Mass, a congregationally sung High Mass; the non-Catholics were present as guests. "Although it was painfully felt that the 'sacrament of unity and of peace' did not join everyone together visibly in the 'communion,' one was nevertheless conscious of a holy community in Him who was being praised." The evening prayers from the

Divine Office of the Society of Christ the King were also prayed jointly in German; they were composed by Father Metzger from the psalms and ancient hymns of the Church. The scriptural readings before each lecture and the evening meditations were led alternately by Protestant and Catholic clergymen.

Father Metzger was so encouraged by the fruitfulness of this second Meitingen conference that he arranged to have a repeat performance on the same topic in Berlin just three months later on November 5 and 6. The Berlin Dominicans put their church and cloister at Father Metzger's disposal. The form of the conference was basically the same, although in most cases the speakers were different. The response here was even greater than at Meitingen. There were sixty-two Protestants (thirty-six were clergymen), forty-seven Catholics (twenty-two were priests), one Orthodox priest, and twenty-seven lay people of unknown religious affiliation—137 in all, including forty-one women. "The discussions that followed the lectures, which were outstanding intellectually, were entirely objective, frank and at the same time irenic. The spirit of the conference was deeply Christian, genuinely brotherly and strongly moved by the common concern for the Una Sancta. 'Results' were not looked for." Father Metzger nevertheless planned for one tangible result. He hoped to publish the lectures jointly in a book entitled *The Church in Ecumenical Conversation*. It unfortunately never materialized.

Lecturing on Una Sancta

Father Metzger's traveling and lecturing to promote the Una Sancta Movement absorbed more and more of his time. Some pictures of his manifold activities through 1941 can be outlined. He lectured on the Una Sancta to clergy conferences (Catholic) in Stuttgart, Karlsruhe, Mannheim, Wiesbaden, and Nuremberg. He also gave public lectures to groups that varied from mostly Catholic to exclusively Protestant in Berlin, Jena, Erfurt, Dresden, Stuttgart, Nuremberg, Wiesbaden, Frankfurt, Munich, Stettin, Hanover, Halle, and Pforzheim—pretty well all over Germany. He reported one or more Una Sancta Circles either functioning or about to be started in all the cities he lectured in—in many instances he doubtless inspired their founding—plus the following: Augsburg, Kassel, Sangerhausen, Potsdam, Wuppertal, Heidelberg, Cologne, Essen, and Koenigsberg—in all, twenty-two cities. All these circles had been started or contacted by Father Metzger by the end of 1940.

He was not content to promote the Una Sancta only in Germany. He strove to spread its idea in the neighboring countries of Holland, France, Poland, and the Balkans, as is attested to by his correspondence with friends in those countries. He attempted to have his writings and other ecumenical materials translated and distributed through a central distribution point among the peoples of those countries. There is no evidence, however, of what success he had, since the war intervened so soon.

That Father Metzger continued his traveling and lecturing for the Una Sancta on a large scale throughout 1941, 1942, and even 1943 is evidenced by brief references here and there in documents, letters, and especially by many individuals who knew him during this period. But neither he nor anyone else has left a detailed account of where he went or what he encountered. This, of course, is not astonishing considering the times: by the middle of 1940 the war was on in full force and became ever more serious; Father Metzger had ever more to fear from the Gestapo, which had already arrested him three times by 1940, and which was beginning to push its oppression of Christianity as well as Judaism to the limit. Even the progress reports of the Una Sancta Brotherhood, which were distributed in mimeographed or typed form, were marked "confidential." The typed application form for receiving the "Report" indicated probably best of all the restrictive atmosphere that existed in Nazi Germany even in something as nonpolitical as Una Sancta activity.

> To the Una Sancta Brotherhood Meitingen
>
> I request on a loan basis the Confidential Report of the Una Sancta Brotherhood.
>
> I pledge myself expressly
>
> 1) to pass on the Report to no one without the express or doubt-free presumed permission of the Una Sancta Brotherhood . . . .

The Flourishing of Una Sancta in Berlin

By August of 1940, Father Metzger found that living in Berlin would be more advantageous for his Una Sancta work. By that time, not only had his various journals and newspapers been suppressed, but he even had to relinquish the direction of his Christ the King Publishing House; the Nazi *Reichsschrifttumskammer* declared him "lacking in trustworthiness."

The amazing response to the Una Sancta conference in Berlin is some indication of the tremendous potentialities in the ecumenical field in Berlin. It was not just its size, but also its status as the national capital, an intellectual and cultural mecca, that made it very quickly a center of Una Sancta activity. In fact, already by 1940, no other city could match the multiplicity of Una Sancta

Circles and activities of Berlin; that was also true twenty-five years later. Both Dr. Kahlefeld and Dr. Schreibmeyer, two respected Catholic theologians of the Oratory in Munich in the sixties, were in Berlin before and during the war years and recalled there being at least four different ecumenical groups that met then.

An interesting description of one Una Sancta Circle that flourished in Berlin for several years during the war was given by the writer and lecturer August Winnig. Shortly after the beginning of the war, he met a Jesuit, Pater Georg von Sachsen, "the oldest son of the last king of Saxony," who introduced him, a Lutheran, to a circle of about thirty Catholic and Protestant laypeople and clerics who met monthly in the home of Frau Kracker von Schwarzenfels. The circle had been founded by Pater Georg and the Protestant, Superintendent Ungnad. The group included Hanns Lilje, later Lutheran bishop of Hanover and outstanding figure in the ecumenical movement, and Hans Asmussen, a leader of the *Bekennende Kirche* and after the war very active in public theological discussions within the Una Sancta Movement. This group broke up in 1943 when Pater Georg died accidentally by drowning and shortly afterward Frau von Schwarzenfels' house was destroyed in an air raid. Father Metzger was also a close friend of Pater Georg and regularly visited this particular Una Sancta Circle. Two years before he died, Pater Georg received a letter from Freiherr von Pechmann, a Protestant, who quoted to him what he had earlier written to another priest, very probably Father Metzger: "If it depended on just the two of us and our closer like-minded colleagues, the overcoming of the division of the Church of our Lord would come within reachable distance, and I could hope to see yet the day on which we would sing together with the joy of worship: praise the Lord oh my soul . . . !"

It was Father Metzger who delivered the eulogy for Pater Georg: "He would have offered his life for his Catholic faith which he carried deep in his heart . . . . How he suffered over the tragic division in the Church of Jesus Christ, which he so wished to see united, as a living testimony of the unifying Holy Spirit." The sermon was delivered June 18, 1943, just a few days before Metzger was arrested for the last time by the Gestapo.

As depressing and terrifying as it must have been to live in Berlin during the war, for those who were willing to risk their lives for principles and people, it must also have been a time of the greatest stimulation. By no means regularly, but at least occasionally, some of the interconfessional circles included Jewish rabbis! It is easy to understand why the Una Sancta Brotherhood and circles were compelled to maintain great caution and secrecy, often meeting in churches in the disguise of liturgical ceremonies. Of course, Father Metzger and many others were constantly engaged in hiding Jews in the Nazi capital. In fact, when Sister Judith Maria, Metzger's secretary, was arrested at the same time as Father Metzger, she immediately assumed they had been discovered in their "trafficking in Jews." On some occasions during the war, there were gatherings not only of religious leaders and thinkers, Protestant, Catholic, and Jewish, but also prominent members of the political resistance, the Goerdeler group. Quite possibly it was in these gatherings that Father Metzger formulated some of the political ideas which helped lead to his destruction.

Father Metzger's ability to meet people and immediately put them at ease and win their trust was a talent that particularly suited him for ecumenical work. Of course, he had long had many contacts with Protestants and was able to gain their trust in both his ability as a Catholic theologian and his sincere concern for their beliefs and rights of conscience. This trust was manifested many times and, in many ways, particularly during the last years of his life. In October of 1940, Father Metzger received a letter from a Protestant pastor, Dr. Hutten of Stuttgart, who was also the Chairman of the Protestant Journalists Organization. He referred to Father Metzger's Una Sancta work when he wrote,

> You have set for yourself a tremendous and trying task, a task which from the human point of view is impossible. However, if anyone is able to accomplish something in the area, then you with your whole manner of gentle discretion, your fine sensitivity, and positive attitude nourished on the biblical fullness are especially well suited.

Father Metzger showed that letter and another to his archbishop, Dr. Gröber, in a continued attempt to win interest in Una Sancta work. The second letter was from a Protestant pastor of Berlin addressed to a Catholic soldier after the Berlin Una Sancta Conference in November of 1940:

> I consider Dr. Metzger to be very well fitted to lead such activities. His tremendous knowledge, his very definite objectivity and his understanding manner in pursuing the line of thought of another down to its very roots have impressed me deeply. He is indeed predestined to lead such intercourse . . . .

Father Metzger once mentioned having been invited by one Protestant minister to preach in his church, the "New Cathedral," in Berlin during the Church Unity Week. The bishop of Berlin, however, suggested that it would be better not to accept the invitation. Father Metzger apparently found himself in a similar position on another occasion. In the same letter to Archbishop Gröber, in which he reported the Berlin Protestant invitation, Father Metzger mentioned in an ambiguous way a situation in Pforzheim where he gave a sermon in answer to one preached by the Protestant City Pastor, Karl Specht, on the Protestant position vis-a-vis the Catholic Church. Father Metzger wrote that his own sermon was very well attended and that afterward Pastor Specht came to him and thanked him for the fruitful answer even though the areas of difference were sharply outlined. Father Metzger did not say in what Church he delivered his sermon, but it would not have made sense anywhere except where the Protestant sermon was delivered, presumably in Pastor Specht's church. To have said as much immediately after describing the Berlin bishop's attitude would have looked like Father Metzger were belittling the wisdom of bishops—hardly political in a letter to his own bishop.

Father Metzger continued his ecumenical work up to the very end of his life. His active life came to an end in the summer of 1943 with his final arrest and imprisonment by the Gestapo, but that is another chapter. The Una Sancta Movement, however, did not stop with the death of Father Metzger, nor with the dissolution of Germany in the spring of 1945. In fact, it enjoyed an unprecedented flowering during the first three years after the war.

CONFLICT WITH TOTALITARIANISM

The story of Metzger's skirmishes with the Nazis began very soon after their rise to power in 1933. Late in that same year he wrote and published a pamphlet, *Die Kirche and das Neue Deutschland* (The Church and the New Germany) in which he again pointed out the strong objections a Catholic Weltanschauung raised against working with the National Socialist system. But Metzger stated that in the interest of peace and the continued preaching of the Gospel he was prepared to accept some feasible modus vivendi. These pamphlets were to be sent to the deans of every chapter of Catholic priests throughout Germany and were to serve as discussion material in clerical circles. However, they very quickly fell into the hands of the Gestapo, which was already checking the mail very closely. Although Father Metzger had signed the pamphlet merely with P (for Brother Paulus), he was arrested—typewriters and mimeographing equipment were also confiscated—and imprisoned from January 23 to 26, 1934, in Augsburg.

> Munich has nevertheless decided that I must be taken into custody. That hits us naturally very hard since mistrust among the people is thereby fostered. And it was just this that I wished to overcome in order to bring about a workable relationship of trust between State and Church!

Somewhat later leaflets of an old article written by Metzger began turning up in the Rhineland. The results of these and other brushes with the party were attacks by party organs and the suppression of the society's *Christkoenigsbote* in 1935 and the little *Alleluja-Rundbriefe*, which went to all the members of the society, in 1937. At the same time, between 1934 and 1938, the police conducted several unsuccessful house searches at Meitingen in an attempt to find evidence of hoarding foreign currency or food.

In 1939, shortly after the beginning of World War II, Metzger was twice arrested by the Gestapo. The first charge was quite humorous; Metzger's Society of Christ the King was suspected of being a "front-organization" for a monarchist party in Bavaria. He was arrested and imprisoned for one day,

September 5, 1939, and in October he was subjected to more questions, and more of the society's material and equipment was confiscated. The following month he was arrested again and imprisoned for a much longer time—from November 9 to December 4—without charge. Two days after his arrest Father Metzger wrote to the state police asking why he was arrested. He was told by the commissioner in Augsburg that he was arrested, along with 120 other men, in connection with the Munich *Bürgerbräukeller* plot (an attempt on Hitler's life), and that his foreign correspondence made him suspect. Metzger's reaction to this accusation, in a letter to Meitingen, was: "*Das ist zu dumm.*" On the first of December he again wrote to the state police demanding to know why he was being held and insisting he had no interest in politics, as was borne out by his activities, which he described. Upon his release Metzger again asked of what he was accused; the answer was that he should be satisfied with being free again.

During this period of imprisonment Father Metzger wrote a large number of letters, two of which merit particular attention. The first was, of course, the letter to Pope Pius XII; the second was a long letter to his fellow prisoners which, after his release, Metzger printed and distributed as Christmas greetings to the prisoners through their chaplains. The following is a small excerpt.

Grace?

A Letter in the Prison Cell

by Br. Paulus

> Perhaps you are confused and shake your head when I write to you with the words of the apostle Paul, "Days of grace have come, days of salvation!"

> Maybe you are thinking: He can talk about a time of grace. He is outside in golden freedom and day by day sees the glorious sun come up, while I in my dim cell . . . .

> Hold on, my friend! I am writing this letter in a prison cell in which for weeks I have been sharing your fate—it doesn't matter why! I know what it means to be cut off defenseless from the outside world, to sit behind a tiny barred window for long days and still longer nights, bereft of all the comforts of life, given a hard cot and set on short rations . . . . I feel it very much in my own body. And yet—will you believe me when I tell you: I have never spent any happier days in my whole life than these?

> How is that possible, you ask .... What makes me happy is something you could have as well as I, the faith in the wise providence of the kind Father in heaven .... The true Christian lives in this faith. And the fact that I can live in this faith, that I therefore can be so happy, that, despite all outward hardships, I have not yet spent a sad hour in this barred cell—is that not in itself a great grace?

On December 7, 1939, Metzger sent the following telegram to the society in Berlin: "Free, Alleluia. Paulus."

Later, in the fall of 1942, when the tide of the war was turning against Germany, Metzger prepared to send a letter to the Führer persuading him to step aside for a government which would prepare the way for an honorable peace. In the beginning of the next year, he showed a draft of the letter to Dr. Matthias Laros:

> Herr Chancellor, if you really love our people and are prepared to give your life's blood, as you have always insisted, then you must step aside and make room for another government which will still be able to conclude a peace which is honorable, since our armies on the borders of the empire still present a considerable force which will not be easily overrun. As the enemy does not wish to and will not negotiate with you, the only alternative, as in every law-abiding nation, is your stepping aside in order to save the nation, even if you must lose your life in the process; now still in honorable battle, later, however, in shame and degradation."[1]

Laros, however, finally disabused Metzger of his naiveté and the letter was not sent; but Metzger eventually did arrange to send a memorandum with a similar purpose to the Lutheran archbishop of Upsala, Sweden, Archbishop Eidem.

On that occasion Dr. Laros warned him not to endanger his religious mission by mixing in politics. But Metzger answered:

---

[1] Metzger, *Gefangenschaftsbriefe* (1947), pp. 78-79. This doubtless is not an exact copy of Metzger's letter, but rather Laros' recollection of it. The original supposedly was burned when the Gestapo arrested Metzger (Interview with Schwester Gertrudis, November 2, 1959), but the prison chaplain Father Peter Buchholz stated a copy of this letter was among the documents of Metzger's trial. "I read these memoranda and stood amazed at the courage of this man." (Peter Buchholz, "*Ansprache anlässlich der Gedenkfeier für Metzger*" [mimeographed], Berlin, April 17, 1946.)

> I have at this time wide foreign contacts. Must I not use them? If the peace of the nations can be prepared for through a servant of the Church, perhaps her least important officially, is that not worth the investment of a life? What that could mean for the standing of the Church in the world today! Don't you realize that there is a crying need at this very moment when everything is hanging in the balance for someone to fight for an endurable peace for his own people and, if necessary, to die?

Father Metzger arranged to have the memorandum personally delivered to the archbishop by Dagmar Imgart, a Swedish convert who for years had shown an interest in Una Sancta affairs and had won the trust of Metzger.

In the personal file of Father Metzger at the Freiburg chancery, a note was recorded by Msgr. Simon Hirt on August 8, 1943. "Herr Direktor Echert of the diocesan Caritasverband reported . . . that Dr. Max Metzger was arrested several weeks ago and is now in the concentration camp at Dachau." On August 20, an entry notes that Dr. Metzger was actually in a Berlin prison rather than Dachau.

Msgr. Hirt then wrote to Bishop Wienken, who was the head of the Commissariat of the Fulda Bishops' Conference, the national organization of the German Catholic bishops headquartered in Berlin. He requested information on where and why Dr. Metzger was arrested and passed on the standard Freiburg chancery characterization of Metzger[14] "who in his work is somewhat impetuous and given to extremes, but on the other hand has great capabilities and a sincere character."

Four days later, on August 24, Bishop Wienken answered that he was aware of Dr. Metzger's arrest and that he had already been to the Reich's Security Headquarters (*Reichssicherheits hauptamt*) several times on his account. The reason for the arrest could not be given to him since the investigation was still continuing. Wienken wrote, "It was simply declared that the rumor current here that Dr. Metzger was arrested because of his helping the Jews and his activity in the Una Sancta Movement did not correspond to the facts." Almost a month later Freiburg, and almost everyone else, was still in the dark as to what the charge against Dr. Metzger was. On September 21, Hirt even inquired of Wienken whether Metzger was still in prison or if he was to be released soon. But the matter was much more serious than that.

Already in 1940, the Swedish woman, Dagmar Imgart, who after having married a German lived in Germany, became interested in the Una Sancta Movement. Later that year or early next, she came into contact with Father Metzger, first through correspondence and then in person. She won Metzger's confidence because she seemed genuinely interested in the Una Sancta Movement and because she traveled back to Sweden once or twice a year and sometimes carried mail between Metzger and Swedish clerics of a religious nature.

Early in 1943, when Father Metzger became deeply concerned about Germany losing the war and the consequences—the remnant of von Paulus' army surrendered at Stalingrad January 31, 1943 —he drew up a memorandum on the state of Germany after the war which he hoped to communicate to his friend Archbishop Eidem of Upsala, Sweden, who, in the event of the imminent collapse of Germany was to forward it to English bishops and through them to the Allied commanders in an attempt to gain mitigated peace conditions for Germany. Metzger explained his plan to Frau Imgart who declared herself prepared to carry the memorandum to the archbishop on her next trip to Sweden. She also very shortly afterward lent Father Metzger a typewriter which she suggested he use when he put his political thoughts and plans on paper so that in the event the document was discovered he could not be proved the author since it was not typed on his machine. It was noted in the German courts after the war that "This machine had a faulty letter. Had Dr. Metzger used it this faulty letter would on the contrary have made it very easy to recognize with which machine his memorandum had been typed. Dr. Metzger had no inkling of these things," when he handed over the memorandum to Frau Imgart in the spring of 1943.

Then in the latter part of that June, Father Metzger received a phone call from Frau Imgart asking for an appointment to talk—this was at his Berlin residence. There was nothing at all unusual about this. She also mentioned that she would bring someone along who was interested in his activities. As arranged, Frau Imgart came during the forenoon of June 29, but she was alone. After the usual sort of discussion about Una Sancta affairs etc. she left, but was very soon back, apparently in the custody of several Gestapo agents under the leadership of Regierungsrat Dr. Roth. Roth then apprehended Father Metzger because they also found his incriminating memorandum still in Frau Imgart's handbag. They were both sent to prison.

The Christkoenig Sisters were concerned about Frau Imgart as well as Father Metzger, for she obviously knew of the contents of the letter and was apparently going to deliver it. They therefore inquired about her. To their horror they eventually learned that she was a Gestapo agent! (Her husband, Otto Imgart, was in 1944 assigned to an SS company at the Bergen-Belsen death camp.) They also learned that Frau Imgart planned to visit Catholic Church dignitaries supposedly seeking help for Father Metzger, particularly from abroad. She attempted several times to get an audience with Cardinal Graf von Preysing in Berlin and did succeed in seeing Cardinal Faulhaber of Munich. However, they and others had fortunately been forewarned by the Christkoenig Sisters.

Father Metzger's arrest was not the sum total of Gestapo activity for the day. Sister Bernharda of the Berlin Christkoenig Sisters was also arrested because of complicity in sheltering Jews. She was held for nine days and then released with the admonition that if she should come into contact with anymore Jews she should report them immediately—the gas chambers and crematoria of Auschwitz were working full-blast at this time. At the same time as the Gestapo action in Berlin, a large bus and several sedans pulled up to the Christkoenig Sisters' motherhouse in Meitingen and dispatched a troop of male and female Gestapo agents who thoroughly searched every building and indiscriminately carried off hundreds of pounds of documentary materials—which were all worthless to them. Dozens of file cabinets were simply carried out to the bus and dumped in. Mimeograph machines, typewriters, etc. were also confiscated.

One person was arrested, Sister Judith Maria, the superior of the Berlin convent and Father Metzger's personal secretary, who happened to be on retreat at the motherhouse. She spent two days in an Augsburg jail and then five weeks in the Berlin prison on Alexanderplatz. She was also charged with assisting Jews. She reported afterward that her Gestapo interrogator was singularly stupid and did not ask her any questions that would have forced her to incriminate herself as far as being Metzger's accomplice. She was kept on as a hostage in an attempt to press more out of Metzger. But it proved superfluous since Father Metzger admitted everything and did not conceal his fundamental disagreement with Nazism. Sister Judith Maria was released early in August and soon afterward had the shocking experience of sitting down on a streetcar directly across from Frau Dagmar Imgart! Frau Imgart feigned nonrecognition.

At the time of Metzger's arrest, it was not at all clear what the major charge or charges would be; everything was kept a state secret. The sisters were able to piece some things together, and for a while it seemed that the sheltering of Jews was the great problem, for the Gestapo agents conducted a series of rapid searches in the neighborhood of Piusstift, the Berlin convent.

Father Metzger was taken off to the notorious Gestapo prison on Prinz Albrecht Strasse where he was kept in a cell with twenty other prisoners. However, the detention was not physically difficult. Among other things, he, like the other prisoners, was able to receive gifts of food, which as a vegetarian

CONFLICT WITH TOTALITARIANISM

Metzger particularly appreciated. In a letter dated July 8, 1943, he gave an exact account of his daily routine.

> 6 A.M. rise and make my bed, wash, daily housework (today mine was emptying pails, etc. but I didn't mind it because it's part of our community life). Then till breakfast time I read my breviary. Breakfast is coffee with bread and margarine or bread and jam. Then I celebrate alone the *Memoria Passionis Domini*, as I used to teach it to others, and this gives me pleasure. I try to put the proper for the day into German choral form, of course without disturbing the others. Then I study St. John in Greek and German. What a privilege to be able to do this in a leisurely way! If I am too tired, I read something lighter. At twelve is our midday meal—one course, quite well cooked. Then I doze for a little while; after that I continue my intellectual work till I am tired and later relax with a game of patience. There is also half an hour's walk in the little garden which always does one good. At 6 P.M. supper and some relaxation, then prayer and bed. Now you can have some idea how I spend my time . . . .

During this time, Metzger's case was investigated, although he received no indictment for months. On August 5, he wrote that his case was clarified to the extent that they had come to the end of his file and that he expected a decision soon. However, the investigation dragged on for over a month and finally on September 8, Sister Judith Maria, who was back in Berlin at Piusstift, received a telephone call saying that she should come to the Gestapo office for church affairs on Meinekestrasse if she wanted to say goodbye to Metzger, for the investigation had been completed and he was about to be transferred to another prison. Sister Judith Maria reported that

> despite the pain that lay between us it was a joyful meeting. The world which was so incomprehensible to these men shined forth in the Christ-happy and Christ-bearing man. Even though locked in and guarded (a Gestapo agent was always present) one enjoyed the precious freedom of the children of God. Brother Paulus was practically undisturbed in the conviction that it must be recognized that he wished to serve the best interests of his people according to his conscience, which of course meant that he had to respect the existing forms and methods of government. He inquired about many of his loved ones, about his Una Sancta friends, about the members of the society and related that he thought he was able to recall them all by name. Among his prison papers we later found prayer leaflets with all the names written on them. He asked about the sick, after each and

> every one and in most heartfelt fashion insisted that all be given a very special greeting. He placed a great emphasis on this. Equally spiritually happy (*gottfroh*) was the leave taking. He was taken back to Prinz Albrecht Strasse and turned over by Regierungsrat Dr. Roth himself along with the assistant, Bandow. The file was closed, their work finished....
>
> Down below outside the door a car was already waiting. Brother Paulus said goodbye, with Bandow insisting that he hurry. Dr. Roth of course followed at a proper distance, solemnly, with his head proudly held high. In his hand he held something upright (perhaps a sheaf of rolled papers?)—at any rate in this situation it seemed like a scepter. He smiled at the sisters patronizingly, maliciously, like one who holds power in his hands. Thus, silently he climbed into the car. This brief event outside the door of the Gestapo building recalled like a flash the scene of Pilate....

A short time later, on September 11, Father Metzger was transferred to Plötzensee prison rather than the Moabit prison as he expected, so as not to overcrowd the houses in the center of the city during air attacks.

During Metzger's time in these two prisons and throughout the rest of his imprisonment he came to know men with varied backgrounds. The descriptions he gives of some of these contacts in his letters indicate again how, by his broadness of attitude, he was so aptly fitted for interconfessional peace work, Una Sancta work. During his first month of imprisonment Metzger's bed was next to that of the president of the German Freethinkers' Union.

> In spite of the gulf which in the eyes of the world divided us, we were nearer to one another than were the others, because of our mutual respect. I could see that he was a man of noble character, and one who was a good friend. I could imagine that in him there survived subconsciously something of the Christian education which had come down through centuries of German history. I would count such a man as among Christ's company more than many a baptized person whose soul has remained untouched by the Spirit of Christ. I have no right to judge of the future fate of any man. It is, however, my belief that it is only those who have fought against their conscience and convictions who are lost in the proper sense of the word, that is, condemned to hell. How many so-called Christians are much worse in this respect than the 'heathen'!

A little later Metzger shared a cell with a radio technician from Vienna: "Again, I imagine, without Church attachment, but a decent fellow and an idealist, so we get on well together." Father Metzger wrote of at least two other contacts across the walls of religious differences. On the day he was to be brought before the court, Metzger awaited his trial in a cellar with six others, a young Frenchman, the son of a Protestant pastor in Marseilles, among them. The young man constantly broke down and then let himself be cheered with the suggestion that he might not receive the death sentence. "He clung to me, his Catholic brother, with whom he felt linked in the one Lord. They came back from their trial one by one with fettered hands, the sign that they had received the death sentence; the only exception was the young Frenchman." One of the men condemned the same day as Father Metzger, but later pardoned, wrote of the journey to the death house prison, Brandenburg: "It will always be unforgettable to me how the Catholic priest prayed the Our Father with us. I thought it never possible that I as a dissenter would ever utter a prayer."

The transfer from the Prinz Albrecht Strasse prison to the one at Plötzensee meant a worsening of material conditions—such things as poorer food, fewer visits and letters, and the wearing, for the first time in Father Metzger's life, of prison clothes. With this move, and the final move to Brandenburg, he also lost his breviary, New Testaments, and other books, and was able to reclaim them only after weeks of writing and petitions. The last two prisons did have the advantage, though, of providing a single cell for each prisoner. On September 30, Metzger spoke of how much he missed the opportunity to offer Mass—during his entire imprisonment he was never allowed to offer Mass—and to study the Bible.

Besides the difficulties inherent in prison life and the anxiety of waiting in ignorance for a trial that would hand down a life-or-death decision, Metzger suffered with other Berlin citizens the horrors of constant air attacks. On August 5, he wrote:

> I am thinking during these days especially of my Berlin friends. After Hamburg we expect to have a night of terror soon, but we are not afraid. Berlin, as you will have read in the newspaper, is to be partly evacuated. The children, at least, are to be preserved for better days.

On the 26th of the same month he remarked: "In these times . . . . every night may bring the end of this earthly life—for we have been having British attacks every night . . . .

On September 22, Bishop Wienken wrote to Archbishop Gröber:

> As an addition to my letter of August 24, I am able to inform you today that according to a statement of the Reich's Security Headquarters the case of your diocesan priest, Dr. Metzger, has already been turned over to the People's Court. [This infamous court had a reputation that easily paralleled that of the Committee of Public Safety under Robespierre.] The charge against Dr. Metzger apparently is high treason.
>
> The superior of Piusstift, where Dr. Metzger lived, tried to visit him in the Ploetzensee prison last week. She was not allowed to and was also told by the prison administration that proceedings for high treason would be instituted against Dr. Metzger before the People's Court. The sister later checked at the People's Court itself and learned that as of last Saturday the files had not yet been received.

The Freiburg chancery answered on September 27,

> We acknowledge your letter concerning Dr. Metzger's situation in Berlin. Since the case seems to be most serious may we inquire whether Your Excellency would see to it that as soon as possible an attorney be acquired for Dr. Metzger who will represent and defend him.

Already on the same day Bishop Wienken wrote again to Freiburg confirming the fear that Metzger's case would go before the People's Court. He also reported that Sister Judith Maria had arranged for Justizrat Dr. Dix to take Father Metzger's case. He went on to remark that "It is inexplicable to me how Dr. Metzger could be guilty of high treason. As far as I knew him from before—have not seen him for almost a year—his activity concerned only the Una Sancta Movement; he avoided all politics." Five days later Bishop Wienken wrote to Freiburg that Dr. Dix had asked him for a description of Dr. Metzger's personality and an evaluation of his work, particularly in the area of social work, but also his activity in the Una Sancta Movement. "May I request that this be done from your office. The address of Justizrat Dr. Rudolf Dix is Berlin W. 8., Behrenstrasse 20."

Archbishop Gröber himself wrote the requested letter and sent it to Dr. Dix:

> Honorable Attorney!
>
> The relatives of my diocesan priest, Dr. Max Metzger, were here just now to report the latest on his situation. I wish to thank you very much for having taken over Metzger's representation. [The well-known Protestant penal law professor, Dr. Holstein, had been rejected by the

Nazis.] I have known Metzger since his gymnasium days when I was his rector in Constance. Perhaps a character sketch of Metzger by me will be of some use to you. Metzger is a man of many great talents, an idealist who has grown ever more estranged from reality. Parish work in the diocese was not enough for him; instead, he preferred social and charitable work and founded a project in Graz with aims and procedures such as only an idealist who was a stranger to the world could pursue. No need was so great that he did not wish to alleviate it; no man was so depraved that he did not approach him as a merciful Samaritan. He was assisted in this by a great talent for speaking and a very outstanding ability for organizing, which however could not prevent catastrophes and the giving up of his foundation in Graz because of financial reasons. Even his very great selflessness could not influence my judgment that he is an idealist of the first water.

Being gifted with a strong energy he was always able to revitalize his foundations and was also able, through his simple, self-denying, priestly example, to influence and win some over to his own ideals. He also continued his social-charitable plans from Meitingen, where he later moved, by lectures, writing and the forming of young men and women who joined his society. Morally Metzger was always above reproach. I have never heard the slightest thing in this regard that could damage him. His ideal appeared to be St. Francis of Assisi, who, following the words of St. Paul, wished to be 'all things to all men,' and thereby forgot about himself. I accidentally heard that about three years ago he had changed his area of activity and was living in Berlin.

A new idea had gripped him once again and absorbed him entirely [in actuality of course he had been driven out of many of his social and journalistic enterprises by the Nazis and therefore was then relatively free to take up Una Sancta work]. He worked for a rapprochement and unification of the Catholic and Protestant Churches and gave numerous lectures. He thereby became even more widely known than before. Through his personality he gained a large number of friends within the Protestant Church both inside and outside of Germany. Already previously as an organizer of international congresses of a purely religious-charitable kind, he came into contact with almost all the countries of Europe. I can recall very well that in one congress that was held in Constance even Spaniards were present, with whom I myself, because I was housing them, became friends. As long as I have known Metzger I have never found him to be involved in anything political except something that was so ideal that it was beyond realization. His consuming passion was always the desire to help others. There was never the slightest trace of the revolutionary who cherishes plans to overthrow the state. If he has now supposedly allowed himself to be drawn into such a thing it is again to be attributed only to a desire to help others and to a love of the Volk. It is characteristic of him that despite his great talents he never gets beyond a certain harmlessness and naiveté. I regard him as a poor judge of humanity who at most could be liable to fall victim and become the instrument of someone else. From a purely psychological viewpoint I have observed in him, despite his selflessness, a certain desire to be accepted. I believe however that he is not aware of this.

Concerning his relation to the German Volk and state it should be noted he has his roots in a loyal German family of teachers. I believe he would be prepared to make sacrifices out of love for the Volk and Fatherland similar to those made for his other ideals. I have seldom known a man who has had such a poverty of means to oppose the existing order as he. He has certainly not become a criminal; at most he has become a dupe, an idealist who wanted to help his Volk and Fatherland but who proceeded from the wrong premises. Unfortunately, I had no opportunity to speak with him in recent months. The last time he was with me I limited myself to denying him permission to give lectures in my archdiocese advocating the union of the two churches—a decision he resented. But I know my exuberant Max who always has his head in the clouds. Please, if you have an opportunity, convey to him my heartfelt greetings—as heartfelt as if I were his father who now inwardly partakes of his suffering and is anxious about his fate. I am completely prepared to do everything for him that might help to save him.

It is a shame about his wonderful talent, his enormous charitable work which he has done for the lowest fellow countrymen. I am convinced that if it is possible again to grant him freedom, having learned from his sufferings and his imprisonment, he could still perform much good for our Volk. He has now fallen from the clouds. He beholds the stony earth before him and will no longer look nor strive towards things which are imaginable only in his idealistic view. I beseech you, most honorable attorney, to do everything you can for him. If you save him, you will not be sparing a criminal from his deserved punishment, but rather an idealist and super-philanthropist from a fate he ought to be spared out of consideration for the reputation he has both in foreign countries and among broad segments of the population. I myself can do no more than to pray for him next Wednesday.

Very sincerely yours,

C

Archbishop.

At first glance it might appear that the archbishop was slighting Metzger, but it must be remembered that at this time he did not know the details of the case. Moreover, he and other Freiburg clerics had long referred to Metzger as an idealist, and he doubtless thought this approach, under the circumstances, was the best calculated to win Metzger some sort of reprieve. Dr. Dix also evidently thought the letter might prove of some help in the trial and wrote as much to Gröber on October 12, two days before the trial. He also mentioned that because the case concerned secret matters, he was not at liberty to divulge the details of the charge.

> Only so much may I say, that the situation is very serious and dangerous and that the possibility of the most extreme punishment is to be reckoned with . . . . From the documents I must infer that an acquittal is excluded. According to the principles of a purely theoretical jurisprudence perhaps there would be grounds for such a plea. But according to the viewpoints which dominate present-day legal doctrine and judicial judgments, and which are also authoritative for the defense, as far as is humanly possible to tell, this will not be possible, and the plea could have the exact opposite effect . . . .

Father Metzger's sister Maria and her husband were allowed to visit him on October 7. On October 9, Dr. Dix visited Metzger to discuss the trial. Metzger had already received the official indictment.

> When I received the indictment, which was objectively drawn, I still had some hope of a verdict which would bear some relation to the facts of the case. But when my counsel came and told me that the trial would take place in a day or two, I realized that the die was already cast. That night I went through my Gethsemane in advance. I also said to the Father, "If it is possible . . . ." I had a quivering heart, but still was able clearly and firmly to decide, "Not my will be done, but yours!" I had offered my life to the Lord for the peace of the world and the unity of the Church of Christ. I did not want to go back on that offer.

On October 12, Msgr. Simon Hirt of the Freiburg chancery office arrived in Berlin as Archbishop Gröber's delegate. Sister Gertrudis came from Meitingen at the same time. The next day both Sister Gertrudis and Sister Judith Maria were allowed to visit Father Metzger once more. Metzger had hoped for such a visit and was deeply moved by it. It was a consolation to him to learn that the two sisters and Dr. Hirt would be present during the difficult hour of his trial and he was astounded to hear that the trial was to be public, for everything had been a great state secret until then.

On October 14, 1943, Father Max Josef Metzger was brought before the People's Court at Bellevuestrasse 15, Berlin W. 9. Dr. Hirt and Sisters Gertrudis and Judith Maria had to be in the courtroom by 8:30 even though Dr. Metzger's case was not scheduled until 11:00. Entrance was only by special permission at the beginning of the day; after that the courtroom was closed. The "public" that filled the courtroom was made up of invited party members of the sixth district and people from the "Labour Front."

In the meanwhile, Father Metzger, along with six other prisoners, waited in the cellar beneath the auditorium of the gymnasium, which was being used as the courtroom. He was fifth on the schedule. His case did not start at 11:00 as scheduled, but only at 3:30. The first four cases took longer than expected; three of them were death sentences.

When Metzger entered the auditorium courtroom it was still quite filled with about four hundred party members, etc. In front was the tribunal beneath a huge swastika. There were five judges, two professional jurists and three laymen, who looked upon their nominations as an honor. The jurists and the prosecutor wore blood-red satin robes and the lay judges Nazi uniforms. The president of the court was Dr. Roland Freisler. "Dr. Freisler, called 'raging Roland' (*rasende Roland*) was known as the most fearful and bloodthirsty of the presidents, who as an experienced and cunning actor played his satanic role at the tribune with a plethora of fanaticism and cynicism." Father Metzger's counsel had warned him of the harsh tone in the People's Court and of the cleverness and capabilities of Freisler. Metzger nevertheless was quite collected and prepared to defend himself in a clear statement, especially explaining the motives of his action. He thought if he were able to do this, and if there were still among the magistrates present "something of the humanity and integrity for which German Courts of Justice were formerly noted," he could at least hope to save his life. He took his place to the right of the tribunal under heavy guard.

If there had been any doubt about the feeling of the court, it was dispelled at the very beginning of the hearing when Dr. Dix asked that the courtroom be cleared so that Father Metzger could freely explain his activities and motives. Not only was this request rejected, but Freisler also interposed that he was man enough to restrain any of Dr. Metzger's political tirades.

The prosecutor read the indictment which charged Father Metzger with "conspiracy for high treason" and "giving aid and comfort to the enemy." A biographical sketch of Father Metzger was read—when it was stated that Metzger had studied theology in Fribourg in Switzerland, Freisler sarcastically remarked that "naturally" German theologians studied abroad. Shortly thereafter he mocked him saying, "So, you have worked in the 'League of the Cross' (*Kreuzbündnis*) ... and then you founded the 'World Peace League of the White Cross.' ... Don't you realize we don't go for so many crosses . . . ." Then mention was made of the pacifist booklet Metzger had written at the time of the first World War, *Frieden auf Erden*, a copy of which lay in front of Freisler. At this point Freisler shouted at Metzger, "How did you come to publish such an article already back then?" Father Metzger very calmly and reservedly answered, "I experienced the want, misery, and horror of war so that for me there was no more pressing task than to work for the understanding of peoples and for peace." Freisler then screamed even louder, "That's a completely other world! Your world doesn't fit in ours! Such nonsense has no place with us!"

At the mention of the Una Sancta Movement Freisler again interrupted to say, very sarcastically: "So then you founded the Una Sancta, and then isn't it right?—There will of course come the Una Sanctissima! Una Sancta, what is that?" Sister Judith recorded:

> The courtroom was breathless as Brother Paulus begins to reply. How like a glorious confession his statement sounded in this "completely other world": "Christ founded only one Church!" But already it was as if all hell would break loose. Freisler raged, stormed, and shrieked: "Una Sancta, Una Sancta . . . Una! Una!! (he seemed almost stricken dumb with fury) That's US! There is no other!"

A little later he screamed, "How do you get the idea to doubt our victory when the whole German Volk is filled with the certainty of victory?" Metzger started to answer by saying, "Reichsminister Dr. Goebbels one time wrote in Reich that every war is a risk and that one never knew how it . . . ." But before he could go any further Freisler flew into another rage and shouted that Metzger was not allowed to quote Goebbels. He insisted that it was a terrible crime to doubt victory, and several times he roared to the courtroom, "We believe in victory and whoever doubts it must be wiped out!"

Metzger later wrote that

> the proceedings soon after the beginning left no further doubt that 'court' would not be conducted here in order to dispense 'Justice'; rather it was a showpiece to make an impression on the people. It soon became very clear to me that all human hope was in vain. At the same time, I felt myself obliged to do what was in my power in order to present the real truth—so to speak—before history, even if it wouldn't be acknowledged in this circle. I had practically no anxieties about the large crowd of listeners—on the contrary. If I had been *certain*—even *after* the judgment—that there existed no hope for me I would have used the opportunity to say everything openly that really ought to have been said in public. However, I felt obliged, and not least out of concern for my Society, to restrain myself at least so as not to destroy my chances for a favorable judgment. But the judgment gavel fell even before I could justify myself. The sea raged—it would have its victim.

The main charge of the prosecutor was the writing and sending of the memorandum on the state of Germany after the war. In itself the memorandum is a very interesting document; it reflects many of Metzger's lifelong concerns such as world peace, social welfare, and religious peace and tolerance. In many ways it anticipated what actually evolved in West Germany, but in other ways it also seemed to go beyond it and in some form included ideas of the later advocates of a United States of Europe. In the document Metzger used a number of pseudonyms, Northland instead of Germany, for example.

> "Northland" (The United Nordic States) is a Confederation of democratically governed free states (Norway, Sweden, Finland, Denmark, Iceland) [really Prussia, Bavaria, etc.]. Every free state within the structure of the Northlandic constitution is independent concerning internal politics, administration, and cultural and social affairs. Foreign affairs are conducted jointly and are reserved to the direction of the Confederation [*Staatenbundes*]. The politics of Northland, both domestic and foreign, is constitutionally firmly founded as a sincere politics of peace on the foundation of moral truthfulness and loyalty and social justice. The politics of peace is grounded internally on the acknowledgment of the eternal moral law, on the recognition of and respect for equal fundamental rights for all citizens, on a progressive social program (security concerning work, earnings and life for all; nationalization of all mines, power stations, railways and large real estate holdings of fields, forests and lakes; a social tax program that

gives consideration to the weak), and a just nationalities and race politics (self-rule of the national assemblies concerning the use of public properties for school purposes, for example). The politics of peace in foreign affairs recognizes and observes to the fullest extent the right to existence of foreign peoples and both advocates and carries out voluntarily a disarmament (to the point of retaining only a police force for the preservation of inner order) "in favor of a supra-national Armed Force which, in the service of a non-partisan organ of the 'United States of Europe,' will be responsible for maintaining a just peace among the nations."

Constitutionally every Northlander inviolably is guaranteed his personal dignity and surety of rights, freedom of conscience, of language and culture, as well as religious practice, freedom to express his opinion and, finally, freedom of personal property and use thereof within the legally clearly defined limits specified by the common good.

All Northlanders who demonstrably share the guilt of the national misfortune and oppression of her people remain, as commonly condemned criminals, for twenty years excluded from all civil privileges (voting, right to public civil office). In all cases until the establishment and confirmation of the moral and constitutional trustworthiness of all functionaries of the anti-national and anti-social parties [National Socialist Party] and their military self-defense organizations [SA and SS] their complicit guilt will be presumed. This list of individuals will be public.

The legal power of Northland will remain until the establishment of the definitive constitution on the basis of a general free plebiscite at a Northlandic Peoples Diet. This is constituted by leading representatives of all professions and classes as well as outstanding personalities from intellectual, cultural, religious bodies who at first will be chosen from the Northlandic Peace Order. The Peace Order is a society of persons from all state organizations and former parties who, in representing the moral, social, and political principles of the new politics of peace to the nation and the world, have proved themselves—and this is particularly important—by having had to bear personal disadvantages from the past system because of their convictions and attitudes.

This political program is set up to deal with the possibility that at the war's end a revolution might break out through which the continuity of justice could not be maintained.

According to Father Metzger's own testimony he showed the memorandum to only one person besides Frau Imgart—his spiritual director. Moreover, he did not make any contacts with persons he thought could later on carry out the specifications of the memorandum, partly to avoid the suspicion of being involved in political activity and partly because he felt that when the collapse came it would not be difficult to find such persons.

Metzger said that he had not intended to do anything that would aid the enemy to the disadvantage of his own people, but that he had sought only what was best for the people; he had reckoned with the possibility that Germany would not be victorious. Needless to say, Freisler stated strongly that the memorandum was degenerate.

The only witness scheduled was Dr. Roth, but he was not called to the stand since Metzger admitted everything—he even spoke of the letter he wrote but did not send to Hitler. The prosecutor then made his summarizing speech in which he emphasized Metzger's two major crimes, pacifist work and doubting victory.

The defense, Dr. Dix, had a very difficult time. Msgr. Hirt, who had witnessed the four foregoing proceedings as well as Metzger's trial, described the defense's situation.

> There could be no talk of a defense in any real sense. The lawyers themselves were very nervous, for they had to fear for their own lives. One attorney from outside of Berlin, who apparently did not know the customs of the People's Court, tried to make a rather free statement whereupon he was energetically set down by Freisler.

When Dr. Dix pointed out that the paragraph used by the prosecutor (91b StGB) in his charge of giving aid and comfort to the enemy did not apply because Metzger had spoken and acted not against but for his people, Freisler sharply rebuked him. "We can take any paragraph we want since the facts of the case are fulfilled even by the mere possibility of an injury." The defense then closed by describing once again Metzger's character and by reading Archbishop Gröber's letter on Metzger. He did not plead for an acquittal, but rather asked that the prosecution's request for the death penalty be denied and that a period of imprisonment be given instead—the length to be left to the decision of the court.

The judges then took ten minutes to make their decision.

> In the short time the judges needed to make their 'decision' I prayed for them that they might act as the instruments of God and serve His

glory. And I was convinced that, after so many had prayed for me, what would happen would in any case lie in God's will and therefore demanded my unrestricted 'yes,' which I was prepared to give.

The judgment was then given: Max Metzger was condemned to absolute loss of honor and death.

> As I heard the death sentence a feeling of proud disdain came over me. I knew that there was no shame but honor in being declared 'without honor' by such a court. I had to control myself in order not to let this feeling show in my expression even more than it involuntarily did. I was totally unimpressed by the sentence.

Freisler added to the sentence:

> This act is so evil and criminal that the accused must be eradicated. I have never until this moment in my career used the word 'eradicate' (!) but I use it here. Such a plague-boil must be eradicated. It does not depend on the interpretation of individuals; if that were the case then someone 175 years old could believe that his sexual activity was normal and natural. The national socialistic state claims total competence and it alone determines what should happen. Moreover, the accused has acted on the basis of doubt, on the premise that Germany could be defeated in this struggle. Only one thought can be in our minds, the belief in final victory and the total dedication of all energies toward this goal. Every person must allow himself to be measured against the German, National Socialistic standard. And it says very clearly that a man who so acts is a traitor to his own people.

Father Metzger was then asked if he had anything further to say. In a serene tone he stated, "I would only like to say once again that before God and my people my conscience is clear; I sought only to serve them."

With his hands chained behind his back, Metzger was led out of the courtroom and back down to the cellar. Dr. Dix was quickly able to arrange a brief meeting there between Msgr. Hirt, the two sisters, and Father Metzger. As they met, Metzger said,

> Now it has happened, I am calm. I have offered my life to God for the peace of the world and the unity of the church. If God takes it I will be happy; if He grants me a still longer life I will also be thankful. As God wills! Give all the brethren and sisters a last greeting and don't be sad. The feast of Christ the King will be a bit difficult. But nevertheless, sing alleluia and remain loyal to Christ your King.

He was then led away still in chains.

Dr. Dix feared that the sentence might be immediately carried out and so arranged to have Metzger petition the same day for a reprieve. Msgr. Hirt dictated a similar plea which Sister Gertrudis signed in the name of the Christkoenig Sisters and brought to the prosecutor, Dr. Drullmann, the following day. He was not much help. He said, "But we cannot deviate from an already drawn up judgment." A second such plea went to the Reich's Minister of Justice.

Immediately after the trial the sisters also telephoned the Freiburg chancery asking that the following *Blitztelegramm* be sent immediately to the State Prosecutor: "Reprieve petition for the priest Dr. Max Joseph Metzger on the way. Request that execution be stayed until decision on petition. Archbishop Gröber." Msgr. Hirt returned immediately to help write the petitions. Two days after the trial on October 14, Gröber sent a whole series of letters. Like the Sisters, he sent one to the prosecutor. He began his letter by stating, "We know that he was guilty of a serious fault against the existing state order, and we condemn his manner of acting in the most emphatic and decisive fashion." He went on to recall the great good Metzger had performed and asked that on this account he be spared the death penalty. At the same time, he wrote to the Reich's Minister of Justice, "I regret his *crime* most deeply. Nevertheless, I dare to direct a petition to you to *dispense mercy instead of justice*" [both italics added] because he is a man given to extremes without realizing the full implications of his actions. "Despite my renewed condemnation of his *crime* [italics added] may I nevertheless recall the great charitable work he has done." He referred to Metzger's parents as "exemplary German citizens" and asked that for their sake Fr. Metzger be spared. He then made what, in view of Metzger's pacifism, seemed to be an extraordinary suggestion. "I hold him capable of atoning for his *crime* [italics added] by the most difficult, heroic death [*Heldentod*] on the front. I ask also that his three sisters, who are loyal German citizens, be considered . . . ."

It might be argued that Archbishop Gröber's several references to Metzger's *crime*, which as he emphasized and re-emphasized, he deplored, and his request for mercy rather than *justice* do not imply he really believed that Metzger was guilty of a criminal act; perhaps he was merely taking that tack, distasteful as it was, which seemed most likely to succeed in helping Metzger. The same might also be said of his stress on the German-ness of Metzger's parents and sisters, which does not prove he was a devotee of German nationalism.

Max Josef Metzger with his parents and two of his three sisters, 1936.

However, too much outside evidence seems to indicate that the archbishop was not involved in duplicity here. Even though Gröber, an early enthusiastic supporter of the Nazis, had become a strong opponent of the Nazis on many points, he never seemed to waiver in his nationalism and patriotism. One of the many indications of this came at the beginning of the war when he addressed a letter to the men called to the colors:

> You belong to the German Volk as its guardian and protector. Blood, language, culture, natural life, and other ties of the most intimate kind bind you to it.
>
> Thus, you live in the Volk.
>
> By the same token, the Volk lives in you. For you are the firm wall of defense that protects our Volk and Vaterland in its most serious trials. All other barriers are down. Only through you can they live and fight, thunder and blaze forth in the battle.

> In your soldierly mission, you offer the Volk all that you prize most highly: time, sweat, strength of will, obedience, love, spirit—and, should fate so decree, your health, your blood, and your life.
>
> It is scarcely possible to give more than this to Volk and Vaterland. And you assume this all-encompassing service as a duty sworn under oath in God's sight! A duty, however, that is not assumed as an unwanted burden but rather, in keeping with the soldierly character, with a deliberate and manly "I will!"
>
> Should one or another of you lose his life, it becomes far more than the ordinary tribute demanded by Death the Conqueror in repayment of man's mortal guilt. It is the ultimate offering to Vaterland and Volk. A soldier's death is, therefore, a sacrificial death. A sacrificial death is a hero's death [*Heldentod*]. The hero's death is death with honor, a wreath of glory to adorn the grave of the Unknown Soldier as a mark of a comrade's gratitude.
>
> In this way you redeem your debt to the German Volk in full. It gave you the heritage of its glorious blood, and you offer it your own precious life's blood in return. You live through the Volk; the Volk lives on through you. And you, in turn, live on in it . . . .

As the war deepened Gröber's patriotic fervor did not cool. On the 1942 Heroes Memorial Day (*Heldengedenktag*) he explained why Germans should find solace in honoring their fallen warriors: "They died for our German *Vaterland*, that is, for something truly wonderful and great, albeit not the very highest and absolutely ultimate good in the scale of values held by the man who believes in God." But not only did they die as patriots: "Yea, God be praised! Our dead heroes died as victors. Seldom in the entire history of the world have armies been so accustomed to victory and so crowned with glory as those in whose ranks these men fought and died." Rejoicing in the fact that these warriors had earned an eternal reward, the archbishop drew the inevitable lessons for those who remained behind, one of which was that "we, too, should fulfill our patriotic duty with Christian fervor."

Even after the war Gröber's attitude did not really change. He argued, "In God's eyes the death for the Vaterland, which is often a most painful death, atones for much and, in the eyes of the All-knowing and All-just, erases whatever remains of sin and guilt on the soul." The hope (in sharp contrast to earlier statements of absolute certainty) was also expressed that these fallen soldiers had found a merciful judgment at the hands of "the Lord of battles." Calling for prayers for the fallen soldiers, Gröber declared,

I hold that such prayer is actually obligatory upon us all. This does not depend upon the success of arms. Even though these warriors were not permitted to mark the victory upon their banners, they nevertheless gave the Vaterland all that they possessed and could give. And they gave it for us—as fathers, sons, or relatives.

Coming in the midst of this train of statements, the letters sent in Metzger's behalf must be seen as reflecting a real horror at Metzger's having transgressed the constituted authority, particularly in a manner that somehow could contribute to military defeat. To Gröber, Metzger was really guilty of a serious crime—it was only his well-meaning idealism that gave cause to pardon him. Gröber's public statements in support of the war plus his fantastic—if not ironic—suggestion that Metzger atone for his sins through a *Heldentod* at the front indicate that he was completely out of sympathy with Metzger's pacifism.

In support of this interpretation is another, almost incredible, letter sent by Gröber on the same day. It was addressed to Rasende Roland himself. Not only does Gröber emphatically deplore Metzger's "crime," but he almost seems to grovel in fear before Freisler. "I have just received the news concerning the proceedings which led to the death sentence for my diocesan priest, Dr. Max Metzger. I deplore most profoundly the crime of which he has been guilty. When in the letter I sent to the attorney Dr. Dix, I described him as an idealist, I did so without having any knowledge of his criminal activities. I consider it important to tell you this because I had absolutely no thought of including his deed in the area of idealism as I described it to you. When I at a most critical time gave a character sketch of the condemned to his attorney, Dr. Dix, it was that as his archbishop I felt myself obliged to do something for him."

One can only stand in astonishment at the lengths to which Gröber went to placate the supposed wrath of Freisler—and this apparently only because of a brief aside Freisler made about Gröber's letter describing Metzger as an idealist: "and likewise his archbishop in a letter which he sent to the defense, and which was read, attested that he was not a criminal, but had called him an idealist. But that is a completely different world, a world which we do not understand." And Gröber's closing remark to Freisler about feeling obliged as Metzger's archbishop to do something seems to indicate an extraordinary weakness of character.

Gröber wrote one more letter concerning Metzger on that October 16. It was to the Papal Nuncio stationed in Berlin—the same figure Hochhuth fictionally brought on his stage in the *Stellvertreter*. Here one can see that Gröber was genuinely deeply saddened by Metzger's fate. But here also, where he has no reason to disguise his real attitude, Gröber showed that he really looked upon Metzger's action as criminal; state authority and the *Vaterland* are overriding concerns even when his personal sympathies are deeply moved. There is absolutely no thought that perhaps Metzger was justified in following his conscience here. "I condemn his political crime, but I have a great pity for him which leads me to try everything which might be of some help . . . . I must leave it to you to ask the Holy Father to take some action on his behalf." The Nuncio's answer was not reassuring; he thought it "very unlikely" that any action on Metzger's behalf would have an impact.

BETWEEN THE FALL OF THE GAVEL AND THE AXE

> As I returned to my cell that evening [October 14] I knelt down and thanked God that He had taken me so intimately into the discipleship of Christ and I prayed to Him to strengthen my heart to the end. I was able to lie down in bed calmly. But the terribly oppressive fetters which I had to wear to bed along with the psychological strain of the day finally brought on such difficulties with my heart that I had to ring and ask that the fetters be removed for a short time so that by relaxing my heart could recover its strength. The guards in Ploetzensee who showed me their sympathy throughout were so concerned that they took the responsibility so that I was able to sleep more or less calmly.

On October 19, Sister Judith Maria was able to visit Fr. Metzger. During the meeting she asked what work he now had to perform. He answered

> For us there is really no more work . . . . I pray and sing, meditate, read and write the small amount that we are allowed. I have been especially struck by the two songs 'In the Midst of Life' and 'What God Does.' They are so beautiful. Sing them along with me. And if death is the gate to life why should I not rejoice if it opens sooner now?

But this was the last visit Metzger received at Ploetzensee. He, along with the other prisoners condemned to death, was transferred from there to Brandenburg-Görden sixty-seven miles away on October 22, apparently because of the bombing raids on Berlin. Metzger had arrived at Ploetzensee on September 12; already on the third of that month there had been a direct hit on Prisoners Building 111. Fortunately—or unfortunately—not one of the three hundred prisoners housed there was killed. Then on the night of September 7, eighteen were hanged. And on each of the next three nights, September 8 through 10, another hundred were hanged and their bodies tossed in piles. Only about a dozen prisoners were spared and shipped to Brandenburg, including Charles P. Sieffert, who later knew Metzger.

The move to Brandenburg meant even fewer visits and letters, a solitary cell, and continued fetters. Metzger wrote that the transfer to Brandenburg was a disappointment to him because the warm and friendly relations he had had with the prison chaplain Father Peter Buchholz had been such a comfort. He was also obliged to realize that that was the last stage and especially that he would not see his loved ones again. However, he soon recovered his equanimity, so much so that he could write about having a decent cell with a beautiful view of the forest and could report that his appearance was so cheerful that the warder on his rounds suspected that something was up.

Archbishop Gröber wrote another letter to Bishop Wienken on October 25, in which he asked that Wienken personally appeal to both the Reich's Minister of Justice and State Prosecutor to have Metzger's sentence changed. Wienken answered him on November 3,

> In the case of Dr. Metzger—your excellency can rest assured—nothing is being overlooked that could contribute to saving his life. A great number of people from both the Catholic and Protestant sides are acting on his behalf in every position which could somehow have some influence on his reprieve. I personally have made several visits on his account. Unfortunately, his deed cannot be undone . . . . We hope—*contra spem*—to God that the many efforts and fervent prayers will despite all finally attain success.

Sister Judith Maria had a very trying task during this time. Even while efforts were being made to obtain a reprieve, she had to try at the same time to make arrangements to obtain the body in case the execution was carried out. She could not wait, for one never knew when the execution would be until it was over and then it was too late, for immediately thereafter the bodies of the executed were put in the crematorium.

Father Metzger's two sisters, Gertrud and Elizabeth, who lived in Freiburg, visited him on November 7. They were very hard hit by the meeting and the hopelessness and despair that hung about the prison. A short time later, on November 15, Sister Judith Maria received permission for another visit. She described it briefly:

> As always, his inner composure was magnanimous and good. A new hope slowly germinated since the angel of death had until then always passed by. The sister was aware of the hopelessness of the situation and of the efforts of good friends even up to Himmler, all of which met with an unyielding no. She tried to indicate something of this with the quiet question, what if the hopes were not fulfilled? With

shining eyes there came the assurance, "If it should be so, then be completely and absolutely assured that I will also go down this path with a joyful yes in my heart." This came out of such a convincing depth that one had to take the words to one's own heart, especially because they radiated so much calmness and surrender.

Except for one other occasion, Sister Judith Maria was unable to obtain permission to visit Father Metzger. Nevertheless, every two or three weeks she would make the 125-mile round trip to talk to the chaplain and through him pass on news to Father Metzger. Occasionally, however, as she stood waiting for the streetcar, she was able to see Metzger, since his cell was in the front of the building directly across from the streetcar stop. He would usually wave with a handkerchief.

The greatness of Metzger's courage as he calmly awaited his execution can be appreciated only when it is realized what a great love of life he had. In a paper dated November 14, he wrote of the fresh shock each time comrades who had arrived at the prison the same time as he were led to the scaffold and he waited, not knowing how long he would be spared. But at least there was the natural hope that sprang up when he saw that once again, he was not among those led to execution. In the end, he said, he had almost a feeling of certainty that he would be preserved from "the worst"

> for, in spite of all supernatural ideas, the unnatural act of being robbed of life does seem 'the worst' fate, however sure one is in faith and will that this passing life is truly not the 'best' life, but rather that the best life is that other life, that eternal life, which God will not allow to be touched by wicked hands.

In another letter written on the 11th he conveyed the same idea, that he had not spent one really downcast hour in spite of the fact that his "heart—so eagerly craving life and liberty—naturally rises up against my will. May God grant me to be faithful unto the end!" And two weeks later he still insisted that he would not yield to depressing thoughts, though they came rather easily to one who had to live and write in fetters.

All his life Metzger had planned and dreamed on a grand scale. Both this train of thought and his optimism continued even in the death house; his memorandum of November 15, 1943, gives an extraordinary example of them. Early one morning he spent quite some time thinking about his vocation, his consciousness of being commissioned; not that he had ever experienced being "called" at a specific time, but he did very early have a strong, clear sense of being commissioned. This feeling of vocation to a great task, he said, was far stronger than he let appear, for he was ashamed, knowing his intellectual and practical limitations, to let others see what great ideas he cherished, what possibilities he saw, in spite of his clear knowledge of those limitations. His particular specialty, in which his whole vocation was rooted, he said, was the universal, the world-embracing. All the concrete tasks he had been given seemed too narrow to him; he even recalled how he had put aside the thought of someday becoming a bishop because it would mean being bound to a circumscribed area. He acknowledged "how little value this Pegasus is as a carthorse," how limitation in any task went against his urge towards the universal. It was in the direction of synthesis, the weaving together and interrelation of thoughts, plans, groups, and places, that his powers lay. And it came over him more than once in those weeks of quiet reflection that he might still perhaps have an opportunity of using his powers, even if in another way than in the past. Perhaps . . . .

> But what is the man thinking of? Must he in the very hour of death make plans—world-wide, secular plans—only to go down into the grave with his plans? Perhaps—*magnum voluisse satis est!* ["To have willed greatness is sufficient!"]—perhaps not. Anyhow, God leads.

Sometime during the next five days, between November 16 and 20, Father Metzger composed a letter to a priest member of the Society of Christ the King, Brother Ambrosius, in which he continued to meditate on the worldwide needs of the Church and his small attempts to do something about them. The letter really does not sound so much like 1943 as it does like 1963, like Saint Pope John XXIII's *Aggiornamento* [bringing the Church "Up to date!"] and Vatican II, both of which would have been wild dreams in Metzger's time.

> If perhaps in a few days I must leave this life—fully prepared in the face of God's will but nevertheless not with a light heart because I still see such great tasks before me and sense undreamed of creative powers within me—I will be filled until the last moment with the concern for the future of the Society of Christ the King which has been given to me by God as a great task and which I must leave behind unfinished—God alone knows how great therein my guilt is . . . .

> As I felt myself called to the work it really was not the ambition to add a new spiritual society to the numberless ones that already existed and also not the drive, which to a certain extent was present, to form an instrument for the great practical plans that was my deepest concern. The essential starting point for the foundation was—perhaps initially in a great deal of unclearness—the awareness of the *needs of*

the Church of Christ, which to a large extent are connected with the *needs of the world* which moved me. The externalization and judicialization of the Church, the loss of the early Christian spirit of penance, of community of service, of love, the self-righteousness especially of those called to the leadership, mechanicalization of an activism, the lack of a living, enflaming spirit, the division of the Church—in no small amount due to this inner lack—all of these needs of the Church demanded a movement of renewal. And it is for this that the Society of Christ the King exists as a necessary instrument which is a model, representative and serving community within the Church and whose goals must be: systematic work on the training of an *essentially* Christian discipleship, of a primitive-Christian movement of sacrifice and love, of a spiritually vital apostolate movement, and this all on the basis of the new appreciation of the Word of God and the Sacrament of the Lord, that is the biblical-liturgical movement; on this foundation then there must be cooperative work in the solving of the great world problems by the founding of a genuine intra- and inter-state social order—in no small measure through the realization of the Una Sancta as the Lord wills it and the world needs it.

I realize how terribly insufficient, almost ridiculously insignificant in view of the great goal, what I leave behind is; not that I wish to seem ungrateful and not acknowledge what spiritual knowledge and radical Christian striving, above all what genuinely charitable works have sprung to life in the Society of Christ the King and still continue . . . .

When I look over what I leave behind, I almost feel like giving up the hope that what appeared before my soul as a revelation will ever be. And yet the Lord God is able to raise up children of Abraham out of stones. He is also able to raise up someone who has greater ability or blessing in what he undertakes then I. Perhaps I must *sacrifice* my life for this so that like the grain of wheat laid in the ground the fruit still blocked through my temporal life will then be able to grow. In any case *I may not* allow the great idea which was given to me *on my account to be buried*, and I must still look to it in death whether another might not be able to unfurl the flag which I let fall from my hand . . . .

I would surely go to my death lightheartedly if I knew that God has fulfilled my last wish, that He had raised up a leader for the Society of Christ the King who would make it into what He has given me a vision of but what was not given to me to carry out.

Metzger's prison life was not wholly given over to making plans and dreaming. During the solitary months, "in spite of the loneliness, which I naturally feel, I am not bored. I study, read, and write . . . even if writing in chains is difficult and can't give the reader much pleasure." Metzger wrote dozens of poems during these months, many of them set to music, and covered every scrap of paper he could get, even the margins of his books, with verses or melodies. Besides his breviary and the Scriptures, Metzger mentions reading Guardini's *Conversion of St. Augustine* and Dostoevsky's *The Possessed*. Of the latter he remarked that one part amused him and caused him to chuckle—and characteristically added, "To chuckle is a grace of which theologians, alas, do not take account!"

Father Metzger also busied himself with the writing of a long theological treatise on the Church. (It was one-hundred thirty-eight pages of very fine handwriting, including 394 footnotes—the writing and reference-hunting alone must have been a wearisome task for someone in fetters.) The treatise was an extraordinarily progressive piece of work for a Catholic theologian of that time. In many ways it is like the descriptions of the Church found in Vatican II. It presents a synthesis of the notions of the Church as the "People of God" and the "Body of Christ," with the emphasis on the former, which can also be seen in Vatican II. The entire basis of his treatise was biblical (over three hundred of the 394 footnotes were scriptural references) and its thrust open and ecumenical. It is a pity that it wasn't published until 1966.[1]

At the same time Metzger made what he hoped would be a good readable translation of St. Paul's Epistle to the Romans—the translation was completed the day before his death.

The time around Christmas seemed to be especially severe for Father Metzger. The cold, hunger, fetters, and unsympathetic guards piled on top of the general atmosphere of despair fostered by the regular executions must have all become especially painful at the time Christians celebrate the coming of new life, of joy, of peace, of love. He wrote shortly after Christmas that neither at Christmas nor afterwards could he shake off his concern when the mass of planes flew over him toward Berlin. He said that for Christmas he sent out in spirit gifts in the form of songs, poems, and a Mass which he composed. "How gladly would I participate!—It is now a *half a year* that I have not been allowed to celebrate *holy Mass*. On Christmas too we were not allowed, but I

---

[1] Möhring, *op. cit.*, pp. 231-302.

joined in a Protestant Christmas service behind the door of my cell and sang heartily with them. Una Sancta!"

But somehow through all the difficulties Metzger never seemed to lose his equanimity and by New Year's had recovered his usual optimism. About two weeks after the new year, he wrote a letter and passed on a poem he had composed for New Year's; its theme was complete acceptance of whatever God sent in this year. He went on to say,

> In God's name! In Him I am, thank God, now as before of good courage. I am confident that God will turn all things to good for me and you, and not last for our people. I experience how good He is to me and how He grants me consolations and inspirations of all kinds . . . .
>
> Even in the isolation from the world I take part in all events with a feverish heart—not least in the fate of our people; what I feel often finds expression in a poem (see enclosure!). Mostly of course, they are religious thoughts that move me so. I have now composed three German People's Masses—one of course I already sent you.
>
> Berlin is always a great source of concern for me; the planes constantly fly overhead past us! But I think, stop—nothing will happen that He doesn't turn to the best if we are prepared for Him. Under these circumstances of course the visit from Sister Judith was a great joy for me.
>
> I do not take any less part in your cares. May my prayer and sacrifice be pleasing to God! Greet all the brothers and sisters, especially the sick.

Father Metzger was not only concerned for his old friends and relatives, but also his newly found, despairing brothers, his fellow prisoners of the death house. Despite the regular executions—usually every Monday there were between 150 and 200 prisoners at Brandenburg, most of them in individual cells. In February of 1944 he wrote, "I remain still a pastor of souls and cannot forget my poor comrades in fate who through the seed of a thought will receive some help." For the sake of these prisoners living between utter despair and some wild hope Father Metzger composed the following prayer of resignation to God's will.

> Holy and almighty God! My Father! I come to you in the great need of my life with confidence in the promise and the blood of your only Son which was poured out for me. With Jesus Christ my Lord and

> Master I cry unto you, Father! If it is possible, let this chalice pass from me! Nevertheless, be it done not as I will but as you will!
>
> Yes, I believe that whatever your wise and gracious providence plans for me, it will be for my salvation. Thus, I give beforehand the unreserved yes of my obedience. In the name of Jesus, I ask you: give me the strength of the Holy Spirit that I may persevere to the end in this trusting obedience! Then I will know that I am and will remain your child and the heir of your eternally blessed life. Amen.

Father Metzger's request that the prayer be printed and distributed among the prisoners was fulfilled by the Sisters, who also distributed it in Berlin. A further small collection of prayers, hymns, and thoughts about death was put together for the same purpose; but this could be completed and printed only after Father Metzger was gone. He also requested specific religious books he thought would help his fellow prisoners in their misery. He even dared at one point to send in a vigorous request to the highest authority that the burden of constantly being in chains be moderated. To no avail, of course.

Ever since his youth in the Black Forest Father Metzger was a lover of nature and animals. He did not lose this quality during his long imprisonment; if anything, it was heightened by the loneliness and isolation of his circumstances. Shortly after his arrival at Brandenburg he wrote that he had a cell with a beautiful view overlooking the forest in front of the airfield.

> I can also see people on the street and am not so completely cut off from the world—the sort of thoughts that come to the mind of one in my situation! But it is good that one lives high up since one is then near to heaven—I wonder if I am near to it. I am, thank God, completely composed and of good courage with the result that yesterday the guard who was making his rounds expressed astonishment that I am so happy. But a child of God never has reason to be sad.

On November 11 he wrote, among other things,

> Even in my lonesome cell I experience some joys . . . . And then—think of it!—I actually received a visitor without official visitor's permit every day at my cell window: the *titmouse* was sent as a messenger from God and you. How did it happen? Despite the rumblings of my stomach, I still cannot decide simply to give up my vegetarianism—after 28 years practice! So, I set the sausage aside to see if I could hold out without the meat . . . . And so, once I stuck it on the edge of the window and inadvertently attracted the birds which I love so much. Isn't that fine?

Two and a half months later he again wrote about the birds appearing at his window. The titmouse came only the one time, but after that a raven came. "Of course, he doesn't bring bread as he did to Paul the Hermit, but rather fetches the meat . . . . Too bad I don't have my Hansi [his canary]!"

Shortly afterwards, on February 10, he wrote to someone else in another letter,

> Think of it! One day there were two of us in my cell. The fellow prisoner was from the 'flyers' [*fliegerei*]—a fly with whom I really became friends. You know that I have a special relation to animals. Do you still recall the vacation in Lychen where I coaxed a butterfly to settle on my finger eighteen times one after another? That was one of the greatest pleasures for me . . . . I really live with the soul in another world. From it flows many powers and thoughts, particularly in loneliness—the poems, some of which I am allowed to send you, also come from there.

On December 28, 1943, Father Metzger received a visit from Father Peter Buchholz, the prisoners' chaplain who had visited Father Metzger regularly at Ploetzensee. Father Buchholz was a man of deep spirituality and humanity and so, especially under the extraordinary circumstances, the two men quickly became intimate friends. Unfortunately, the priest assigned to the chaplaincy at Brandenburg was a small-hearted man with whom Father Metzger found no spiritual kinship. Consequently, this visit by Father Buchholz was a special consolation for Father Metzger.

After a great deal of difficulty Sister Judith Maria was able to obtain permission for one more visit on January 4. When she arrived at Brandenburg, she was told it could only be a short visit because the guard did not have much time—although he proceeded to stand and gossip a long time with the guard at the gate. When Father Metzger was finally brought, he came with a slip of paper on which he noted everything he wanted to ask about. Sister Judith wrote,

> The joy was indeed great, but the time was so short that it just barely sufficed to settle matters. He was not allowed to receive anything. The guard in general was very much the cold official . . . . It was in general a short, if at the same time heartfelt and, as it even then appeared, last personal greeting. And his greeting again, as always, was sent to all the loved ones.

Bishop Wienken wrote to Archbishop Gröber on January 8, saying that he understands that Father Metzger "is calm and composed as he awaits the coming things [*den kommenden Dingen*]. The last decision on the reprieve petition has not yet been given." A week later Gröber wrote that he just learned that Metzger still was in chains and asked if Wienken could intercede to have this general regulation relaxed since with Metzger there was neither the possibility of his committing suicide nor attempting to escape. "As I understand, the Holy Father personally has interceded for him, for which I am extraordinarily thankful."

A few weeks later, on February 3, Wienken reported that the request to exempt Metzger from wearing chains was denied. Only in very special cases could this rule be relaxed, and the fact that Metzger was a priest and that there was no danger of suicide or an escape attempt was not sufficient. He also related that he had just heard the day before that Father Metzger was in good spirits. Then he used exactly the same sentence to describe Metzger's attitude that he had a month before: "He is calm and composed as he awaits the coming things." This could be coincidence, or the phrase might have become almost a stock-in-trade expression, since he mentioned that the same was also true of a Father Wachsmann who recently arrived at Brandenburg—apparently also from the Freiburg diocese.

Ironically, Metzger did not need the official's permission to relieve himself of the weight of the chains at least part of the time. He lost enough weight to be able to slip one hand out of the fetters during the night and thus relax somewhat.

February 3 was Metzger's fifty-seventh birthday. He apparently had a relatively pleasant time since he wrote that "on my birthday I was very happy to receive the letter my sister and brother-in-law wrote on New Year's Eve. Thank them and send them my warmest greetings. God granted me several joys on my birthday. I feel that I am remembered in love." Father Metzger composed a short poem on his birthday. It is one of very many that indicated his acceptance of God's will. Like almost all of his poetry it was in rhyming verse.

> What is it that you now wish from me, oh Lord? To suffer wordlessly as a sacrificial lamb? To battle to the end as a defender of the right? I do not know—tell me your desire!
>
> Only not cowardice, nor weakness of faith and weariness! You have not in vain given me a heart Full of storm and stress and feverish thirst, Zealous only for the highest, inflamed by it . . . . Lord, send your Spirit!

Do not leave me any longer blind! I do not wish to avoid your hand of wrath—just so that it serves your greater glory. I place myself at your disposal as your child.

A little over a month passed and then the following letter arrived for Father Metzger.

Dear Max!

I can address you this in recollection of our long-passed days in Constance. So much lies between then and now. And so many difficulties. But in God's name! The difficulties also have their great spiritual and religious value even that most difficult. Hope still always lives in me. Your sister visited me ten days ago. All is well with her. I pray for you and yours.

Your old [*Ihr alter*]

Conrad [Gröber]

Although there are no documents available to indicate when the reprieve petition was finally denied, this letter would seem to indicate that Gröber had pretty well given up hope by the beginning of March, even though he says, "*Es lebt in mir immer noch die Hoffnung.*" [There still always lives hope within me.] It is interesting to note that he became intimate enough to address Metzger as Max—not enough to use the *du* form. Even though in thought, feeling, and action Gröber was the opposite of Metzger he apparently felt drawn enough to him, or driven enough by the tragic circumstances and his felt duty as his bishop, or both, to write him this personal, somewhat awkward, farewell.

Charles P. Seiffert, a German Catholic journalist who was imprisoned by the Gestapo in December of 1941 and subsequently condemned to death, knew Father Metzger at Brandenburg. Because highly placed friends were constantly working on his behalf, Seiffert was able to stave off execution until he was finally freed by American troops on May 15, 1945. By mistake he was on three different occasions led out to be executed, only to be returned to his cell. By the time he was finally freed, he had lost half his weight and was told that although he was only forty-eight years old he looked seventy-five. He had been one of the dozen that had lived through the mass executions in September 1943 at Ploetzensee and were removed from there to Brandenburg just before Metzger was transferred to Ploetzensee. Nine years after the war he wrote to Sister Gertrudis and described his contact with Father Metzger.

At the end of October 1943, many replacements arrived. They were spread out between Houses I and II; I was in House II. During the so-called free hour—about a thirty-minute walk in the courtyard—one section walked clockwise and the other counter-clockwise about a meter apart. Despite the sharpest observation it was always possible to converse in passing with, so to say, closed lips. The replacements were mostly Viennese; that was the first time. Among these replacements there was one fellow sufferer who, because of his upright bearing, his carefree look, and his almost white hair, despite a youthful face, made a deep impression on me. One always tried to speak with those for whom one felt a spiritual kinship. The clothing of course made us all alike, and often it was weeks before one realized that in these walking rags there was a general. At first, I judged the new fellow sufferer to be an actor, a great dramatic performer. He said to me, I am a Catholic priest, which made me happy. I soon learned his name; Father Metzger, born in Schoepfheim, chaplain in Karlsruhe, Pforzheim, pastor in Kenzingen in Breisgau. I was born in Karlsruhe in Breisgau and went to school in Pforzheim. Since 1943 my mother lived in Kenzingen with her sister.

It was soon understood that at the walk we would not walk in the same row; we could have walked behind each other, but at a three-meter distance. Father Metzger after a while was transferred into my section on the ground floor. Our cells were just a few meters from each other. I soon learned the reason for his death sentence. We could talk together when every four weeks we were taken to the showers. All the fellow sufferers said "*du*" to each other. There were no distinctions among us . . . .

Once by the shower I asked Dr. Metzger: "Are you afraid of death?" His answer: "No, I am not afraid of it. How is it with you?" I overcame my fear of death years ago, was my answer. But I would like to avoid having my head chopped off by criminals. He: "Exactly the same with me. However, if it has to be, then with head held high."

In our view of death, we were alike. But many did not think as we. They dragged themselves around the courtyard and hung too tightly on to life and on to the world. We did not give up, rather we hoped for the rapid collapse of the system.

One time our conversation in the courtyard caused a great to-do. The chief guard, who was keeping the watch then, screamed at Dr. Metzger that he always felt it necessary to whisper something secretly to the others. As we immediately afterwards again passed each other we both laughed. [From his boyhood days in the Black Forest Father Metzger had not changed much in this regard either.]

In general, the guards were very good. Some suffered in their fate. We were never mishandled or berated. So, a few chief guards screamed now and again.

We thought nothing of it. The newcomers always attempted to ask (in passing one another, naturally) "How long have you been here?" When I gave my length of time, I could see in the faces of most of the others a glimmer of hope. I was the longest in the death cell—two years, seven months, and fifteen days.

On February 23, 1945, I was shipped with eighteen other fellow sufferers to Halle while another two hundred remained. There were several among them who had known Father Metzger. After almost four days of continual travel, we found ourselves with many others packed into the bottom hold of a ship. I was asked who this tall man with the white hair was. We were all agreed that Father Metzger, although perhaps many did not know what he was, had a calming influence on all the fellow sufferers. I had often observed him walking and looked to see if I could not make out a halo. His picture in the book [the edition of the prison letters] and the way he really looked during the last months are actually quite different from each other. His hair became whiter and his face grew thinner and from his eyes there came a light that was almost unearthly. In the picture in the book Father Metzger is a priest who was standing in the middle of life. In the last weeks he gave the impression of a man who stood above life, whose soul was transfigured, who indeed bodily still lived on the earth, but whose spirit already stood before the blessed heavenly Father.

The constant hunger brought me to the edge of hunger insanity. We were only spirit and hardly possessed a body anymore. The pull of gravity appeared to be broken; only the will lived on. It could not have been other with Dr. Metzger.

He believed in or hoped for his reprieve. My experiences throughout my long imprisonment were already so great that I did not believe in it. I prayed every evening for him. Unfortunately, I had something like a sixth sense. I always knew, at least during the last year, on Saturdays who I saw for the last time. I knew that one day I would have to part with Father Metzger. I believe his day of sacrifice was a Monday and on this day the walk fell out. On the next day he was missing;

> I was in deep darkness. But I knew that he had gone on his last way with great strength. Father Scholz [the chaplain] confirmed this several days later.
>
> I lived through about five thousand executions around me. Among them a number of Catholic priests were known to me. There was, however, only one Dr. Metzger among them. None was an example as he was. None lived so unaffectedly as he.
>
> One felt only bodily imprisoned. The spirit was in complete freedom and despite the death sentence one lived in the cell released from all earthly things. Only upon receiving pen and paper in order to write one's next of kin did one have to return to the everyday— and that was painful. I perceive from reading his letters that it was the same with Dr. Metzger as with me. He was concerned about his brothers and sisters; about himself he was not concerned. We were proud because our blood was the seed of the freedom of the nations. Dr. Metzger and I were cheerful at our meetings and we tried to tease our guards as often as possible, just as we had teased our teachers as youths.
>
> For most there was a great deal of time to be able to recognize that death, or the departure, is a reward. The manner of death was not congenial, but it wasn't painful for it took hardly a second. Above all, we treasured this death much more than the '*Heldentod*' [Hero's Death] for the erstwhile house painter.
>
> ... In the last weeks he impressed me as a saint, and that he was, in my deepest conviction —he is so in all eternity.

One last time Father Buchholz was able to visit Father Metzger, on April 12, 1944. The visit, in a way, was a particular joy to Father Metzger since he had not been allowed any visitors for months. The sisters were also happy about the visit as it gave them an opportunity to perform some last little acts of love for Father Metzger. They sent along with Father Buchholz a chocolate bar they had received as a present and an apple from their garden which they had preserved very carefully—it was spring already—plus a few slices of bread. These were all precious little things in those days and circumstances.

Father Buchholz's visit was on Easter Wednesday and so Metzger was in a joyful mood, despite the fact that he had been unable to celebrate or even attend Mass during Holy Week or on Easter—or any time since his arrest ten months before. He was, however, brought communion every week or two.

Father Metzger showed Father Buchholz the three Easter hymns he had composed—words and music—and sang one through for him. The alleluia must have rung strangely in that building. He gave Father Buchholz a number of things he had written, including his long theological treatise on the Church. All in all, it was a joyous occasion. Father Buchholz later remarked: "When the chaplain visits the prisoners, especially those who have tasted the fear of death for months and are torn between hope and dread, he is the giver of consolation, but with Dr. Metzger it was he, not I, who was the giver, and I who received from him."

The next day, Metzger was so struck by a restlessness that he asked the chaplain if he was on the next execution list. He said no. It was apparently on that day that the list was made up. Thirty executions were ordered for the following Monday—but only twenty-nine names were specified. Who the thirtieth was to be was not even known in the tight circle of executioners. Only on Monday afternoon, April 17, did one of the judges remark to the chaplain that one of his *confreres* was on the list: Dr. Metzger.

He rushed to inform Father Metzger. Calm and composed, like an ancient stoic, he received the news, laid his pen down, and asked for Holy Viaticum. After the reception of communion, he sat on his cot and said, "Now, Lord Jesus, I come quickly." The two farewell letters which Metzger was then allowed to write were never recovered. Shortly after three "he was led to the place of execution, upright as in his best days." At 3:26 P.M., Monday, April 17, 1944, Max Josef Metzger, Brother Paulus, like Paul of Tarsus, was beheaded. His executioner afterward told Chaplain Buchholz: "Never have I seen a man die like that."

About the same time the sisters at the motherhouse in Meitingen were saying the prayers for the dying, as they had been doing every Monday for years, for prison executions were usually on Mondays and the condemned often had no one to pray for them. When they received news of his execution, they sang a *Te Deum*.

Sister Gertrudis wrote a general letter to all members of the Society two days after the execution.

> My Very Beloved Brothers and Sisters!

"The Lord carries us through all Good Fridays and one day Easter will remain." I wrote something like this to Vater Paulus[2] in the last letter I was allowed to write—on Good Friday. For him it has now become true. On Monday, April 17, he was allowed to enter into heaven and celebrate the eternal Easter feast. We wish to rejoice over this. Now he is permitted to see with the eyes of God and participate in the councils of the most Holy Trinity and he will from there show us the way God has planned for us. It must be a great joy for him again to meet Brother Gottwills and Brother Franz who with him had brought the work to life.

Concerning what has struck us all, my beloved, I cannot in Father's name say anything more beautiful than what the gospel for the day of his return home says to us: "Now you have sorrow, but I will see you again and no one will take your joy from you again."

And I repeat what at the departure after the condemnation he commissioned us to say to you: "Give all the brothers and sisters a lasting greeting and tell them to remain loyal to Christ the King."

On the day after the execution Sister Judith Maria traveled to Brandenburg to make arrangements for the burial. She, of course, had long before made a number of requests to have the body released to her. Fortunately, she was able to obtain the permission of the local city authorities to bury Father Metzger in Brandenburg. But at the same time as she received the notice of the execution from Dr. Dix, she was told by him that the body would not be handed over because of a new general rule against delivering the corpses of condemned, since the bombing destruction was so great. She said nothing of this and hoped that the Brandenburg officials would know nothing of this new regulation yet and would keep to their agreement.

That Friday, April 21, 1944, at eleven in the morning, Father Metzger was buried with prayers quietly murmured by Chaplain Jochmarm in the old city cemetery in Brandenburg (forty-two miles from Berlin). Just a very few people were present. He was buried next to Father Wachsmann—the student chaplain also from the Freiburg diocese who Bishop Wienken in February had reported had arrived at Brandenburg at the beginning of January; he was executed that February because of some remarks he made in a student circle. Prison officials brought Father Metzger's body in a hearse and lowered it into

---

[2] "Father" is not a title given to priests in Germany; this is obviously meant as their "founding father," their spiritual *Pater familias*.

the ground. "It was a rainy, gloomy day. But as the casket sank into the earth, suddenly the sun burst out!"

Several weeks later the sisters received from the People's Court the following "Account for the Punishment of Max Josef Metzger because of Preparation for High Treason."

1. Fee for execution - Par. 49. 52. D. GKG	RM 300.00
2. Expenses: Postal fees - Par. 721 D. GKG Prison costs for the time 29 June 1943 to 16 April 1944, 293 days at RM 1.50 per day - Par. 727 D. GKG	RM .12 RM 439.50
	RM 739.62
3. Amount covered by condemned's own money	RM 368.36
Remainder to be paid (E. G. StA. Nr. 119/44)	RM 371.26

After the final collapse of Germany, the sisters wanted to transfer Father Metzger's body from its rather isolated spot. Of course, they would have preferred to have transferred it to Meitingen, but because of transportation and different occupation zone problems this proved impossible. They decided to move the remains to a Berlin cemetery near Piusstift. Sister Judith Maria again made all the arrangements. On September 13, 1946, at seven in the morning, the disinterment took place. It was necessary to transfer the remains to a casket that would be safe for travel.

> Only after the transfer was I allowed to see him. Father still had upon him the cross that I was allowed to send at that time along with a stole. He was still very recognizable by his noble forehead and his hair. The hair in front was slightly soiled; apparently it had been soaked in blood. His long form almost did not fit in the normal casket. It was not an unhappy experience, as I feared; my image of Father is in no way disturbed . . . . But now I am assured and the haunting thought that we could have been deceived even at the last moment is banished.

After the body was driven to Berlin it had to wait until the eighteenth of September for the burial. It took place at 11:00 in the St. Hedwigs Friedhof. The chapel held only two-hundred persons and was overcrowded long beforehand; consequently, the eulogies and final prayers were given outside so that the one-thousand people present could all hear, answer all the prayers in German and sing the hymns. Father Buchholz delivered the eulogy, and the crowd was addressed by the *Bürgermeister* of the Wedding Section of East Berlin and several other officials, including Pastor Horn who spoke in the name of the great number of Protestants present. There had already earlier been a large memorial celebration in Berlin sponsored by the Christian Democratic party, the political party that embraced both Catholics and Protestants. It was held on April 19, 1946—Good Friday.

Perhaps one of the most balanced assessments of Father Metzger's life came from Msgr. Hirt several years after his death.

> If the judgment about the personality and the effectiveness of Max Metzger is not uniform—he was anything but an average man—his upright, strong, and courageous conduct in the face of National Socialism and his last effort for the cause of peace among nations and confessions as well as his truly heroic bearing in the harshest of imprisonments and in the face of death demand acknowledgment and wonder. He offered up everything, including man's dearest treasure, his life, for the cause of peace.

On April 27, 1968, Father Metzger's body was transferred for a final time from East Berlin to Meitingen by Augsburg. After a commemorative celebration there was a large procession to the local Meitingen cemetery with the casket, where Bishop Josef Stimpfle of Augsburg, attired in joyful Easter liturgical vestments, made these remarks:

> We have brought the mortal remains of a 'Doer of the word' (James 1:22), of a pioneer in the biblical, liturgical, and ecumenical movements to their final resting place.
>
> It is a bitter tragedy—a participation in the bloodwitness of the Lord and his disciples—that Dr. Max Josef Metzger, who in the conviction of his conscience and from the purest of motives wished to prepare the way for an understanding between the world powers, had to lose his life under the National Socialist regime in Germany.
>
> Here in Meitingen at the cradle and the center of his life's work, where the Society of Christ the King which he called into existence works further in his spirit in modern style, here he now rests.
>
> The figure of Dr. Max Josef Metzger and his name are inseparably bound up with the Una Sancta work which here in Meitingen and from here throughout our country has been carried on through prayer and sacrifice, through word and writing for the reunion in faith. The

Una Sancta Brotherhood which he founded, the ecumenical conferences which he held here in Meitingen, the urgent plea to Pope Pius XII to call a general council with the goal of the reunion of all Christians [which, of course, gloriously happened under Pope St. John XXIII, in Rome, 1962-65] were the work of a prophetic spirit.

For the unity of the Church and for the peace of the world he offered up his life to God on the scaffold on Monday after Easter week, April 17, 1944, in the Brandenburg-Görden prison. "Nothing," he wrote in his testament, "nothing could give my life a more meaningful ending than if I could be allowed to give it up for the peace of Christ in the Kingdom of Christ . . . .

Dearly beloved brothers and sisters, one could think here at the grave of Dr. Max Josef Metzger that "a torch of ecumenism has been extinguished." But no, the torch of his example lights further the way for us. This torch must burn on in and through us! Dr. Max Josef Metzger was in fact only a steward of that which another had given him. He was conscious of his being one commissioned. It was Christ who had lit the fire of ecumenical work in him. He was a torchbearer of Christ. This burning light must not go out. We must carry it farther. We may not disregard the call of the deceased in this hour. Our active responsibility for the reunion of Christians is demanded!

FINAL REFLECTIONS

UNA SANCTA

You Christians! Have you forgotten that word
Which the Lord spoke to you before his last agony?
Do you in bold self-will disregard
What he spoke to you in his holy testament?
"That all be one! One shepherd and one flock!"
That was his high priestly plea;
That His divine mission would be credible
Through holy unity, a fruit of the breath of the Spirit . . . .
The pagans no longer point to you in astonishment
Because you love one another as they had never seen
They point at you with despising fingers
You who have rent the bond of unity!
You read: "One Lord! One Faith! One Baptism!"
In your churches you preach the Scriptures,
But the battle of words of your men of God
Strikes the ear of the heathen as a scandal.
"One Lord!" Before Him you should bend your knee,
Praising Him in one spirit from out of your heart!
For the cross and resurrection you should witness
Before all the world with the voice of one Church!
I am astonished: you still find the leisure to wrangle
On the day of God's wrath and the day of Judgment!
"*Metanoia!*" The Master calls: "Do penance!"
Do you not see the bloody signs in the heavens?
"One body! One Spirit! With one holy bread
Nourished," the divine pledge of the unity of love!
The Una Sancta rests on the command,
Which in the Lord's Blood found its seal.

Paulus in vinculis [Feast of St. Paul in Chains]
January 18, 1944

FOREWORD TO PART 2
"STANDING ON THE SHOULDERS OF GIANTS"

It was truly an inspired choice for Professor Leonard Swidler to choose to make the Una Sancta Movement of Max Josef Metzger his research topic for his PhD thesis. This research led to the publication of his first book, *The Ecumenical Vanguard* in 1966 and his follow-up book about Metzger, *Bloodwitness for Peace and Unity* in 1977, which has been republished in this volume. Perhaps it was the same inspiration that led me also many years later to learn more of Metzger—discovering he was a real prophetic catalyst in the whole movement of ecumenism in the mid-twentieth century, and someone who indeed gave his life for this cause. Reading Leonard's book on Metzger encouraged me greatly on my personal path of discovery. It helped me to seek to learn more about the man and the movement he engendered in wartime Germany, a movement which continued and blossomed after his martyrdom in 1944. It also prompted me to seek to make personal contact with the Christkoenig Institute which Metzger founded in Meitingen in Germany, and to be sent, by the Sisters, selections of his poems written in times he spent in prison. This gave the inspiration to set some of these poetic texts in a Song Cycle called "*Gefangnisgedichte*" or "Prison Poems," which led to a performance of these poems for the hundredth anniversary of the founding of his community in Germany in 2019. Finally, it inspired me to create a full-length Oratorio dedicated to him, "Metzger," which includes twenty-seven of his texts. We aim to have the premiere of this work in a Cathedral in the City of Brandenburg and in Brandenburg-Görden prison itself, where Metzger was martyred.

To my knowledge, my ancestry is not connected with Germany; I am an American-born Irishman of Catholic background and practice who has developed a deep interest and love for ecumenism. Much of this interest stems from understanding the Irish history of division between Catholics and Protestants which was the background to my father's life in Northern Ireland. This led me to compose music in support of Christian Unity which I was able to have performed by a joint Catholic-Protestant choir in Northern Ireland and later in the Republic. It was the same interest in ecumenism that brought me to learn of Metzger and to decide to set some of his prison poems to music in the song cycle described above. To write a work in German as a non-German with rudimentary German language I had picked up as a student was quite a challenge, but there is something special about a non-German writing for or about Metzger.

Leonard Swidler wrote about him in the 1970s and I also, musically, in the 2000s. Although Metzger was German, and did not, as far as I know, ever visit either England, Ireland, or the US, his legacy goes far beyond Germany, both to the Church and indeed to the world of international politics. As I will try to show, Una Sancta, the movement of Christian reconciliation he engendered, carried on even more powerfully after his martyrdom in 1944. It reached its zenith perhaps in its participation and influence on the 1960 Munich Eucharistic Congress which was christened "the dress rehearsal for Vatican II." The Council which followed in 1962 led to the establishment of the Pontifical Secretariate and then Council for Christian Unity which in turn opened the door for the possibility of real reconciliation between Christian Churches split at the time of the Reformation. This work led to the historic signing of the Joint Declaration on the Doctrine of Justification between the Catholic Church and the Lutheran World Federation in 1999 and the later agreement on this doctrine by Anglican, Methodist, and Reformed Churches. The roots of the Reformation were being healed! One can trace all these developments back to the pioneering zeal and deep passion for the unity of Christians sought by Fr. Max Josef Metzger in wartime Germany. It is not to say that this breakthrough might not have been possible otherwise, especially with the post-war intermingling of Catholics and Lutherans in traditional confessional states (*Cuius regio eius religio*)[1] and the sharing of church buildings or the joint experience of suffering of Pastors of both confessions in the concentration camps such as Dachau. It was, however, Max Josef Metzger who helped to "create this wave" and brought passion to this challenge and made it all into a movement for change. This change too, as I will try to show, had its effect on post-war German politics and the creation of the Christian Democratic Party—the CDU/CSU. For the first time this party had Christians of both religious backgrounds working together. This Party has led Germany for fifty of the seventy-four years since the foundation of the Federal Republic of Germany in 1949,

---

[1] "*Cuius regio eius religio*," meaning the principal of "whose realm, their religion," which had developed from the Peace of Augsburg in 1555. This effectively divided German-speaking states into Catholic and Lutheran Confessional states.

helping to establish it as a powerhouse of Europe and a backbone of the European Union. Una Sancta gave much of the inspiration for this development politically by bringing together the two Confessions during wartime.

Something of this history caught the fertile imagination of Leonard and Arlene Swidler, encouraging them to cross the Atlantic and research Una Sancta and Metzger's life and influence while its memory was still current and then to present it to the English-speaking world in this book. Without Leonard and Arlene's work we would know so much less about his life and work. Leonard felt that he was standing on the shoulders of a giant. Therefore, in this postlude to Leonard's republished work, I feel I am also "standing on the shoulders of giants" in reconciliation between faith traditions. It is a great honor for me to seek to continue to share the enduring story of Max Josef Metzger and Una Sancta.

Dr. Cormac O'Duffy

Christmas 2022

Special Acknowledgements

The Sister at the Christkoenig Institute who originally gave me so much unique archival material, especially about the CDU memorial meeting in Berlin in 1946, was Sister Gertraud. This history was practically unknown to any Metzger biographer. She also gave me the words of the hymns and songs for the Oratorio which had been neglected and unsung since the 1930s. Sadly, Sister Gertraud passed in 2023. We loved her, and now she is buried next to Metzger in the graveyard in Meitingen. She has done her work well and we are blessed!

Sister Anne Marie Superior of the Christkoenig Institute of Meitingen provided the photos of Metzger that appear in this book and great support for the events at the "Alleluia" Memorial to Metzger in April 2024 at the Brandenburg prison where he was martyred. A great debt of gratitude is owed to her and all the Sisters who have helped keep Metzger's spirit and memory very much alive.

POSTWAR DEVELOPMENT OF UNA SANCTA

Parish Church St. Menas in Koblenz-Stolzenfels of
Fr. Matthias Laros, Leader of Una Sancta.

German children return to the ruins of Berlin, 1945.

After the great turbulence of the Second World War, the late 1940s was a time for picking up the shattered remains of postwar Germany. The huge displacement of German refugees, particularly from the East, meant great demographic changes in areas that had previously remained nearly all Protestant or all Catholic since the time of the Reformation.

Displacement of Populations

As Swidler relates, "the purely Catholic communities in Bavaria in 1910 numbered over 2,300; after the Second World war this sank to 9. Where in 1910 there were 244 purely Protestant communities today [1966] there are none."[1] Every area of Germany was required to take a quota of displaced persons without regard to their religious denomination. The displacement of populations, together with common wartime experiences in such places as concentration camps, prisoner of war camps, and refugee centers, created a soil where possible religious reconciliation between the different Christian Churches also could take place. In these circumstances both Catholic and Protestant Churches lent buildings to each other for services, something that would have been unthinkable previously—a practice that continues even today in the joint use of church buildings.

Growth of Una Sancta to a People's Movement

This period gave birth to an unprecedented growth of Una Sancta, which during the war had effectively been purely an underground movement and very much subject to Gestapo surveillance. Martyrdom of Christian leaders, such as with the execution of Metzger, created a new "seedbed for the church."

Dozens of new Una Sancta Circles sprang up throughout Germany. Everywhere in the crucible of mass suffering that came with the last years of the war and the years of want and deprivation that immediately followed it, bonds of unity between Christians were being formed. On the far-flung battlefields and in the concentration camps Protestants and Catholics learned to know each other as they had never had an opportunity to do before. They learned that much more joined them together than separated them. Dachau, where thousands of Catholic and Protestant clergymen were imprisoned, was particularly

---

[1] Leonard Swidler, *The Ecumenical Vanguard* (Pittsburgh, PA: Duquesne University Press, 1966), 168.

fruitful in generating ecumenical friendships between priests and ministers. An additional impetus in breaking down the walls of ignorance between the masses of Catholic and Protestants was given by the twentieth century "wandering of the nations."

Many areas of Germany before the war were purely Protestant or purely Catholic, or nearly so. After the war practically none were. Some ten million Germans were driven from their homes in the East and settled in Western Germany. Naturally no heed could be paid to religious affiliation in the herculean task of settling and assimilating the refugees. As a result, every area was now religiously mixed; Protestants learned that Catholics did not have cloven hooves, and vice versa. The refugees of course had no churches when they were moved into areas where they had no religious colleagues. Building new churches was out of the question for years; whatever funds were available for construction had to be directed toward providing adequate shelter for the millions of homeless persons. The only solution possible in this chaotic crisis was to make the maximum use of those churches which did exist—regardless of confession. This is exactly what was done; hundreds of Protestant churches were put at the disposal of Catholics, and the other way around. As a result, Catholics and Protestants came to know each other just by the simple process of rubbing shoulders going in and out of the same church, by cooperating with each other on the level of the sacristan's or sextant's work.

It suddenly became a rather common thing to have Protestant and Catholic theologians appear on the same platform to discuss matters of faith. Various Una Sancta Circles sponsored conferences that brought Catholics and Protestants together in retreat-like situations, much as Metzger had done at Meitingen. Articles on—or in a spirit of—ecumenism appeared with great frequency in all levels of periodicals and newspapers. The Una Sancta Movement suddenly became a popular movement, having deep roots due to its early beginnings and sufferings during the wartime, and attracting a wide variety of lay and clerical members. It was not unlike the sudden growth of ecumenism that took place much later in the wake of Vatican II in the United States.

In the midst of this ecumenical spring, Father Metzger still played a central part through his Sisters of Christ the King at Meitingen. The superior, Sister Gertrudis, very painstakingly re-established the Una Sancta contacts that had all been destroyed by the Gestapo and the war. Then in 1946 the *Una Sancta* newsletter started to appear from Meitingen; it was edited by Dr. Matthias Laros, a friend of Father Metzger. It was small and was written mainly by Dr. Laros, but it served as a sort of focal point for the movement. In the early

1950s the editorship was taken over by Dr. Thomas Sartory, a young Benedictine priest from Niederaltaich Abbey. It then became a full-fledged quarterly with solid scholarly articles by Protestant, Catholic, and Orthodox theologians, and a subscribership of over ten thousand—Protestant, Catholic, and Orthodox.

Matthias Laros, who was asked to take over the leadership of Una Sancta at Meitingen, wrote that, while the Brotherhood had worked previously in an isolated and less organized fashion, "there had arisen now in the broad masses of people ... an elemental will toward a final ... fruitful elimination of the division of faith."[2] Over the period from 1945 to 1950, the Una Sancta Brotherhood grew to where it was estimated there were up to ten thousand active participants in the movement.[3] Groups varied in size from ten members to some numbering over two hundred; Berlin itself had several Una Sancta Circles. When an Una Sancta evening was announced in Berlin, with speeches being given by alternatively Catholic, Lutheran, Orthodox, and Baptist speakers, the church, which had a capacity of 2,500, was "filled to overflowing half an hour ahead of time."[4] Similar meetings attracting hundreds of people were held in Frankfurt and Munich. In the northern town of Eberswalde over a thousand crammed into the largest venue available for talks by Protestant, Catholic, and Free Church speakers. "Ecumenical weeks" were organized where lectures were given by Protestant and Catholic theologians. These were especially popular throughout the Rhineland where priests and pastors presented to each other courses of their own theologies on such challenging subjects as papal infallibility and the Augsburg Confession.

---

[2] Matthias Laros, *Una Sancta - Einigung 1 Rundbrief*, September 1946, quoted in Swidler, op. cit., 171.

[3] Edward Grüber, "Im Zeichen," 215, quoted in Swidler, *Ecumenical Vanguard*, 175

[4] Swidler, Ecumenical Vanguard, 176.

Karl Adam on the Reassessment of Luther

Evangelical Lutheran Markuskiche in Stuttgart, place of Karl Adam's lectures on Una Sancta in 1947.

In Stuttgart, the famed Catholic theologian and University Professor Karl Adam gave a series of lectures on "Una Sancta from the Catholic Viewpoint" over three nights, April 27–29, 1947, to overflowing crowds at the Lutheran Markuskirche. Sensing the zeitgeist of the postwar period he deduced, "it cannot be doubted that at the present moment, under the shattering impact of two world wars, at least in the sense that the unreality of mere polemic is being abandoned, that Luther on the one hand and the papacy on the other are being seen in a clearer and more friendly light, and that real efforts are being made, by Christians everywhere, to being about if not an *unio fidei* [union of faith] at least an *unio caritatis* [union of heart]."[5] Adam then proceeded to describe Luther, not in the former way as an arch heretic, fallen monk, or even psychotic, but rather as a man of great brilliance and a sharp incisive mind, who was horrified by sham holiness.

---

[5] Karl Adam, *One and Holy* (New York, Sheed and Ward: 1951), 7. This was reprinted as *Roots of the Reformation* (Steubenville, OH: Coming Home, 2000), 7.

Dr Karl Adam (1876-1966), theologian and
leader in the Una Sancta Movement.

To Adam, if Luther had brought these gifts to the service of the church and remained a faithful Catholic, "he would be forever our Great Reformer, our True Man of God, our teacher and leader, comparable to Thomas Aquinas and Francis of Assisi. He would have been the greatest saint of our people, the re-founder of the Church in Germany, a second Boniface."[6] His lectures were repeated later in Karlsruhe and later published both in German and English. When the book was later published with the title *Una Sancta in Katholischer Sicht*, he dedicated the book to the memory of Fr. Max Josef Metzger.[7]

Guiding Principles of Una Sancta

One particular meeting in the Benedictine Abbey of Niederaltaich helped to bring the whole movement into clear focus. At a joint Catholic–Protestant retreat held in August 1946 the participants came up with three defining principles for Una Sancta work:

> 1. In the effort toward mutual understanding there must be preparedness to learn from one another to practice Christian love.

---

[6] Adam, *One and Holy*, 26

[7] Karl Adam, *Una Sancta in Katholischer Sicht* (Dusseldorf, Patmos-Verlag: 1947).

2. In the striving towards Christian truth it is necessary that the divisive points be clearly seen. A union must not result at the expense of truth.

3. The actual Union is the Work of God. God however works in history. Great historical events, great common needs can become in the hands of God decisive means of his grace when the hour is ripe. We can and must already now prepare ourselves for such a working of God's grace by taking the first two steps and by a sincere prayer for unity.[8]

Benedictine Abbey of Niederaltaich, Bavaria, the venue for Una Sancta meetings.

The Stuttgart Una Sancta Circle sponsored an Una Sancta conference at the Benedictine Abbey of Neresheim, with many important Christian leaders attending, including Hans Asmussen, President of the Chancery of the Evangelical Church in Germany, and a member of *Die Sammlung* together with Catholic University professors from Tubigen University. At this event two lectures were given, one by a Catholic and one by a Protestant, in memory of Max Metzger, "founder and blood martyr of the Una Sancta Movement."[9]

---

[8] Swidler, *Ecumenical Vanguard*, 120.

[9] Ibid., 181.

Youth Gatherings and Publications

Olympic Stadium, Berlin, venue for the Una Sancta youth gathering, October 1946.

While many renowned Church leaders and theologians from different confessions continued the intense sharing that Una Sancta involved, much larger gatherings were held for youth. On October 27, 1946, between three and four thousand students gathered for an ecumenical celebration at the Berlin Olympic Stadium as a public demonstration for all baptized youth.

Cologne University, venue for a large Una Sancta youth demonstration for Christian unity.

A similar demonstration took place by several thousand students at Cologne University.[10] From some quiet, almost clandestine meetings in wartime Germany, after the war Una Sancta grew into a national movement, with a wide variety of gatherings, meetings, conferences, lectures, and demonstrations for Christian unity. According to Laros, who became the official leader of Una Sancta at the invitation of Sister Gertrudis after the death of Metzger, it was now a "people's movement." It had developed into publishing where a wide variety of publishing houses now spread the word across Germany. Una Sancta headquarters themselves in Meitingen produced their own *Rundbrief*. It was estimated that over fifty thousand copies of this circular were distributed nationwide sharing their ecumenical vision and latest developments.

Visibility of Una Sancta and Konrad Adenauer

Konrad Adenauer, leader of Christian Democratic Union (CDU) and first Chancellor of West Germany.

Swidler comments that anyone who was "*au fait*" of religious activities in postwar Germany would have been aware of the work of the Una Sancta Movement.[11] It had gained the highest level of support from leaders of the church of all confessions, the German Catholic Bishops Council, and even the listening ear of the Vatican. One person who was *au fait* with the very visible

---

[10] Ibid., 186

[11] Ibid., 198

effects of Una Sancta was the committed Catholic politician from Cologne, soon to become the leader of the new Christian Democratic Union Party (CDU) and first Chancellor of postwar Germany and visionary of the future European Union, Konrad Adenauer.[12]

In the authorized biography of Adenauer, author Paul Weymar describes the pioneering politician seeking to ensure the base of the new party did not have confessional splits or schisms between different Catholic or Lutheran members. Weymar writes of Adenauer's insistence, often after acrimonious debate, on a strict parity and equality between the confessions. As he drove across Germany, Adenauer would often write in his notes such comments as "good cooperation between the confessions, Una Sancta atmosphere"—or else "tension must be eliminated, X too aristocratic."[13] Una Sancta, however, was not a political movement. According to Swidler, apart from the mixing of politics and religions, there was no treatment of political issues in any of its early literature. Metzger always sought to clarify to the Nazi authorities that his movement was not political; however, in seeking to draw together the two historical streams of German Catholicism and Lutheranism, he was in fact preparing for a growing river, if not a flood, that would spread across all of Germany. In the postwar years it would inspire, if not invade, both social and political realms. Adenauer was friends with Una Sancta leaders such as Robert Grosche (1888–1967), who was the Dean of Cologne. They had extensive talks about the future of the city and society, and Grosche supported the aims of Adenauer to found the CDU without himself actually joining it.[14]

Another lifelong colleague of Adenauer was the Jesuit Max Pribilla, whose experiences in World War I inspired him in his ecumenical vision, leading him to a leadership position within Una Sancta. Adenauer was in contact with other Una Sancta leaders, including New Testament scholar Fr. Otto Karren. The leader of Una Sancta after the death of Metzger, Matthias Laros, kept up regular correspondence with the Chancellor. In March 1951 he sent a copy of his latest book, *The Word of the Lord for This Time* (*Die Botschaft des Herrn*

---

[12] Konrad Adenauer, *Memoiras 1945-53* (Chicago: Regnery, 1965), 244.

[13] Paul Weymar, *Adenauer: His Authorized Biography*. (New York: Dutton, 1957), 172.

[14] Marcel Albert (Gerleve), "Robert Grosche: Stadtdechant von Köln (1888-1967)," Portal Rheinische Geschichte, https://rheinische-geschichte.lvr.de/Persoenlichkeiten/robert-grosche/DE-2086/lido/57c6d803506a94.74616954

an diese Zeit), with a note saying he would be preaching on the message of "One Shepherd, One Flock."

Later, in January 1952, Laros wrote again to the Chancellor, congratulating him on the ratification of the Schuman Plan for the integration of the French and German coal and steel industries. This development would make the outbreak of war between these two traditional enemies practically impossible. Laros told him of the "deep sympathy in Catholic Circles" for this work and to share that he had a "host of people praying for him."

The Word of the Lord for This Time by Laros, gifted to Konrad Adenauer.

Fr. Matthias Laros (1882–1965), Una Sancta leader and friend.

Adenauer replied to Laros by saying, "I have read with great joy that large groups of the Catholic population of our homeland share intimately in my work with their prayers. May the Lord God bless our work." Adenauer had regular correspondence with many Una Sancta leaders over the time of his chancellorship. To Asmussen, Metzger's colleague from Berlin's Una Sancta Circle and head of the Lutheran Church after the war, Adenauer wrote to commemorate his "beneficial work as a pastor" and his "resolute and sympathetic commitment to the idea of cooperation among all Christians in our country." Asmussen had also at this time become a member of the CDU.[15]

The Growth of Christian Democracy: Stegerwald to the CDU

Adam Stegerwald, 'Founding Father' of the idea of Christian Democracy, former Prussian Prime Minister.

Adam Stegerwald (1874–1945) was regarded by many as the founding father (*Unionsgedanke*) of the movement for Christian democracy in Germany. He served in many roles as Prussian prime minister, Christian trade unionist, and leader of the left wing of the Center Party. At a meeting of the Congress of Christian Trade Unions in Essen in November 1920 he had pointed out the difficulty in a lack of confessional harmony in the politics of Germany: "What is needed is a union of constructive forces in both the Catholic and the Protestant camps … a strong Christian national people's party, which

---

[15] Information from the Archive Section of Adenauer Haus, Rhondorf Bad Honnef, June 13, 2019.

Protestants cannot create by themselves because they lack the necessary unity and Catholics also are too weak to organize themselves."[16]

The end of the war in 1945 provided the first real opportunity for such a political movement to be realized. There existed no party capable of bringing the two confessional sides together. The old Center Party in the eyes of Protestants was looked at as a purely partisan party of Catholics, who indeed formed a minority of the German electorate in the Weimar era. On the other hand, the Protestant Church was after the war no longer associated with the Hohenzollern monarchy and now sought to be free from the terrible legacy of the German Christians of the Hitler era. The cry was coming from many quarters across Germany for a party that crossed confessional lines.

---

[16] Quoted in Arnold Heidenheimer, *Adenauer and the CDU* (The Hague: Martinus Nijhoff, 1960), 7, referenced in Geoffrey Pridham, *Christian Democracy in Western Germany* (New York: St. Martin's Press, 1977), 26.

POSTWAR DEVELOPMENT OF UNA SANCTA

Election poster of the Catholic Center Party,
showing its challenge to left- and right-wing groups.

The Founding of the CDU in Bad Godesberg, December 1945

CDU poster with different church spires, with the message, "the gathering of all Christians on a level plane."

In the months immediately after the end of the world war, a wide variety of Christian political groups had developed across Germany, such as the Christian Democratic Party in Frankfurt and the Christian Democratic Reconstruction Party in Schleswig-Holstein. These groups finally coalesced after a nationwide conference of Christian Democrats held in Bad Godesberg in December of 1945, adopting formally for the first time the name Christian Democratic Union. By January 1946 Konrad Adenauer had become one of its leaders. The CDU were all adamantly anti-Nazi:

> National Socialism has plunged Germany into a catastrophe that is without parallel in her long history. It has covered the German name in the eyes of the whole world with shame and humiliation. All this would not have overwhelmed us if wide circles of our nation had not let themselves be governed by an avaricious materialism. In this way far too many fell victim to National Socialist demagogy which promised each German a paradise on earth.[17]

---

[17] Leo Schwering, *Frühgeschichte der Christlich-Demokratischen Union* (Berlin: Kommunal-Verlag, 1963), 193, quoted in Pidham, *Christian Democracy*, 215.

They all believed in Christian principles as the basis for Political life. "The Christian outlook on life must again replace the materialistic outlook, and instead of the principles resulting from materialism must come the principles of Christian ethics."[18] To do this they felt the need to create a confessional bridge and to break out of previous confessional ghettos in order to bridge divisions in German society and to build a joint vision of a free Federal State based on principles of social justice.

The CDU Meeting in Berlin 1946 to Honor Fr. Max Metzger

Sister Judith-Maria of the St. Pius Stift, Community of Fr. Metzger.

---

[18] Schwering, *Frühgeschichte der Christlich-Demokratischen Union*, 178-79.

On April 10, 1946, just four months after the CDU had been established, a leader of the CDU in Berlin wrote to Sister Judith Maria, Head of Fr. Max Metzger's Christ the King Institute at Pius-Stift, Berlin. She had been visiting Fr. Max during his final months in prison and was later responsible for his reburial in St. Hedwig's Cemetery in Berlin. She was responsible for the Una Sancta work in Berlin. He wanted to tell her about a special meeting the new CDU was holding in Berlin with the aim of "crossing the denominational divide."

They had asked Lutheran pastor Walter Dress of St. Annen Kirche in Dahlem, Berlin—a Center of the Confessing Church that had opposed Hitler—to give the address. He was a professor of history at Humboldt University and was brother-in-law to Dietrich Bonhoeffer who had also, like Max Metzger, been executed by the regime for his stand. Dr. Dress wished to celebrate the life, testimony, and martyrdom of Fr. Max, and the CDU wished for Sister Judith and Una Sancta to be represented and to bring materials to the talk.

Saint Joseph Catholic Church in Wedding, Berlin, location of the talk honoring Fr. Max Josef Metzger.

Mercedes Palast Berlin, a former cinema seating over 2,500 people, location for Pastor Dress's memorial to Max Josef Metzger.

Dr. Max Josef Metzger.

The Address of Pastor Walter Dress

This is the text of Pastor Dress's speech.

> One year ago, when the anniversary of Dr. Metzger's death was the first year, we had to be silent. Now we may and want to commemorate [his death] publicly. We know and testify that he was one of the noblest and most vocal champions of peace among peoples, of the freedom and dignity of man, of the right of the Spirit and the faith of Christendom. In the conflict two years ago, on April 17, 1944, he was offered by the Bloody Court as a sacrifice. If I am allowed to speak at this hour and at this event to express what moves us all in the memory of him, then at first I must express my gratitude for God's having me meet him … a man whose winning friendliness grew out of the goodness of a heart conquered by Christ, and who at the same time grew so strong through his faith that no world power could divert him from the path which his prophetic conscience allowed him to take.

Dr. Max Josef Metzger experiences World War I.

> The experiences he had had to make as a Division Chaplain in the war that broke out in 1914 taught him to detest and hate the war. He was always an active person and had to turn his findings into action: [In prison, he had occasionally found this being more difficult to cope with than the imprisonment itself.] Immediately he set to work to create a peace movement and sought to promote the reconciliation of peoples. It was in line with these thoughts, insights, and far-sighted plans that later the reconciliation of the Christian denominations became the very purpose of his heart, the very meaning of his life and work, and the aim of his hopes and prayers.

Interior of Mercedes Palast, the Wedding, Berlin venue for the memorial of Max Josef Metzger by Pastor Walter Dress.

Fr. Max Josef Metzger celebrating Mass at his home Church of St. Wolfgang's, Meitingen.

Fr. Max Josef Metzger in his study in Meitingen.

Based on such insights, Dr. Metzger started the brotherhood Una Sancta. It was not intended to be a new organization alongside other organizations; rather, he wanted to emphasize the fact that the Lord Himself calls all who confess Him their Master and who regard the division of Christendom as a problem and a challenge, should be encouraged to persevere in the prayer for the realization of unity and to cultivate a fraternal encounter with the Christians of the other denominations. The call Dr. Metzger made found a wide echo. He soon succeeded in bringing together in many places consortiums of Christians from different churches and communities who received his thoughts, led to responsible debates, and clarified a number of contentious issues. The work, which has begun so auspiciously, which was then greatly hampered in the last months of the war and finally, like so many other things, was interrupted, has since been resumed. Because we have in recent years learned a lot as Germans and as Christians—we know it must [now] be continued. Dr. Metzger has left us a legacy of particular importance; which we must not let be forgotten…. At the time of his death, the Dr. Metzger could not yet have understood how his immense suffering at the time could inspire us [in the future] to be fruitful as a people, and as Christians.

Reaction to the Meeting at Mercedes Palast and St. Joseph's Parish, Berlin

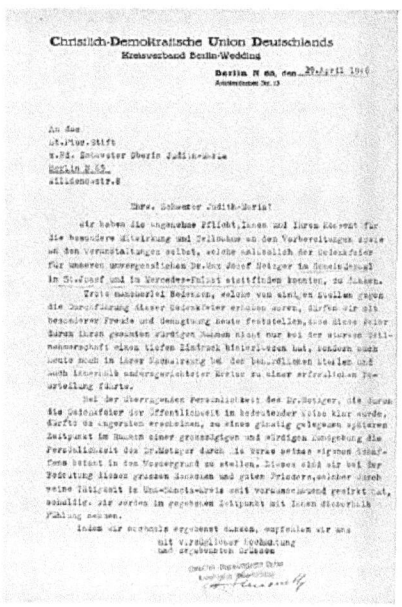

What were the effects of the meeting? It might be hard to assess, but as soon as the meeting was concluded, the same day, the CDU Berlin-Wedding representative wrote again to Sister Judith, thanking her and the St. Pius-Stift Convent for their contribution and participation as well as for the events themselves. The writer noted that the commemoration was held in a very dignified manner that had left a "deep impression" on all those who attended at both the Parish Hall of St. Joseph and later at the Mercedes Palast. They noted that the event was well received by the authorities and in wider circles. The CDU representative suggested, given the outstanding personality of Dr. Metzger, that there could be another such event that would emphasize more Fr. Max's creativity. They felt they owed it to this great priest who had achieved such far-sighted work through Una Sancta Circles. What is remarkable is that these two rallies in the German capital were not organized by the Una Sancta Brotherhood but by a new political party that had only been established three months previously, the Christian Democratic Union.

The Achievement of Una Sancta and the CDU/CSU

Program for the Celebratory Concert dedicated to the memory of Fr. Max Josef Metzger, Good Friday 1954.

Una Sancta went through various phases until its work was recognized in the Vatican with the foundation of the Pontifical Council for Promoting Christian Unity and the first agreement between Catholics and Lutherans since the Reformation in the Joint Declaration on the Doctrine of Justification. This historic document was signed by representatives of both churches in Augsburg in 1999. It is hard to see how either of these events might have happened without the driving zeal and pioneering work of Fr. Max Joseph Metzger and his Una Sancta Brotherhood.

The Rev. Martin Junge, general secretary of the Lutheran World Federation, embraces Bishop Munib Younan of the Evangelical Lutheran Church, president of the Lutheran World Federation, front center, during an ecumenical prayer service at the Lutheran cathedral in Lund, Sweden. At right, Pope Francis embraces Archbishop Antje Jackelén, primate of the Lutheran Church in Sweden. At left is Bishop Anders Arborelius of Stockholm and Cardinal Kurt Koch, president of the Pontifical Council for Promoting Christian Unity. (CNS photo/Paul Haring)

The Legacy of Fr. Max Josef Metzger

In concluding his thoughts at the Mercedes Palast in the April 1946 meeting, Dr. Dress challenged those in attendance to follow Fr. Max's example: Dr. Metzger himself was a man who lived in and out of prayer. That was the secret of his personality. And he was a praying man, praying for God's will because he was at home in the Scriptures. He himself points out in one of his writings the biblical joy "in the Catholic Church." The letters he wrote in the prison prove on every page—one might almost say, in every sentence—how the Bible became the most personal possession.

> He took from God's hand what God offered him abundantly and was therefore able to give away and comfort, strengthen, and raise many those [who were with him] in prison. Metzger worked and fought as a German Christian friend of peace during the war: he was daring, completely ready to commit his whole person for the thing he knew as right and true, bravely and without any evasion even in front of the court [that sentenced him], a court which was nothing but a diabolical

farce; what can we do in this hour of remembrance as we pledge that we will strive to emulate his example and inherit his inheritance? What was true in his own life was the belief and knowledge in the promise of the Holy Scripture: If this mortal will put on the incorruption and this mortal will put on the immortality, then it will be fulfilled the Word that is written: "Death is swallowed up in victory. O death, where is thy sting? Hell, where is your victory?! Thank God, who gave us the victory through ours Lord Jesus Christ."

Fr. Max Josef Metzger outside the chapel of the Johannesheims in his native Meitingen.

UNA SANCTA IN GERMANY TODAY

The Example of the Munich Una Sancta Circle

As has been recounted, Una Sancta spread across Germany and Switzerland during the war period of 1939–1945 and flourished in the postwar period. Today, it is no longer as active, and only one Una Sancta cell still remains, the Una Sancta group in Munich. Gudrun Steineck is the chairperson of the working group of the Munich Ecumenical Circle (*Vorsitzende der AG Ökumenische Kreise*). She explained that "the other groups in Berlin and Hamburg have now sadly ceased operating," and that "there needs to be a new influx of youth to the work to help it to grow again."

The story of the Una Sancta group in Munich is fascinating, continuing the quest of Max Josef Metzger and others for Christian unity in spite of difficulties and opposition. I will now seek to give a short account of the Una Sancta Circle in Munich, a circle that is still functioning today, eighty-four years after its founding in 1938. I will use, as a source, a talk given by Gudrun to the international ecumenical community in Burg Rothenfels in 2005.

Gudrun joined Una Sancta in 1980 and felt immediately at home in her Lutheran faith, inspired by Heinrich Freis, who explained the importance of understanding ecumenical theology as a passionate desire for truth. In spite of obstacles and occasional despair at the task of church unity, his words to her, "Never stop starting," have inspired her to the present day. At the time of writing this account she was still active and was looking forward to the next Una Sancta circle meeting later that year.

The circle in Munich began in 1938 and was a private circle with mixed religious services, Bible studies, and theological reflections, leading to a crystallization of ecumenical aspirations. The original meeting house was that of Maria von Bornstedt in Gauting, near Munich. It was founded by Christians who did not wish to put up with "the stumbling block of divided Christianity."

The group members had connections with well-known theologians, both Catholic and Lutheran. They met amid all the difficulties of the Nazi era, in which all assemblies were banned. Meeting together was therefore "life threatening." A wide group of influential people attended, including the Jesuit Alfred Delp, the Benedictine Hugo Lang, the Confessional Lutheran pastor Hans Asmussen, the evangelical pastor August Rehbach, and Vicar Walter Hildmann. From different backgrounds, they all expressed uninhibited cordiality and friendship with each other. Many who attended had to leave their homes during Nazi times and were imprisoned or even later executed.

Cardinal Faulhaber of Munich, who was a very outspoken critic of Nazi policies and ideologies, helped make their meetings possible. He provided a fixed, secure place and time to meet together so that the existence of the circle would be unknown and therefore not endangered. The group survived the war, found a new location, and was open to all in need in the postwar period. Their bonds of fellowship had been strengthened through shared suffering and by the loss of those who had been martyred, particularly Max Josef Metzger and Alfred Delp.

In 1948, the group sought to organize an all-German meeting and chose the location of Konstanz, located at the end of Lake Bodensee in southern Germany. They sought participation from Old Catholic, Evangelical, Catholic, and Orthodox Christians, as well as the Swiss Una Sancta group and Russian exiles in Paris. Unfortunately, the initial meeting was derailed by a *monitum* from the Holy Office in Rome that forbade Catholics from participating without Rome's express permission. However, after a flurry of telegrams and the help of Bishop Jaeger of Paderborn (who had his own Una Sancta Circle of ecumenical theologians), permission was granted.

The work continued to flourish, including contacts with ecumenical movements in the US, England, and Holland. In 1956, the group found a new home in a Christian youth center at Rothenfels Castle, overlooking the Main River near Frankfurt under the direction of Heinrich Kahlefeld, Thomas Sartory, and Rudolf Stälin. This continued to be its meeting place until relatively recently. The meeting place has now returned to Munich.

The highlight of all the ecumenical events initiated by the Munich circle was its participation in the Eucharistic World Congress, which was held in Munich in 1960 and will be described in more detail below.

The event began under difficult circumstances. Although Lutheran Bishop Stälin viewed the Una Sancta event as strategic for Christian unity, Cardinal Wendel found the twenty proposed Catholic theses of the Munich Una Sancta group "too suspicious." They were intended for distribution to the nine thousand participants attending meetings arranged by Una Sancta in all available rooms at Munich University, the site given for their participation in the Congress. As we shall see later, the Congress was a prelude to the ecumenism that was to develop in the heart of the church at the Second Vatican Council.

The 1960 Munich Eucharistic Conference and Una Sancta

It had been described as the dress rehearsal for Vatican II.[1] With the participation of a million people, it was the first major international event to take place in Germany since the end of the war in 1945. Such was the concern of the authorities about such a swell in the population of Munich that the Bavarian Interior Minister declared a state of emergency and ordered an extra group of five thousand police to see that the lines of the mass gathering were orderly.

Cardinal Joseph Wendel of Munich had wished to bring the Congress to Munich for a long time. He gained an opening with Pope Pius XII, who had previously resided in Munich as Papal Nuncio. After his death, the Cardinal found support in newly elected Pope John XXIII. He had already announced the advent of the Second Vatican Council and, according to an article published by Domradio, the Pope later described the Munich Congress as a "dress rehearsal for the Council."[2]

The Congress, like the Council, was ripe with liturgical innovation, and Munich itself became the scene of a wide variety of forms of worship. In the Hofbräuhaus, the cradle of Bavarian tavern culture, Bishops distributed the bread for an agape celebration. The foundations for Todesangst-Christi-Kapelle (chapel) were laid at the Dachau concentration camp, and the Bonn Professor of Theology Fr. Joseph Ratzinger (later Pope Benedict XVI) summarized the Congress by saying that "the Masses became a community." Optimism had been engendered in a community that was just starting to experience peace and hope for the first time since the end of the war.[3]

---

[1] Christoph Renzikowski, "Generalprobe für das Zweite Vatikanische Konzil," Domradio (July 30, 2010), https://www.domradio.de/artikel/kirchlicher-kongress-war-1960-erstes-mega-event-nach-dem-krieg.

[2] Ibid.

[3] Ibid.

Perhaps the greatest innovation of the Congress—which was also taken up by the Vatican Council to follow—was the welcome given to the Una Sancta Circle of Munich and its speakers, making it the first time since the Eucharistic Congresses started in June 1881 in Lille, France, that the Congress had had an ecumenical dimension. It brought to the Congress (in the words of Brother Roger of Taizé) "the scandal of the separation of the Churches" and gave an impassioned plea for unity in belief. Professor Heinrich Fries said that the clarion call of ecumenism could be heard in the official church for the first time.[4]

The Congress itself marked the first chance of the Church to gain a foothold on the public stage since the Nazi period, opening a door for the renewal of the liturgy. However, the breakthrough in ecumenism went way beyond the walls of the church and had an effect on politics and society, with its desire for the assurance of peace and stability following the tragedy of the war. This seemed to be summarized by Professor Hans Küng, who later remarked,

> No peace among the nations without peace among the religions. No peace among the religions without dialogue between the religions. No dialogue between the religions without investigation of the foundation of the religions.'[5]

The importance of the Congress was understood by Chancellor Adenauer, who attended the Congress on the final day. He had also attended the only previous Eucharistic Congress in Germany in Cologne in 1909. In an address sent to the opening of the Munich Congress he wrote,

> In 1939, the disaster of the Second World War began in Germany. These wounds have not closed to this day. Europe—indeed, the whole world—is still suffering. In the wake of this war, materialistic atheism went on an offensive all over the world and has stood at the heart of the European Continent since 1945, even threatening its spiritual core.... Since the end of the war, a new element in the political image on the German people has been the cooperation of the members of the two Christian denominations, the Catholic and the Protestant, in public life. It was almost a creative act, a departure from a paralysis that had lasted for centuries, when the Union of Catholic and Protestant Christians, who had to suffer together under National

---

[4] From a description of the Congress given to the author by Gudrun Steineck, Vorsitzende of the Oekumenische Kreise in Hofheim, Bavaria.

[5] Hans Küng, Quotes, *Goodreads*, https://www.goodreads.com/quotes/157789-no-peace-among-the-nations-without-peace-among-the religions.

Socialist persecution, formed after the collapse.... May the Eucharistic World Congress in Munich strengthen these forces, make them resilient and let them continue to radiate.[6]

Adenauer was aware of how Una Sancta had helped to develop this new sense of unity between the churches with its effect on politics and society in the formation of his Christian Democratic Party, which for the first time had politically united Catholics and Lutherans in one unity party. Now it was time, when Una Sancta was at its zenith, to bring its cause for church unity to the heart of the Church itself and on into the Vatican Council.

Una Sancta in Munich

At the time of the Congress there were five hundred members in the ecumenical Una Sancta group in Munich. It was still a movement gathered in small groups for discussions, conferences, sharing, and fellowship in the style Metzger had created; it had not had an ecumenical breakthrough with the wider general public.

When the Congress was announced, a preparatory circle from the group presented the organizers with an application to be included in the event. There was much communication back and forth with Cardinal Wendel of Munich, who was organizing the Congress, before approval was finally given. However, due to the objections of the Conservative Canon Lawyer from Munich University, Professor Karl Mörsdorf, permission was then revoked, but with the help of many friends, the objections of Mörsdorf were overruled. It now seemed Una Sancta as a movement for church unity was now "weatherproof" and could face any storm.

Because of the delay caused by the objection, however, the original location of the larger Bayernhalle for the presentation of Una Sancta was no longer available. Una Sancta had the use of the Auditorium Maximum and the Atrium of the University. In this location the Una Sancta group of Munich was able to welcome the nine thousand visitors to their events in all available spaces, along corridors, stairs, and floors. It was only with the use of some gentle persuasion that they managed to seat all the bishops who wished to attend. A member of Una Sancta who attended the meetings counted as many as two hundred bishops who were able to be directed to the reserved seats. The program listed talks by Abbot M. Heufelder, OSB, of the Niederaltaich

---

[6] Bulletin of the Press and Information Office of the Federal Government No. 139 (July 29, 1960), 1381, https://www.konrad-adenauer.de/seite/29-juli-1960.

Monastery, who gave the introduction and closing word; Dr. Otto Karrer of Lucerne, who gave the talk "Eucharistic Thought among Our Separated Brethren"; and Father Thomas Sartory from Niederaltaich, who gave a talk on the Last Supper while music was supplied by the John of Damascus Choir of Essen. Another highlight was the contribution given by Una Sancta in Meitingen, where the Una Sancta Movement had begun. All of this led to a friendly interaction that moved the assembly, culminating in the Orthodox chants of the Essen Choir. The day after the Congress, Lutheran Bishop Wilhelm Stählin described it as a "world event." The Una Sancta group had prepared a booklet on ecumenism with articles by many influential writers and speakers. All the eight thousand copies of the texts were quickly snapped up by the participants, and for the three following years back orders were shipped out to inquirers until finally only one copy was left with the organizers.

The Vatican itself stated that the Munich Congress opened the door officially for ecumenical encounter and reconciliation. In a publication given by the Vatican in preparation for the Dublin Eucharistic Congress of 2012, which itself had a whole day apportioned to the question of ecumenism, they wrote,

> The first thirty-seven International Eucharistic Congresses did not deal with the themes of ecumenism and interreligious dialogue, except at the Congress of Jerusalem in 1893—although only partially and in a manner quite different from our approach today. The time had not yet come, but we can hope that coming years will see a greater openness to the essential link between the Eucharist and the communion of the Churches. If by its very nature the Eucharist manifests and realises the *forma ecclesiae*, it represents not only the goal, but also the way and means of attaining visible communion between the Christian Churches.
>
> It was at Munich in 1960 that ecumenical relations began to take on their full importance at Eucharistic Congresses. Hardly had the preparations for the Second Vatican Council begun when Blessed John XXIII decided to establish the Secretariat for the Promotion of Christian Unity. From then on, in the ecclesial context of Vatican II the movement towards Christian unity became part of the agenda of Eucharistic Congresses. This was followed in more recent times by interreligious dialogue, which has received such great attention in the

Church since the first meeting at Assisi called by Pope John Paul II in 1986.[7]

After the Congress and the Vatican Council, the "fire fell" and a spiritual blaze was kindled with the help of Una Sancta groups in Berlin and Hamburg. The Munich group continued to explore theological issues concerning Christians and Jews. In these encounters, the group followed a set of principles developed by Josef Tomé in 1941 that they continue to find valuable for their ecumenical work today.[8]

Guidelines for Ecumenical Encounter, by Josef Tomé (1941)

First, look at what the denominations have in common.

See how history might have changed things today. (For example, in a parish letter from 1956, there was a quote from Cardinal Faulhaber forbidding mixed marriages. Now the good pastors are happy; the marriage is a Christian marriage, and the children are brought up as Christians.)

Do not fight the other denominations but seek ways to get alongside them.

Fight against the Pharisaic tendency to seek comfort in your own ranks and denomination.

Have reverence for the other denominations.

Compare ideal with ideal and reality with reality.

Blame the breakup on your own denomination first.

Get to know the other denominations through personal encounters and through their literature.

---

[7] "Pastoral Visit to Perugia and Assisi: Address of John Paul II to the Representatives of the Christian Churches and Ecclesial Communities Gathered in Assisi for the World Day of Prayer," https://www.vatican.va/roman_curia/pont_committees/eucharist-congr/documents/rc_committ_euchar_doc_20090609_fisionomia-congressi_en.html

[8] Information gathered from a talk given by Gudrun Steineck on the occasion of a meeting of the International Ecumenical Fellowship (IEF) in Burg Rothenfels in 2005, by kind permission of the author.

> Do not try to convert others to your denomination.
>
> Do not talk about the return of the other denomination to your church, but expect the bridging of the opposites, moving forward, maturing, and developing of both denominations together.

Una Sancta has been the principal driving force in German, and subsequently world, ecumenical endeavors. The vision that Fr. Max Josef had in Meitingen in 1939 has carried on past his own martyrdom, and, in this process, the work and vision of the Munich Una Sancta group has been clear. The influence carried on right up to the changes at the Vatican Council and the Pontifical Council for Promoting Christian Unity and to the words and direction of the Popes and other denominational leaders today. In his encyclical on Christian unity "Ut Unum Sint," Pope Saint John Paul II said,

> It is absolutely clear that ecumenism, the movement promoting Christian unity, is not just some sort of appendix which is added to the Church's traditional activity. Rather, ecumenism is an organic part of her life and work, and consequently must pervade all that she is and does.[9]

We await the day when Fr. Max is finally announced as Blessed Max Josef Metzger or Saint Max Josef, Saint of Ecumenism, and all others too are venerated for the work they did to fulfill the Priestly Prayer of Jesus "that they may be one."

---

[9] Pope Saint John Paul II, "Ut Unum Sint: On Commitment to Ecumenism," https://www.vatican.va/content/john-paul ii/en/encyclicals/documents/hf_jp-ii_enc_25051995_ut-unum-sint.html, par 20.

AFTERWORD

HE WAS A MUSICIAN!

METZGER'S LEGACY LIVES ON IN MUSIC

By Cormac O'Duffy

While Metzger's writings and compositions have been discussed at length throughout this book, you may be surprised, as I was, to learn he was also a musician and a poet. I discovered Metzger's music as I researched what led to the breakup in the churches caused by the Reformation and how ecumenism had developed in the twentieth century to heal the wounds of that epochal time.

Signature of Fr. Max Josef Metzger (Br. Paulus) saying,
"God be with you all … Yours, Br. Paulus."

The Search for Christian Unity

My interest in Christian unity led me thus to examine German church history and indeed to visit Wittenberg, the place of the 95 Theses of Luther. As I understood how the Reformation divided Germany, I also saw how the effects of the two world wars had started to reshape this inheritance. Germany was no longer split up into strictly Lutheran or Catholic states, as it had been. In the midst of these times, there were wonderful writers in Germany who had started to examine the circumstances of the Reformation without partisan polemics or apologetics, to see what had been faults on both sides; they analyzed the deep misunderstandings and the exaggerations that often come when parties fall out with each other. The names of these writers included Adolf Herte (1887–1970), Joseph Lortz (1887–1975), Karl Adam (1876–1966), and later Bishop Jaeger (1892–1975) of the Diocese of Paderborn and his Lutheran colleague Bishop Wilhelm Stählin (1883–1975) of Oldenburg. It included leaders of the Confessing Church such as Hans Asmussen. Finally, the debate found its way to the new institution of the Pontifical Secretariat and subsequent Council for Christian Unity and the Vatican Council's own work for Christian unity with its founder Cardinal Augustin Bea (1881–1968).[1] They had all through their scholarly and pastoral work helped to make the possible greater understanding and reconciliation between Lutherans and Catholics.

Joseph Lortz, Author of
the Reformation in
Germany

Pastor Hans Asmussen,
Evangelical Church
Leader

Cardinal Augustin Bea,
Founder of the Pontifical
Council for Christian Unity

The Prophet of Ecumenism?

As a priest, Father Metzger had written a letter from prison to the Holy Father Pius XII asking for a new work of Christian reconciliation:

> Church history and world history alike will raise a memorial to that wearer of the triple crown who begins this work on a generous scale, and to the one who may perhaps finish it later.[2]

---

[1] Notes of these are given in Jerome-Michael Vereb, C.P., "The German Theater of Ecumenical Activity," in *Because He Was a German! Cardinal Bea and the Origins of the Roman Catholic Engagement in the Ecumenical Movement*, 67–120 (Grand Rapids, MI: William E. Eerdmans, 2006).

[2] Lilian Stevenson, *Max Josef Metzger* (London: S.P.C.K, 1952), 54–55.

METZGER'S LEGACY LIVES ON IN MUSIC

Christ the King Institute, Meitingen, Germany.

Who was this priest whom many would come to know as the "prophet of the ecumenical movement"? My interest in Metzger led me to try to make personal contact with the Christian institute Metzger had founded in the small town of Meitingen, near Augsburg, in Germany. I discovered that the Christ the King Institute was soon to celebrate the centenary of its founding by Metzger in 1919. It was still involved in ecumenical dialogue and youth work, although many of its Sisters and Brothers were now advancing in years. Sister Gertraud Roßmann was their archivist and sent reading materials to me in connection with their "Brother Paulus," as they called Max Josef. When I received the package, it was a selection of his compositions. I found out that Max Josef had been a talented musician—a composer and poet.

"Freundschaft"

One poem Sister Gertraud sent to me was called "Wenn Zwei" or "Freundschaft," meaning "When Two" or "Friendship." As a composer myself, I immediately took an interest in Metzger's writing, which seemed to be so lyrical, and started to compose a suitable melody of my own for his words. Little by little, I discovered that Metzger had written a whole series of poems while in prison and that some indeed had been published in the UK in the 1950s. These poems included some written in the prison at Brandenburg- Görden in the weeks and months before his execution on April 17, 1944. These *Gefangnisgedichte* (Prison Poems) had been published in England by Irish peace activist and member of the International Fellowship for Reconciliation Lilian Stevenson in her biography *Max Josef Metzger*. My curiosity prompted me to order a copy of the book, an old green text, formerly from the Library of Manchester. As I read them, both in English and in German, I grew to love them and felt an urge to set several of them musically as a song cycle.

The Meitingen Concert, November 3, 2019

I knew Metzger was also a composer, but I did not have any access to his melodies. I also knew from the literature sent by Sister Gertraud that the hundredth anniversary of the founding of their community was due to take place in 2019. I had the idea to set these poems as a song cycle and then see if I could find a choir or orchestra who would *secretly* prepare a concert of these poems for the anniversary year and then present them to the Sisters of the Institute! It was a big challenge! I started to make contacts in Augsburg and then with the leader of the men's choir in Meitingen itself and, all of a sudden, I found a groundswell of enthusiasm for this notion. Although I had had a performance of my Requiem for Dresden in Dresden in 1985, this new work was unconnected. I was now setting poems of a German martyr in 1944 to music and preparing to present them to his community!

The project was not kept a complete secret from the Sisters of the Institute, but on November 3, 2019, an ecumenical choir drawn from the Meitingen Catholic parish of St. Wolfgang and the Lutheran Church of St. Johannes together formed a ninety-member "Una Sancta" ecumenical choir. Together with a group of locally organized musicians and orchestra players, they gave the first performance of these historical prison poems of Max Josef Metzger. The event was filmed and broadcast locally and blessed by the future Bishop of Augsburg, Bertram Meier. God works his wonders to perform!

METZGER'S LEGACY LIVES ON IN MUSIC

Poster for the Meitingen Concert, November 3, 2019.

The Una Sancta Choir of Meitingen.

Udo and Helene, soloists in the Meitingen Concert.

American Premiere at St. Matthew's Lutheran Church, Charleston, February 2020

Subsequently the music has been performed in America by a professional choir. The first of these performances was with the Taylor Festival Choir and members of Charleston Symphony Orchestra at St. Matthew's Lutheran Church in Charleston, South Carolina. The church rang out 133 bells to celebrate the 133 years since the birth of Metzger in Schopfheim in 1877. These two events in Germany and the United States created a deep bond of friendship between the producers and performers and the Sisters in Meitingen.

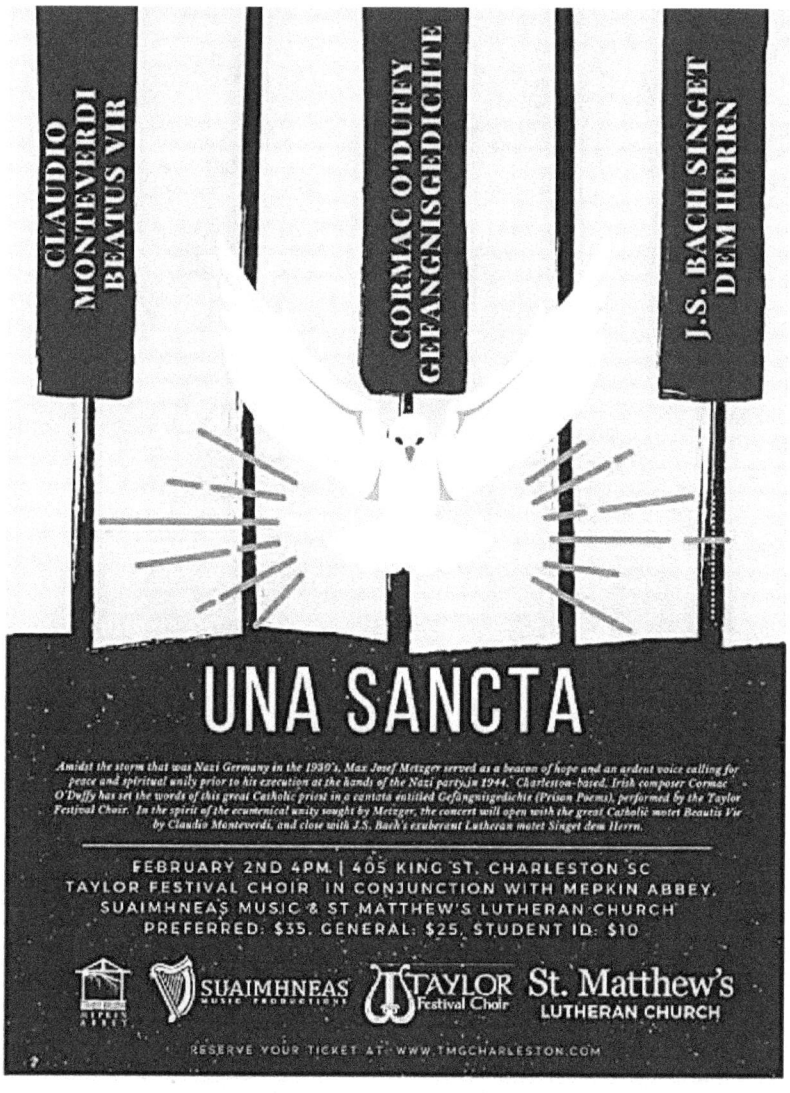

Poster for the Una Sancta concert in Charleston.

The composer at the piano of St. Matthew's, Charleston.

Fr. Joe Tedesco, Superior of Mepkin Trappist Monastery,
who gave thanks for the American performance of *Gefangnisgedichte*.

METZGER'S LEGACY LIVES ON IN MUSIC

The Making of the Metzger Oratorio

Subsequent to the German and American premieres of *Gefangnisgedichte*, new texts were sent to me from Meitingen by Sister Gertraud. One of the first was a beautiful poem celebrating the New Year of 1944. The text was written on a letter from Brandenburg-Görden prison near Berlin, where Fr. Max had been awaiting his execution.

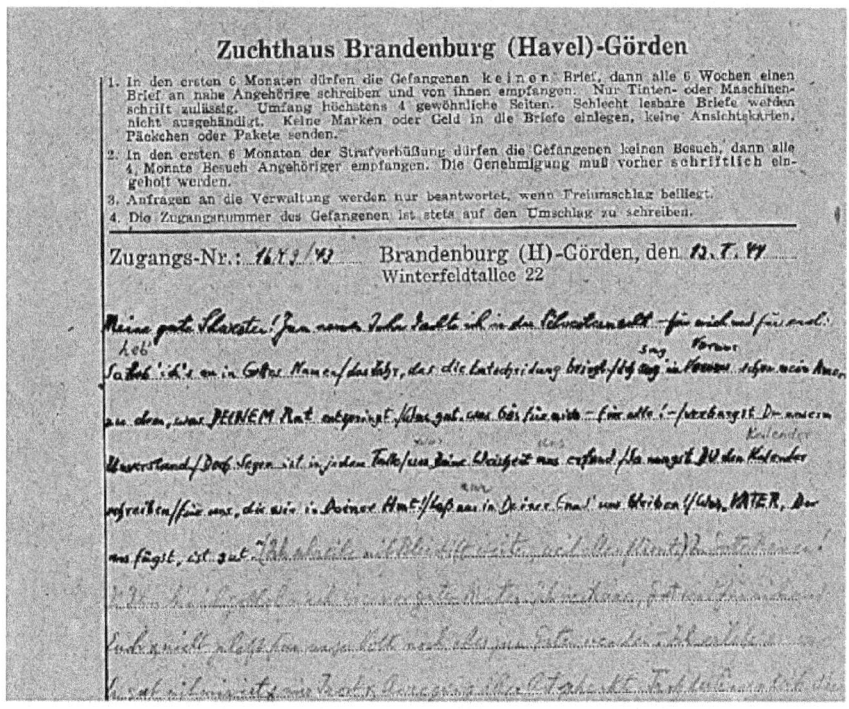

The text of the Poem "*Neujahr*," written on New Year's Eve 1944 and sent on January 13, 1944, to the Christ the King Institute in Meitingen. (Notice the text of "*Neujahr*" inked in on the second line of the letter, beginning with "*So heb' ich's an in Gottes Namen ...*").

Brandenburg-Görden Prison 1933–45.

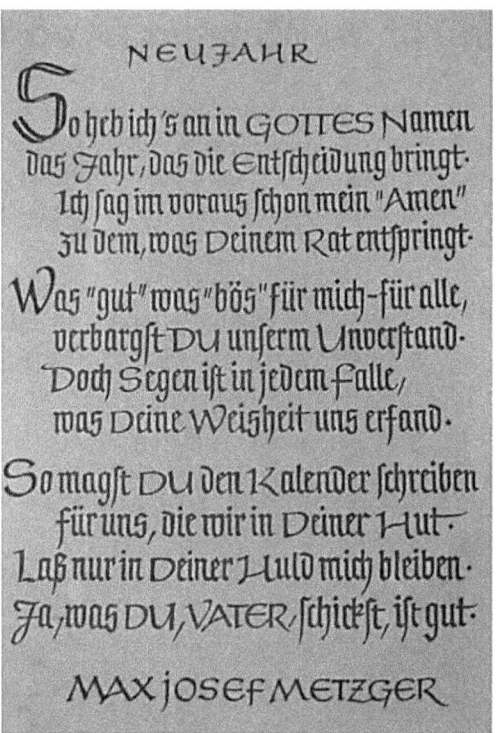

Text of *"Neujahr"* by Max Josef Metzger.

After the Catholic priest and martyr Dr. Max Josef Metzger was sentenced to death in Berlin on October 14, 1943, and was taken to Brandenburg-Görden prison to await execution, he wrote in a letter on January 13, 1944, "I study, read and write, I write poetry and compose, even if I can't put everything on paper." On New Year's Eve 1943 he wrote a poem to encourage his Christkoenig congregation in Meitingen. He called the poem "New Year." Three months later, on April 17, 1944, Dr. Max Josef was executed. *"Neujahr"* was the first part of several "Hymns and Songs" of Metzger that became Part One of the oratorio. I received a copy of this poem in December 2020 and set it to music. On New Year's Eve 2020, exactly seventy-seven years after Brother Paulus (as he was known to his congregation) first wrote his lines, tenor Udo Scheuerpflug gave a special premiere of the song to the sisters of Dr. Max Josef Metzger's congregation in Meitingen. Local filmmaker Josef

Gogl filmed this special event.[3] This composition marked the beginning of what was later to be known as the Metzger Oratorio.

Further Texts of Metzger from Sister Gertraud, Christ the King Institute

"Bin ein junges Blut" from Liederschatz des Weissen Kreuzes.

---

[3] Max Josef Metzger, *Gedicht 'Neujahr' mit musikalischer Untermalung* von Cormac O'Duffy, YouTube, uploaded on December 15, 2021, https://m.youtube.com/watch?v=Wbl20ln5J2k.

The Liederschatz des Weissen Kreuzes songbook of 1924.

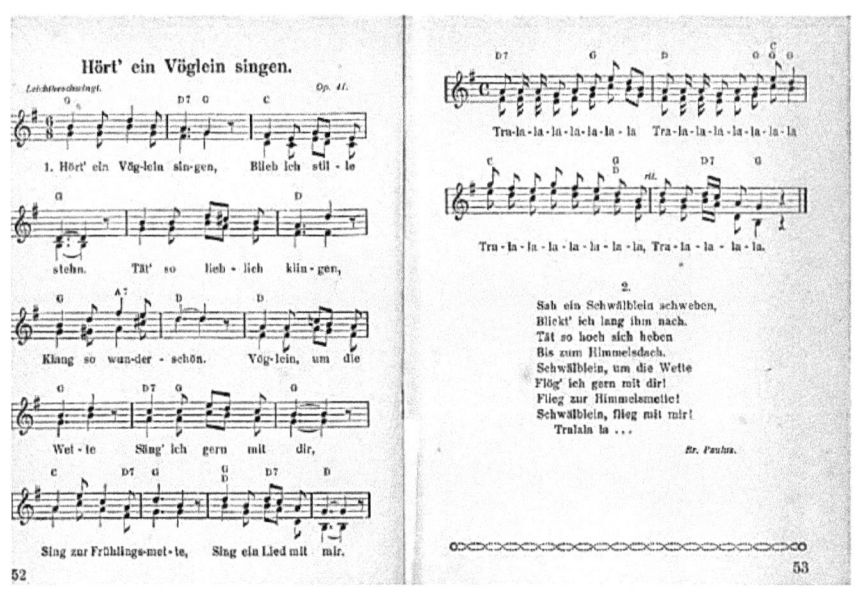

"Hört ein Vöglein Singen" from the Liederschatz des Weissen Kreuzes songbook.

Hymns and Songs from the Community of the White Cross, 1924

New texts were sent to America by Sister Gertraud. They mostly represented the earlier part of Fr. Max's life and his enjoyment of the seasons, bird songs, dancing and singing, friendship, and love of country, as well as his deep faith. They had been published as the *Treasures in Song of the White Cross*—the name of Metzger's Community—in 1924. He described the purpose of the songs in his introduction:

> Love urges song. That is why the song is part of the essence of the White Cross. The Alleluia song of love for God, the kind Father, the merciful Son, and the empowering Holy Spirit. The jubilant alleluia of enthusiasm for the wondrous works of God in nature and in human beings. The alleluia of joy in enjoying the delicious joy of God on a happy journey and in brotherly fellowship. The strong-hearted alleluia in the trial and need of body and soul. The alleluia of supplication for God's mercy on us and on all the brethren around us. Carefree Alleluia children's song and willingly serious Alleluia evening prayer of mature age. Whatever struggles in the rich soul of a man who lives in God and strives for God for a strong form, seeks its deepest expression in song, the simple children's song, the simple, artless way of the folk song, in special high times and times of need.

In setting these poems, I sought to keep to the style of Metzger, and on two occasions used the original melodies written by Metzger for the composition.

The Institute in Meitingen and Its Members

Members of the Christ the King Institute in Meitingen.

The Institute buildings in Meitingen, still used today.

Fr. Max Josef with members of the Christ the King Institute.

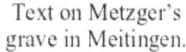

Text on Metzger's grave in Meitingen.

Metzger's grave in Meitingen.

Oratorio Structure: Parts One and Two

The oratorio is divided into two parts: "Part One: Hymns and Songs" and "Part Two: The Prison Poems." Part One begins and ends with words "*Ich habe mein Leben Gott angeboten, für den Frieden der Welt und für die Einheit der Kirche*" (I have given my life to God for peace in the world and for the unity of the Church). These are the same words that are written on Metzger's grave in Meitingen. Coupled with these are two other sayings of Metzger: "*Keine Verkündigung wirkt so überzeugend wie das Leben und Lieben überzeugter Christen*" (No preaching is more convincing than the lives and loves of convinced Christians), which is heard at the opening. At the end of Part One, with the repeat of the words from the gravestone are the words "*Als ich am Abend in meine Zelle kam, habe ich mich hingekniet und habe Gott gedankt, daß er mich so in die Jüngerschaft Christi hineingezogen hat, und ihn gebeten, mir das starke Herz bis zuletzt zu bewahren*" (When I came to my cell in the evening, I knelt down and thanked God for drawing me thus into the discipleship of Christ and asked him to help me keep my strong heart to the end).

The Prison Poems

The second part of the Oratorio was in fact written first and consists of the poems written by Metzger during his three imprisonments. Between Parts One and Two there are altogether twenty-seven of Metzger's texts.

For Peace and Unity: Letters from Prison.

Lilian Stevenson's collection of Metzger's poems in German and English, 1952.

"Christian Witness in a Torn World: Letters from Prison 1934–1944."

The 2022 performance of "*Gefangnisgedicht*" of Max Josef Metzger at Mepkin Abbey, South Carolina, USA.
L-R: Robert Taylor, Cormac and Fiona O'Duffy, Fr. Joe Tedesco, OCSO Superior Mepkin Trappist Monastery, Ellen Dressler Morryl, Producer, Bishop Jacques Fabre, CS and Bishop Robert Guglielmone, Bishops of Charleston, Rev. Tory Liferidge, Grace Reformed Episcopal Church
Photo credits: Doug Deas, The Catholic Miscellany, Diocese of Charleston, USA.

THE FUTURE

April 17, 2024, will mark the eightieth anniversary of the martyrdom of Fr. Max Josef Metzger. To celebrate this occasion plans are being made to bring a choir from the United States to Berlin and Dresden followed by a special performance in the States. This will be the first time the complete oratorio will be heard in both countries.

The "Alleluia" Memorial, Brandenburg, April 17, 2024

At 3:26 p.m. on April 17, 2024, a small group of people will gather at the execution hall of the Brandenburg Görden Prison, a penal institution situated about ninety kilometers west of the German capital of Berlin. Their gathering place had a notorious reputation as the prison of victims of the Nazi dictatorship during World War II. The prisoners (of whom sixty percent were incarcerated for political reasons) were of varied European origin—from France, Belgium, and what had been Czechoslovakia, as well as from all parts of Germany. The conditions were inhuman, with programs of sterilization and castration, long-term detention, and finally execution.

In 2024, among those gathering will be representatives of the main German churches, Catholic and Lutheran, local pastors of churches and fellowships, and some overseas guests and leaders of peace movements. In addition, there will be some local political figures, all who will come to pay tribute to the deceased. They will be gathering to mark the eightieth anniversary of the execution of a Catholic priest. At exactly 3:26 p.m., the time of the execution, a flute will be heard within the walls of the prison, imitating the bird song beloved of this priest and martyr, while a solo singer will sing a simple hymn called "Alleluia."

The words of the hymn will be those of the prisoner, written just about a week before his execution. They were written in celebration of Easter, which had passed on April 9, and were given by the priest to the prison chaplain, Fr. Peter Buchholz, on April 12. Both the chaplain and the priest were able to share the hymn of Easter joy together. Years later, the chaplain remarked that normally, a chaplain gives words of consolation to a prisoner, but in this case, he felt he had been given consolation by the faith of the prisoner. The words he wrote declared that death was not to be feared and that light and darkness must vanish as the Easter sun has risen.

Tod! Wo ist dein' Macht geblieben?

Höllenfürst wie bist du klein!

Alles Dunkel muß zerstieben

Vor der Ostersonne Schein!

A small memorial with the text of the "Alleluia" poem will be unveiled in the area with some prayer cards with the text for future prison visitors to reflect upon. The meeting will conclude with prayers being offered by the Christian leaders in attendance, whose presence represents the great contribution made by the priest and the group he founded to the development of ecumenism between Catholics and Protestants during the war and in the postwar period.

Several days later, on the morning of April 21, a larger group will gather in the same area. They too will have speeches and some music to recognize the contribution that the priest made to the development of Christian democracy in the postwar period. Wreaths will be laid to his memory by political figures from the different German political parties represented. Messages of support from high-ranking officials will be read. They will then make their way along the street named for the priest and Görden Allee to the center of Brandenburg and enter one of the main cathedrals of the city, which has hosted wonderful ecclesiastical musical events for hundreds of years. They will carry with them a larger plaque inscribed with the "'Alleluia" text with the name and dates of the author of the text.

When the group arrives at the cathedral, they will be greeted by the minister and then will attend a short service of dedication while the plaque is placed on the cathedral wall. Prayers will be said for Christian unity before the service ends with the singing of the "Te Deum." This is the hymn that was sung eighty years previously when news of the execution reached the religious community founded by the priest in Meitingen, near Augsburg.

Later that evening, the same church will be filled with the sound of voices and musical instruments. The cathedral now will be brightly lit and celebratory. After playing a hymn of praise for all present to sing, the musicians will then present for the first time a large choral work together—an oratorio which will contain twenty-eight texts written by the same prisoner. The final chorus of this work will have the same words of Christian triumph that have been brought from the prison—the "Alleluia." After the chorus is sung, now with a fully harmonized orchestral setting with brass and percussion, the covering over the plaque will be removed and a bright light will enable those attending to see the poem as a lasting tribute to his memory.

Who is this man they are celebrating with prayer, music, and "Alleluia" song?

This man is Father Max Josef Metzger (1887–1944) priest, peace worker, founder of the Christ the King Institute and the ecumenical Una Sancta Brotherhood.

Father Metzger was initially laid to rest in the Brandenburg City Cemetery on Karl Sachs Straße with a service officiated by Chaplain Jochmann. It was said that the day was dark and gloomy, but as the body was laid in the grave, the sun burst out. Over a year later, on September 18, 1945, the body was transferred to St. Hedwig's Cemetery in Berlin. There, Fr. Metzger's life was celebrated with over a thousand people present. The prison chaplain who had been with Fr. Metzger in his final week gave the eulogy, and Protestant Pastor Horn gave some words of remembrance on behalf of the Protestant community present. Previously, the Christian Democratic Union political party had given two memorial services in Fr. Metzger's honor at St. Joseph's Church in Wadding and in the Mercedes Palast Cinema. Finally, on April 27, 1968, Fr. Metzger's body was reinterred in the graveyard in Meitingen, the home of his Christ the King Community.

At Fr. Metzger's final service, the Bishop of Augsburg exclaimed, "We may not disregard the call of the deceased in this hour—our active responsibility for the reunion of Christians is demanded."

There is no doubt that celebrating the legacy of Fr. Max Josef Metzger on the eightieth anniversary of his martyrdom in 2024 is merited. The world has traveled a long way from the period of the Kulturkampf in the time of the emperor and the horrors of the Jewish and Christian persecution of World War II. Germany has emerged as a powerful force for good in the modern world. The age-old divisions between the churches are no longer a source of antagonism and separation, as Christians have moved a long way toward the unity that Max Josef Metzger sought and prayed for. As he said (and as the choir will sing in the oratorio), he gave his life for the "peace and the unity of the church." His political legacy was recognized right from the start of the Christian democratic movement in Germany. Though he did not live to see the fruits of his labor, it would be hard to explain the growth of either Christian ecumenism or Christian democracy without his legacy.

Truly, we can speak with him his own words and, by so doing, thank him for his testimony of faith, courage, and sacrifice:

Alleluja! Singt die Weise	*Alleluia! Sing the Story*
ostermächtig laut ins Land!	*He is risen, mankind to save!*
Alle Welt den Sieger preise,	*All creation praise the victor*
der aus dunklem Grab erstand!	*Risen from darkness and the grave.*
Sonne überwand die Nacht:	*Christ has triumphed o'er the night*
Christ' hat neuen Tag gebracht.	*And a new day brought to light*
Alleluja! Alleluja!	*Alleluia! Alleluia!*

ABOUT THE AUTHORS

Leonard Swidler, PhD

Dr. Leonard Swidler is the founder and president of the Dialogue Institute and a recently retired professor of Temple University's Department of Religion where he taught for 56 years. At Temple and as a visiting professor at many universities around the world, he has mentored a generation of US and international scholars in the work of interreligious dialogue. He has proposed a "Universal Declaration of a Global Ethic," based on various religious and ethical communities, ethnic groups, and geographical religions, encouraging work and discussion in drafting their own versions of a global ethic. Professor Swidler is the author of more than 100 books, including *The Power of Dialogue: Jewish–Christian–Muslim Agreement and Collaboration*; *Authentic Humanity*; and *Jesus Was a Feminist*.

Cormac O'Duffy

Cormac O'Duffy is an American-born son of an Irish Tenor. Having spent most of his life in Ireland and the UK, he holds a BMus degree from University College Dublin, teaching qualifications from Middlesex University, and an MA and PhD from Mary Immaculate College and the University of Limerick. He is known for his musical compositions, including 'Hear O Israel,' which tells the story in Oratorio style of the return of the Jewish people to Israel. It was performed in Jerusalem on the 40th anniversary of the State. More recently, his work includes an Oratorio called 'Mary,' which was performed at Mepkin Abbey in Charleston, SC.

Cormac has long been interested in the life of Fr. Max Josef Metzger, learning much from Professor Swidler's work. He has written an Oratorio with 27 texts of Metzger, premiering in 2024 at the place of Metzger's martyrdom. Cormac has written a book on the life of Bishop John England with Msgr Edward Lofton and a book on the history of hymns. He and his wife, Fiona, have four children and two grandbabies.

Meet iPub Global Connection

A Hybrid Boutique Publishing House and Forum for Scholars, Writers, Educators, Artists, Dreamers, Thinkers, and Survivors

With every piece of content we publish, we help someone somewhere. The company, the team, the authors, the contributors, our community, and everyone else in between—we are determined to publish our way to a better tomorrow. It is possible!

iPub Global Connection is the brainchild of Sandi Billingslea. Originally built to showcase the distinguished academic library of works by Sandi's brother Dr. Leonard Swidler, close to a decade later, iPub Global has grown into so much more.

We spotlight voices in our community in print, digital, video, and audio formats—and we are always looking to add to the chorus. The evolution of success is found in seeing where one wants to go and then recognizing one's own ability to build unique pathways to get there. We see those builders as the future, making choices with critical clarity of mind and a love for humanity, sharing losses, embracing successes, and cheering others on, so that all the world can see, "It is possible!"

iPub Global Connection, LLC
www.iPubGlobalConnection.com
1050 West Nido Avenue
Mesa, AZ 85210
info@iPubGlobalConnection.com

Come and visit our website to stay up to date on your favorite writers and subscribe for news on new releases, events, and promotions: www.iPubGlobalConnection.com.

Join the conversation at Facebook.com/iPubGlobalConnection.com.
Join our community at iPubForum.com.

Publisher's Acknowledgements

This book was published with special thanks to:

Ann Marie Bahr	Esther Elizabeth Suson
Jessica DiDonato	Joe Stoutzenberger
Elyse Draper	Henry Whitney
Rob Robinson	Brenda Van Niekerk

We are grateful for your contributions.

Please show support for our authors by sharing this book with your friends and family, writing reviews everywhere books are sold, and joining our community. www.iPubGlobalConnection.com.

READ MORE FROM DR. LEONARD SWIDLER   iPub

SCAN ME! TO REQUEST YOUR FREE COPY

THE DIALOGUE DECALOGUE
Ground Rules for Interreligious, Interideological Dialogue

 WWW.IPUBGLOBALCONNECTION.COM

www.ingramcontent.com/pod-product-compliance
Lightning Source LLC
Chambersburg PA
CBHW050901160426
43194CB00011B/2243